<< cjnow! >>

The Course Companion to *Criminal Justice Today* Online

Frank Schmalleger, Ph.D.

Prentice Hall

Upper Saddle River, New Jersey 07458

Publisher: Dave Garza
Senior Acquisitions Editor: Kim Davies
Managing Editor: Mary Carnis
Production Editor: Adele M. Kupchik
Director of Manufacturing and Production: Bruce Johnson
Manufacturing Buyer: Ed O'Dougherty
Composition: Denise Brown
Creative Director: Marianne Frasco
Cover Design Coordinator: Miguel Ortiz
Editorial Assistant: Lisa Schwartz
Marketing Manager: Chris Ruel
Marketing Assistant: Joe Toohey
Director of Marketing Communication and New Media: Frank Mortimer, Jr.
Marketing Coordinator: Adam Kloza
Printer/Binder: Banta, Harrisonburg, VA
Cover Image: Scott Petty
Cover Design: Lafortezza Design Group
Cover Printer: Banta, Harrisonburg, VA

Prentice-Hall International (UK) Limited, *London*
Prentice-Hall of Australia Pty. Limited, *Sydney*
Prentice-Hall Canada Inc., *Toronto*
Prentice-Hall Hispanoamericana, S.A., *Mexico*
Prentice-Hall of India Private Limited, *New Delhi*
Prentice-Hall of Japan, Inc., *Tokyo*
Prentice-Hall Singapore Pte. Ltd.
Editora Prentice-Hall do Brasil, Ltda., *Rio de Janeiro*

Prentice Hall

10 9 8 7 6 5 4 3 2 1
ISBN 0-13-090761-8

Dedication

This book is dedicated to new media visionary and Pearson Education whiz-kid Frank Mortimer (A.K.A. "Company Man") whose ideas, professional dedication, and technological prowess have shaped every aspect of the online package this guide supports.

Thanks also to virtual reality architect Craig Marcus for using his considerable technical skills in the development of this project.

<< contents >>

Part 2 POLICING

Part 3 ADJUDICATION

Part 4 CORRECTIONS

Part 5 SPECIAL ISSUES

<< to the student >>

This small book is part of a revolutionary approach to learning about crime and the American system of criminal justice. *CJNow!* is a guide to the sixth edition of Frank Schmalleger's comprehensive online digital textbook, *Criminal Justice Today*. It's purpose is to point the way to enhanced learning opportunities that are available to you using the Internet. This guide leads to a wealth of online multimedia criminal justice learning materials that are just waiting to be heard, viewed, read, and explored.

Although you can hold this brief volume in your hands, the materials to which it points are all Web-based. The advantages of Web-based e-books over their print counterparts are numerous—such as ease of accessibility, lower cost, integrated sound and video, and interactive activities. But one advantage stands out from all the rest. It is this: Online books can be continuously updated. Frequent updates make the online version of *CJNow!* a living book, brimming with dynamic up-to-the minute content. All of the chapter opening stories, news events, crime and justice statistics, studies, and court cases that you will find at the e-book site are built upon the latest information available and are always current.

Still, the online materials go one step further. They provide full integration of crucial course materials with government and private Web-based resources. The online site can help you fully explore the Web so that you can easily find information of interest to you—be it from the U.S. Supreme Court, the *Sourcebook of Criminal Justice Statistics*, or a small town police department.

The online site that this guide supports includes all of the following features:

- **Electronic syllabus.** Check here to see if your instructor has created an online syllabus. If so, refer to it to keep track of reading assignments, test dates, term papers, and other coursework. The electronic syllabus posted by your instructor may also contain links to other Web-based media, such as online lectures, and to sites chosen by your instructor for you to view.
- **Audio chapter introductions.** Hear the author introduce each chapter. Audio chapter introductions require Real Player™ or Windows Media Player™ software.
- **Chapter learning objectives.** Set your study goals for each chapter with chapter-specific learning objectives. Use these objectives to maintain your focus on important materials as you read through the text.
- **Practice review questions.** Prepare for tests and assess your knowledge of critical content with online review questions. Use these true-false and multiple-choice questions to test yourself as often as you want—and watch your scores improve.
- **Electronic homework.** Respond to online essay questions and e-mail your answers to your instructor for grading. Electronic homework makes it possible for you to demonstrate your knowledge of core concepts while it helps save trees!
- **Chapter summaries.** Review chapter materials with online summaries of key points. Bulleted summaries allow for quick and easy access to critical content and can help you remember important chapter information.
- **Web Quests!** Work your way through comprehensive Web-based chapter projects, and learn how to do criminal justice research on the Internet. Web Quests! make studying enjoyable and open the door to a wealth of electronic information.
- **WebExtras!** Visit sites that are closely related to the materials you are reading about. WebExtras! provide a virtual criminal justice tour of the Internet, with visits to police, courts, and corrections sites on the Web.

- **Library Extras!** Read carefully selected documents from the Bureau of Justice Statistics, the National Institute of Justice, the Bureau of Justice Assistance, the Federal Bureau of Investigation, and other agencies at the *CJNow!* electronic library. Library Extras! are constantly updated to bring you the latest in criminal justice research and data.
- **Crime and justice news.** Stay up-to-the-minute with late-breaking crime and justice news from APB News online. Continually updated stories, integrated throughout the *CJNow!* Web site, provide complete coverage of current events in the crime and justice field.
- **E-mail announcements** of late-breaking crime news. Sign up for e-mail announcements from APB News online, and have the latest in breaking crime news delivered right to your desktop every day. E-mail announcements are a convenient and easy way of keeping abreast of events in the justice field.
- **Careers center.** Use the careers feature to find the best-paying jobs in the justice profession. If you aren't sure that you want to work in the justice system, the careers center can help you decide your future.
- **Message boards.** Discuss criminal justice issues with students and professors from across the country and around the world. Our boards allow you to read and post messages whenever you are connected to the Internet.
- **E-mail discussion list.** Join our e-mail discussion list, and stay abreast of what other students are talking about. E-mail discussions are a handy way to stay current on issues in the field and to share your thoughts with others. You can also begin an e-mail study group to review text materials with students in other colleges.
- **Dr. Frank Schmalleger's Cybrary.** Find what you're looking for on the Web with Dr. Frank Schmalleger's cyber-library of criminal justice links. Containing over 12,000 crime and justice sites in its fully searchable database, the Cybrary is well known on the Internet as "the world's criminal justice site directory."
- **Electronic glossary.** Use this Web-based glossary as a ready-made study aid to help in understanding key concepts and other text materials. Our glossary includes standardized terminology from the criminal justice, criminology, law, and corrections fields.
- **Twenty-first century criminal justice.** Learn what the criminal justice system of tomorrow will look like, and see how the principles that underlie today's system will influence the justice system of the future.
- **The U.S. Constitution.** Review the full text of the U.S. Constitution, including all amendments. Use this feature to research the constitutionally protected rights of those facing processing by the justice system.

As you use this guide, remember that the "What You Should Learn" sections found at the start of each *Quick View* Chapter are designed to let you know at a glance what you should pay close attention to as you study the online chapters at the *CJNow!* Web site. You should also read the Learning Objectives that accompany each chapter online. The "What You Should Remember" sections found at the conclusion of each *Quick View* Chapter are intended to help you retain important material from the online chapters at the *CJNow!* Web site.

Part 1

<< crime in america >>

Chapter 1

WHAT IS CRIMINAL JUSTICE?

Chapter 2

THE CRIME PICTURE

Chapter 3

THE SEARCH FOR CAUSES

Chapter 4

CRIMINAL LAW

Chapter 1

quick view

<< what is criminal justice? >>

Outline

- Justice and Criminal Justice
- American Criminal Justice: The System
- American Criminal Justice: The Process
- Due Process and Individual Rights
- Criminal Justice and Criminology

What You Should Learn

- How media reports of crime have led to increased public concern about criminal activity.
- The differences between the individual rights and social control perspectives.

- The nature of justice, and the different types of justice discussed in the online book.
- The structure of the criminal justice system, and the differences between the consensus and conflict models of the justice system.
- The meaning of due process of law, and where guarantees of due process can be found in the American legal system.
- The difference between the academic disciplines of criminology and criminal justice.
- The definitions of key terms that appear in boldface throughout this *Quick View* chapter. Definitions can be found online at http://www.cjnowonline.com.

Hear the author introduce this chapter at *CJNow!* online.

Justice and Criminal Justice

Most students who major in criminal justice seek to dedicate their professional careers to crime fighting. That was not true in the case of Benjamin Nathaniel Smith, a 21-year-old former criminal justice major at Indiana University in Bloomington. On Fourth of July weekend, 1999, Smith went on a 36-hour drive-by shooting spree that spanned the states of Illinois and Indiana. When it was over 2 people were dead and many more injured. Smith's targets appear to have been Hispanics, blacks, Orientals and Jews.[1]

Hate crime experts believe that Smith saw himself as a soldier in RAHOWA—the racial holy war movement that is driving members of some underground groups into committing a wide variety of hate-motivated crimes.[2] During his time at IU-Bloomington, Smith had become well known for his habit of littering the campus with racist leaflets and for discussing his racist views openly in class.[3]

Smith's shooting spree ended on the evening of July 4, 1999. As officers pursued him down a highway in southern Illinois, Smith apparently tried to kill himself—firing two shots into his body as he drove. Soon afterward his vehicle crashed into a tree. As officers surrounded the car and struggled with Smith, he managed to fire one more shot—this one into his own heart. Officers were able to positively identify their quarry when they saw the tattoo "Sabbath Breaker" on Smith's chest.

Another infamous crime, the Columbine High School massacre, in which 13 students died and 20 more were injured, also took place in 1999. The shootings, which happened on April 20, 1999 in Littleton, Colorado, were the work of 18-year-old Eric Harris and 17-year-old Dylan, both of whom were students at the school.

Crimes like these—where seemingly random violence unexpectedly claims the lives of well-meaning citizens going about their daily routines—have shaken American confidence in the criminal justice system, and have greatly enhanced the fear of crime that so many Americans have come to feel. Because of such shocking crimes, a growing fear of crime persists—even amidst today's falling official crime rates. Such crimes also challenge long-cherished beliefs about **social control** in American society, and call into question a number of basic values centered on the family, children, violence in the media, public safety, and social equality.

The Focus of The Online Book—Individual Rights and Public Order

The online book that this guide supports focuses on the American system of criminal justice and the agencies and processes that constitute it. It has an orientation that is especially valuable for studying criminal justice today. For many years the dominant philosophy in American criminal justice focused on guaranteeing the rights of criminal defendants while seeking to understand the root causes of crime and violence. During the last decade, however, a growing conservative emphasis has concerned itself with the interests of an ordered society and with the rights of crime victims. This now popular perspective has called into question some of the fundamental premises upon which the American system of criminal justice rests. In attempting to balance both points of view, the materials presented in the online text are built around the following theme:

> There is increasing recognition in contemporary society of the need to balance (1) the respect accorded the rights of individuals faced with criminal prosecution against (2) the valid interests of society in preventing future crimes and in reducing the harm caused by criminal activity.

> While the personal freedoms guaranteed to criminal suspects by the Constitution, as interpreted by the U.S. Supreme Court, must be closely guarded, so too the urgent social needs of local communities for controlling unacceptable behavior and protecting law-abiding citizens from harm must be recognized. Still to be adequately addressed are the needs and interests of victims, and the fear of crime now so prevalent in the minds of many law-abiding citizens.

Figure 1-1 represents this theme diagrammatically. Most people today who intelligently consider the criminal justice system assume either one or the other of these two perspectives. The online text refers to those who seek to protect personal freedoms and civil rights within the criminal justice process as **individual rights advocates.** Those who suggest that under certain circumstances involving criminal threats to public safety, the interests of society (especially crime control) should take precedence over **individual rights**, are called **public order advocates**. The online textbook looks at ways that the individual rights and the public order perspectives can be balanced to serve both sets of needs.

Perspectives On Criminal Justice and the Theme of *Criminal Justice Today* Online

Although the emphasis on individual rights, which rose to ascendancy a few decades ago, now appears to have been eclipsed by calls for social and individual responsibility, the tension between the two perspectives still forms the basis for most policy-making activity in the criminal justice arena. Rights advocates continue to carry on the fight for an expansion of civil and criminal rights, seeing both as necessary to an equitable and just social order. The rights perspective holds that it is necessary to allow some guilty people to go free in order to reduce the likelihood of convicting the innocent.

In contrast, law and order advocates want ever-greater police powers. They claim that the criminal justice system has coddled offenders and encouraged continued law violation. Society, they say, if it is to survive, can no longer afford to accord too many rights to the individual or place the interests of any one person over that of the group.

As we begin the twenty-first century, the trick, it seems, is to balance individual rights and personal freedoms with social responsibility and respect for authority. The online book from which this guide is derived has two basic purposes: (1) to describe in detail the criminal justice system, while (2) helping students develop an appreciation for the delicacy of the balancing act now facing it. The question for the future will be how to ensure the existence of, and effectively manage, a justice system which is as fair to the individual as it is supportive of the needs of society.

Figure 1-1 The theme of this book: Balancing the concern for individual rights with the need for public order through the administration of criminal justice.

Social Justice

One popular dictionary definition of justice says that it is "the principle of moral rightness, or conformity to truth."[4] Of special concern to anyone seeking justice are **criminal justice** and **civil justice**—both of which are aspects of a wider form of equity termed **social justice**. Social justice is a concept that embraces all aspects of civilized life. It is linked to notions of fairness and to cultural beliefs about right and wrong. Questions of social justice can arise about relationships among individuals and among parties (such as corporations and agencies of government), between the rich and the poor, between the sexes, among ethnic groups and minorities, and about social linkages of all sorts. In the abstract, the concept of social justice embodies the highest personal and cultural ideals.

Civil justice, the first subcomponent of social justice, concerns itself with fairness in relationships between citizens, government agencies, and businesses in private matters—such as those involving contractual obligations, business dealings, hiring, equality of treatment, and so on. Criminal justice, in its broadest sense, refers to those aspects of social justice which concern violations of the criminal law. Visit *CJNow!* online to learn more.

American Criminal Justice: The System

The Consensus Model

Those who speak of a **system of criminal justice** usually define it as consisting of the agencies of police, courts, and corrections. Each of these agencies can, in turn, be described in terms of their subsystems. Corrections, for example, includes jails, prisons, community-based treatment programs such as "halfway houses," and programs for probation and parole. Each subarea contains still more components. Prisons, for example, can be described in terms of custody levels, inmate programs, health care, security procedures, and so on. Some prisons operate as "boot camp" facilities, designed to "shock" offenders into quick rehabilitation, whereas others are long-term confinement facilities designed for the most hard-core criminals who are likely to return to crime quickly if released. Students of corrections also study the process of sentencing through which an offender's fate is decided by the justice system, and examine the role of jails in holding prisoners prior to conviction and sentencing.

The systems model of criminal justice is characterized primarily by its assumption that the various parts of the justice system work together by design in order to achieve the wider purpose we have been calling *justice*. Hence, the systems perspective on criminal justice generally encompasses a larger point of view called the **consensus model**. The consensus model assumes that all the component parts of the criminal justice system strive toward a common goal and that the movement of cases and people through the system is smooth due to cooperation among the various components of the system.

The Conflict Model

The **conflict model** provides another approach to the study of American criminal justice. The conflict model says that criminal justice agency interests tend to make actors within the system self-serving. Pressures for success, promotion, pay increases, and general accountability, according to this model, fragment the efforts of the system as a whole, leading to a criminal justice *non*system.[5] Learn more about the differences between the consensus and conflict models at *CJNow!* online.

American Criminal Justice: The Process

As we have said, the criminal justice system can be described *structurally* in terms of its component agencies: police, courts, and corrections. Whether system or nonsystem, however, the agencies of criminal justice must process cases which come before them. *Functionally*, the components of the "system" may work together well or they may be in conflict. An analysis of case processing within the system provides both a useful guide to the online book and a "road map" to the criminal justice system itself. Beginning with the investigation of reported crimes, Figure 1-2 illustrates the processing of a criminal case through the federal justice system.

Due Process and Individual Rights

Imposed upon criminal justice case processing is the constitutional requirement of fairness and equity. Guaranteed by the Fifth, Sixth, and Fourteenth Amendments to the U.S. Constitution, this requirement is referred to as **due process**. The due process clause of the U.S. Constitution is succinctly stated in the Fifth Amendment, which reads "No person shall be . . . deprived of life, liberty, or property, without due process of law." The constitutional requirement of due process mandates the recognition of individual rights in the processing of criminal defendants when they are faced with prosecution by the states or the federal government. The guarantee of due process is found not just in the Fifth Amendment, but underlies the first ten amendments to the U.S. Constitution, which are collectively known as the Bill of Rights. The Fourteenth Amendment is of special importance, however, for it makes due process binding upon the states—that is, it requires individual states in the union to respect the due process rights of U.S. citizens who come under their jurisdiction. Table 1-1, which is available online, outlines the basic rights to which defendants in criminal proceedings are entitled.

The Role of the Courts in Defining Rights

Although the Constitution deals with many issues, individual "rights" are open to interpretation. Many modern rights, although written into the Constitution, would not exist in practice were it not for the fact that the U.S. Supreme Court decided, at some point in history, to recognize them in cases brought before it. The well-known Supreme Court case of *Gideon* v. *Wainwright* (1963)[6], for example (which is discussed in detail online in Chapter 9), found the Court embracing the Sixth Amendment guarantee of a right to a lawyer for all criminal defendants and mandating that states provide lawyers for defendants who are unable to pay for them. It is important to note, however, that while the Sixth Amendment specifically says, among other things, that "In all criminal prosecutions, the accused shall enjoy the right to . . . have the Assistance of Counsel for his defence," it does *not* say, *in so many words*, that the state is *required to provide* counsel. It is the U.S. Supreme Court which, interpreting the Constitution, has said that. While it is often impossible to avoid ideological conflicts when interpreting the law, it is also realistic to think of the American system of justice as representative of *crime control through due process*. It is the **due process model** of law enforcement infused with the recognition of individual rights which provides a workable conceptual framework for understanding the American system of criminal justice—both now and into the future.

Criminal Justice and Criminology

Although criminal justice has historically been viewed as a technically-oriented field of study, it has recently taken its place alongside other academic disciplines in the social sciences. **Criminology**, on the other hand, has long had a firm academic base. Criminology is the interdisciplinary study of the causes of crime and of criminal motivation. It combines the academic disciplines of sociology, psychology, biology, economics, and political science in an effort to explore the motivation of the offender and the social and economic conditions which give rise to criminality. The study of criminology is central to the criminal justice discipline, and courses in criminology are almost always found in criminal justice programs.

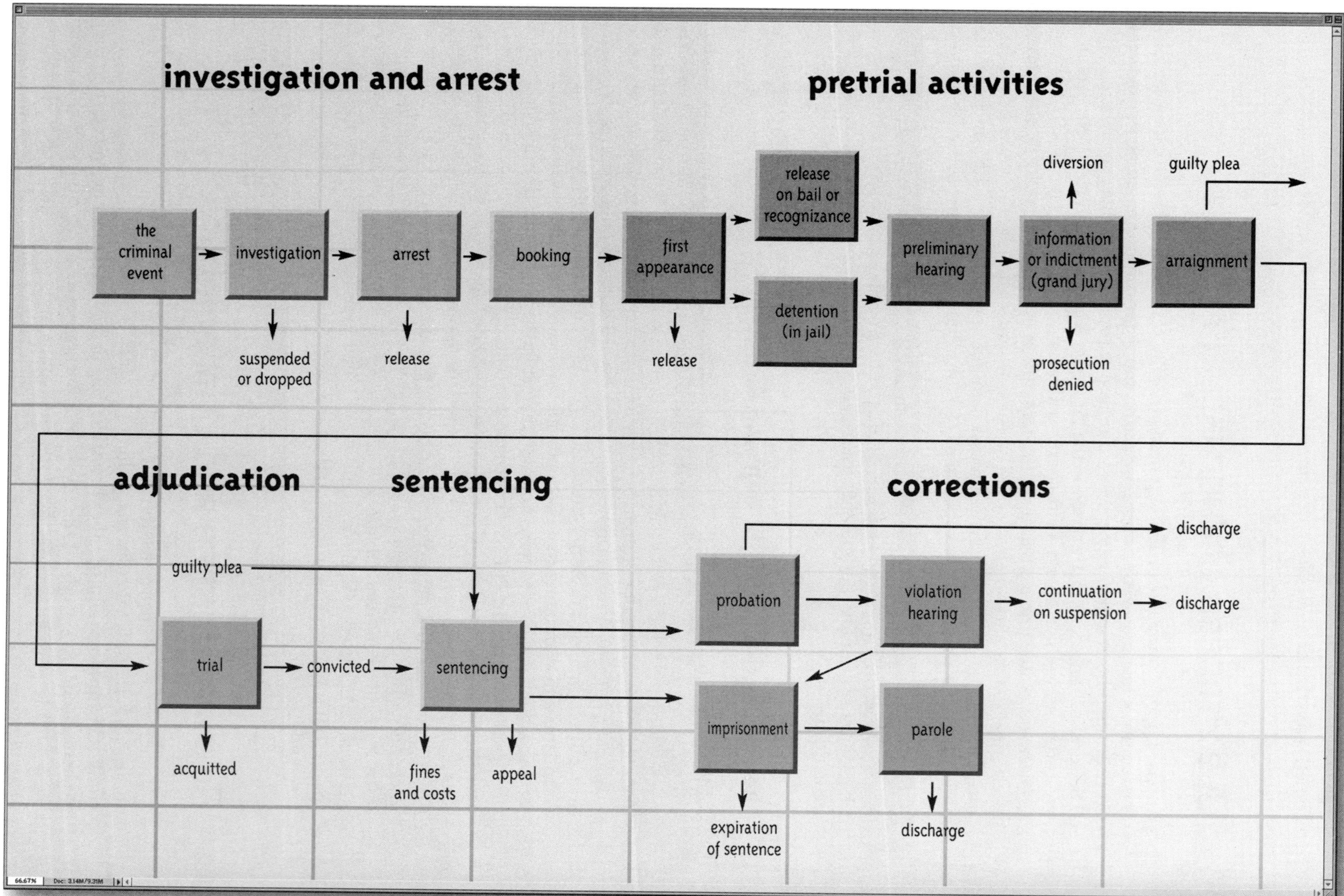

Figure 1-2 Criminal case processing: Adopted from U.S. Department of Justice, *Compendium of Federal Justice Statistics 1989* (Washington, D.C.: Bureau of Justice Statistics, 1992), p. 3.

Today criminal justice is well established as an academic discipline and is offered as a major course of study in well over 1,000 colleges and universities across the country. Freda Adler, a well-known criminal justice academician, notes that "[f]rom an obscure discipline scorned by most academics with only two small doctoral programs as recently as 1970, criminal justice has exploded to 350,000 undergraduate majors at colleges and universities."[7]

What You Should Remember

- A recent spate of personal violence has left Americans in fear of crime and personal victimization—even amidst today's falling official crime rates. Media reports of such crimes have led to doubts about long-cherished beliefs concerning social control in American society and have called into question a number of basic values centered on the family, children, violence in the media, public safety, and social equality.
- This guide, and the online book that it supports, build upon the theme of individual rights versus social control—or the need to balance the Constitutional rights of those facing criminal prosecution against the interests of society in preventing crime and controlling offenders.
- Justice is an overarching term that refers to the principle of moral rightness. The online book supported by this guide distinguishes between criminal justice and civil justice—both of which are aspects of what we have called social justice.
- The criminal justice system consists of the police, courts, and corrections.
- The criminal justice system can be described either in terms of a consensus model or a conflict model.
- The U.S. Constitution requires that the criminal justice system operate according to the principle of due process of law, which mandates the recognition of individual rights in the processing of criminal defendants.
- While the academic discipline of criminal justice is largely concerned with the administration of justice agencies, criminology is the interdisciplinary study of the causes of crime and criminal motivation. Both fields, however, share much in common.

LIBRARY EXTRAS!

Library Extras! are suggested readings that are available digitally to readers of this guide. They may be accessed at the *CJNow!* Web site.

Library Extra! 1-1. *The Challenge of Crime in a Free Society: Looking Back Looking Forward* (USDOJ, May 1998).

Library Extra! 1-2. *Perspectives on Crime and Justice: 1996–1997 Lecture Series* (NIJ, 1998).

Library Extra! 1-3. "Race, Crime, and the Administration of Justice: A Summary of the Available Facts," from *The National Institute of Justice Journal* (NIJ, April 1999).

Library Extra! 1-4. *Women in Criminal Justice: A Twenty-Year Update* (NIJ, 1998).

Library Extra! 1-5. The Violent Crime Control and Law Enforcement Act of 1994.

ENDNOTES

[1] "Weekend of Terror," APB News online, July 5, 1999. Web posted at http://www.apbonline.com/911/1999/07/05/chicago0705_02.html.

[2] Amy Worden, "FBI Eyes Link to Hate Shootings, California Fires," APB News online, July 7, 1999. Web posted at http://www.apbonline.com/911/1999/07/07/hate0707_01.html. Citing David Goldman, executive director of Hatewatch.

[3] "Gunman's Racial Outrage Was Building," APB News online, July 6, 1999. Web posted at http://www.apbonline.com/911/1999/07/06/chicago_suspect0706_01.html.

[4] *The American Heritage Dictionary on CD-ROM* (Boston: Houghton Mifflin, 1991).

[5] One of the first published works to utilize the nonsystems approach to criminal justice was the American Bar Association's *New Perspective on Urban Crime* (Washington, D.C.: ABA Special Committee on Crime Prevention and Control, 1972).

[6] *Gideon* v. *Wainwright*, 372 U.S. 353 (1963).

[7] Fox Butterfield, "A Newcomer Breaks Into the Liberal Arts," *The New York Times*, December 5, 1998.

Chapter 2

quick view

<< the crime picture >>

Outline

- Introduction: Sources of Data
- The Uniform Crime Reports
- The National Crime Victimization Survey
- Emerging Patterns of Criminal Activity

What You Should Learn

- How crime statistics can be useful in social policy creation.
- Some of the limitations inherent in statistical reports of crime.
- The names and characteristics of the two major national comprehensive crime data-gathering programs in operation in the United States today.

- The major differences between those two data-gathering programs.
- The eight major crimes found in the Uniform Crime Reports (UCR).
- The definition of "hate crime."
- The difference between the UCR's Part I and Part II Offenses.
- The meaning of the term "clearance rate."
- Details about the National Incident-Based Reporting System (NIBRS) and how it differs from the Uniform Crime Reporting Program.
- The definitions of key terms that appear in boldface throughout this *Quick View* chapter. Definitions can be found online at http://www.cjnowonline.com.

Hear the author introduce this chapter at *CJNow!* online.

Introduction: Sources of Data

The online version of this chapter provides a statistical picture of crime in America today. It does so by examining information on reported crimes from the FBI's *Uniform Crime Reports* (UCR), as well as data from the door-to-door National Crime Victimization Survey (NCVS) conducted by the Bureau of Justice Statistics (BJS). While reading through the online chapter, however, it is important to keep in mind that statistical aggregates of reported crime, whatever their source, do not readily reveal the human suffering, lost lives, lessened productivity, and reduced quality of life that crime causes. Although every murder victim, for example, led an intricate life and had a family, dreams, and desires, his or her death at the hands of another person is routinely recorded only as a numerical count in statistical reports. Such information does not contain details on the personal lives of crime victims, but represents merely a numerical compilation of reported law violations.

Crime Data And Social Policy

Crime statistics render a comprehensive picture of crime in this country. If used properly they can provide one of the most powerful tools for social policy creation. Decision makers at all levels, including legislators, elected public officials, and administrators throughout the criminal justice system, rely on crime data to analyze and evaluate existing programs, fashion and design new crime-control initiatives, develop funding requests, and plan new laws and crime-control legislation. The "get-tough" policies of the 1990s, for example, were in large part based upon the public's perception of increasing crime rates and the measured ineffectiveness of existing programs to reduce the incidence of repeat offending.

Collecting Crime Data

National crime statistics come from two major sources: (1) the FBI's Uniform Crime Reporting Program (UCR), and (2) the Bureau of Justice Statistics' National Crime Victimization Survey (NCVS). The most widely quoted numbers purporting to describe crime in America today probably come from the FBI's *Uniform Crime Reports* and depend upon reports to the police by victims of crime. In contrast to the UCR, the Bureau of Justice Statistics' (BJS) National Crime Victimization Survey (NCVS) relies upon survey data and personal interpretations of what may (or may not) have been criminal events. Another source of crime data can be found in offender self-reports based upon surveys that ask respondents to reveal any illegal activity in which they have been involved.

The Uniform Crime Reports

Development of the UCR Program

In 1930 Congress authorized the attorney general of the United States to survey crime in America, and the FBI was designated to implement the program. The original UCR

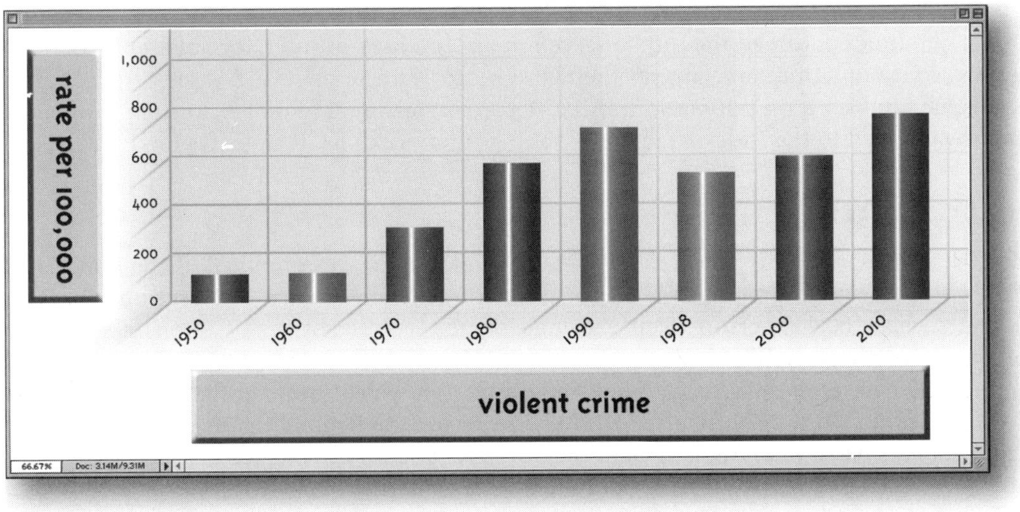

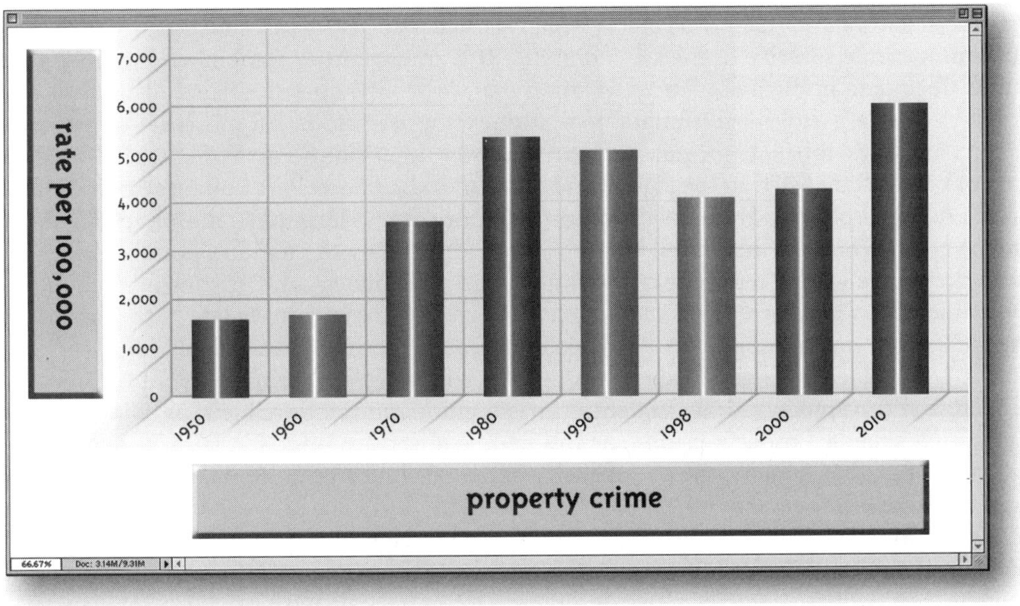

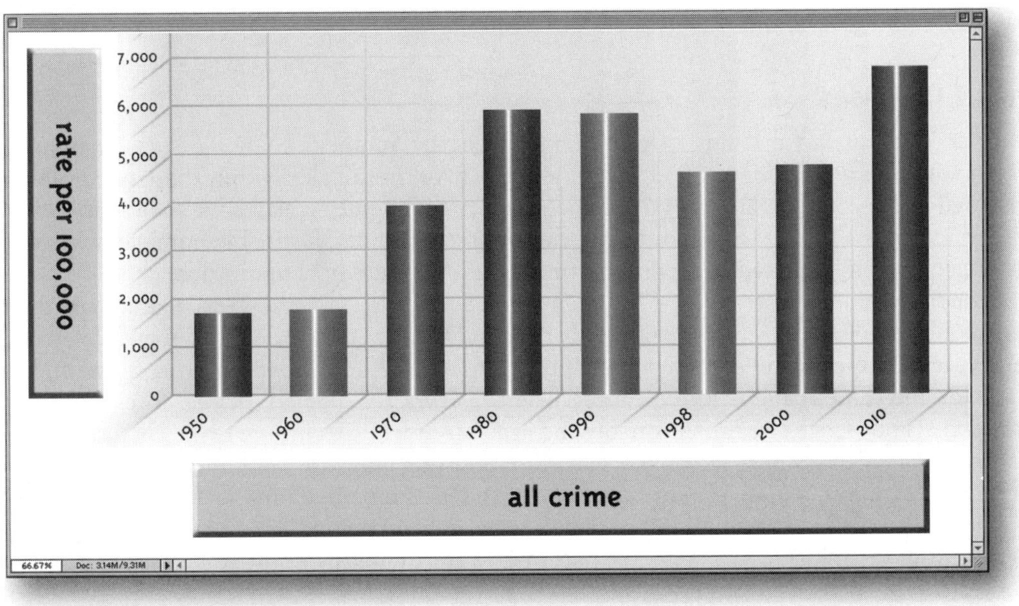

Figure 2-1 Actual and projected rates of crime in the United States per 100,000 inhabitants 1950–2010. *Source:* Federal Bureau of Investigation, *Crime in the United States* (Washington, D.C.: U.S. Government Printing Office, various years); James Alan Fox, *Trends in Juvenile Violence: Report to the United States Attorney General on Current and Future Rates of Offending* (Washington, D.C.: Bureau of Justice Statistics, 1996).

Program was designed to permit comparisons over time through construction of a **crime index**. The Index summed the total of seven major offenses-murder, forcible rape, robbery, aggravated assault, burglary, larceny-theft, and motor vehicle theft-and expressed the result as a crime rate based on population. In 1979, by congressional mandate, an eighth offense-arson-was added to the Index. Table 2-1 online summarizes UCR statistics for 1998.

Historical Trends

Most UCR information is reported as a *rate* of crime. Rates are computed as the number of crimes per some unit of population. National reports generally make use of large units of population, such as 100,000 persons. Hence, the rate of rape reported by the UCR for 1998 was 34.4 forcible rapes per every 100,000 inhabitants of the United States.[1] Rates allow for a meaningful comparison over areas and across time. See Figure 2-1, which shows both historical rates of crime and projected rates through 2010. When viewing the figure, keep in mind that official crime rates are based upon the FBI eight major crimes and do not include drug offenses.

UCR Terminology

Figure 2-2 shows the UCR crime clock, which is calculated yearly as a shorthand way of diagramming crime severity in the United States. It is important to remember, however, that crime clock data imply a regularity to crime that, in reality, does not exist. Also, while the crime clock is a useful diagrammatic tool, it does not use rate-based measures of criminal activity and does not allow for easy comparisons over time. Eight "Part I offenses," also called "major crimes," are listed in the right-hand margin of the figure. Part I offenses are: 1) murder, 2) rape, 3) robbery, 4) aggravated assault, 5) burglary, 6) larceny, 7) motor vehicle theft, and 8) arson. The sum total of all Part I offenses, divided by the nation's population, comprise the UCR's widely reported **crime index**, which facilitates comparisons of crime rates over time. Since, however, arson was added as a Part I offense relatively late in the history of the UCR program, it is sometimes excluded from official crime index calculations.

The crime clock distinguishes between two categories of Part I crime: **violent** (or **personal**) **crime** and **property crime**. Violent crimes include murder, forcible rape, robbery, and aggravated assault. Property crimes, as the figure shows, are burglary, larceny, and motor vehicle theft. Other than for the use of such a simple dichotomy, UCR data do not provide a clear measure of the severity of the crimes they cover.

A commonly used term in today's UCRs is **clearance rate**. The clearance rate of any crime refers to the proportion of reported crimes that have been "solved." Clearances are judged primarily on the basis of arrests and do not involve judicial disposition. Once an arrest has been made, a crime is regarded as "cleared" for purposes of reporting in the UCR Program. Figure 2-3 shows clearance rates for all Part I offenses.

Part I Offenses

Murder is the unlawful killing of one human being by another.[2] UCR statistics on murder describe the yearly incidence of all willful and unlawful homicides within the United States. Included in the count are all cases of nonnegligent manslaughter which have been reported or discovered by the police. Not included in the count are suicides, justifiable homicides (that is, self-defense), deaths caused by negligence or accident, and attempts to murder.

Broadly speaking, the term **rape** has been applied to a wide variety of sexual attacks and, in popular terminology, may include same-sex rape and the rape of a male by a female. Use of the term **forcible rape** for statistical reporting purposes by law enforcement agencies, however, has a specific and somewhat different meaning. The *Uniform Crime Reports* defines forcible rape as "the carnal knowledge of a female forcibly and against her will." According to the *Uniform Crime Reporting Handbook*, which serves as a statistical reporting guide for law enforcement agencies, says: "By definition, sex attacks on males are excluded [from the crime of forcible rape] and should be classified as assaults or 'other sex offenses,' depending on the nature of the crime and the extent of the injury."[3] Although not part of UCR terminology, some jurisdictions refer to same-sex rape as **sexual battery**.

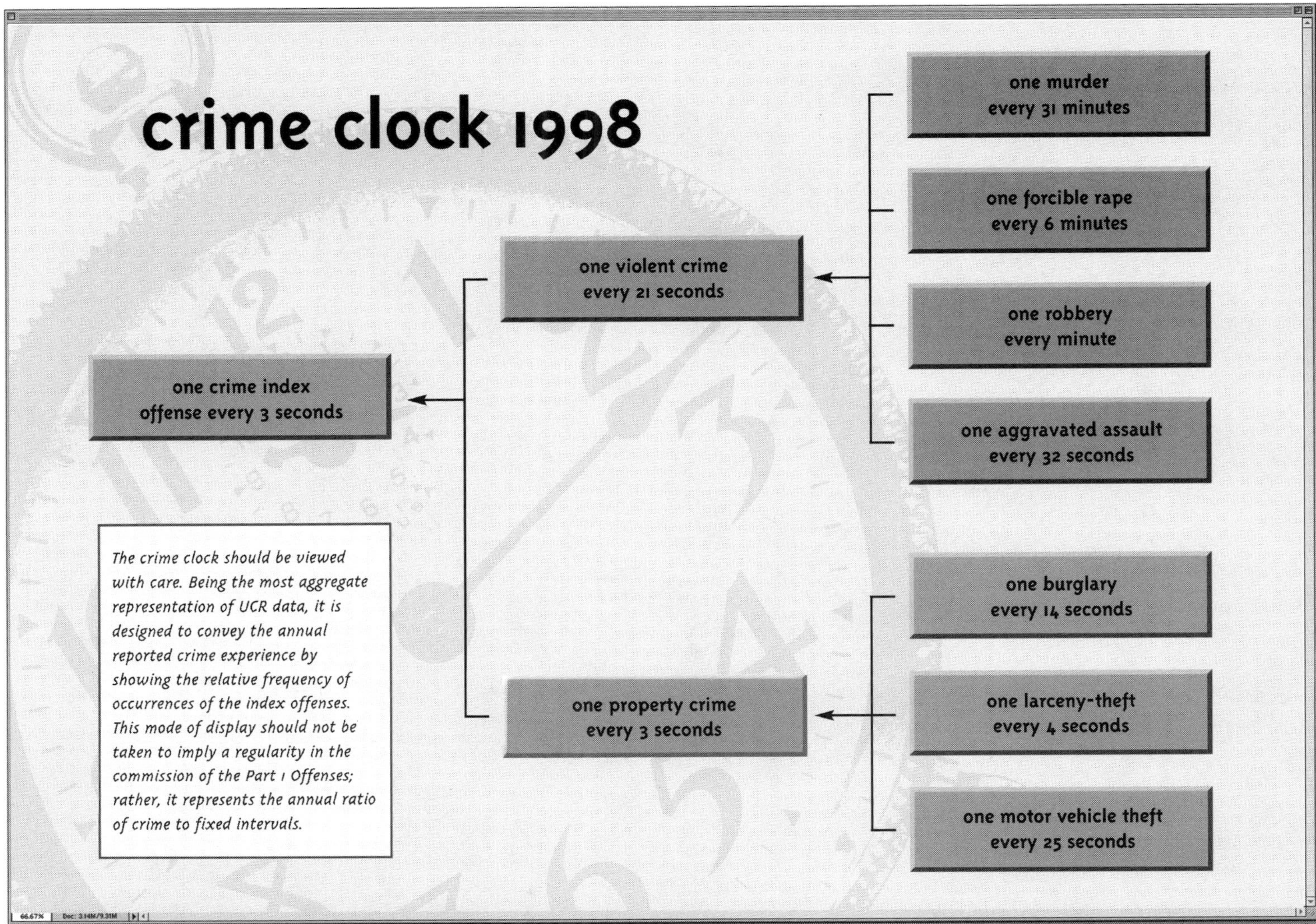

Figure 2-2 FBI crime clock, 1998, showing the frequency of major crime commission. *Source:* Adapted from Federal Bureau of Investigation, *Crime in the United States, 1998* (Washington, D.C.: U.S. Government Printing Office, 1999).

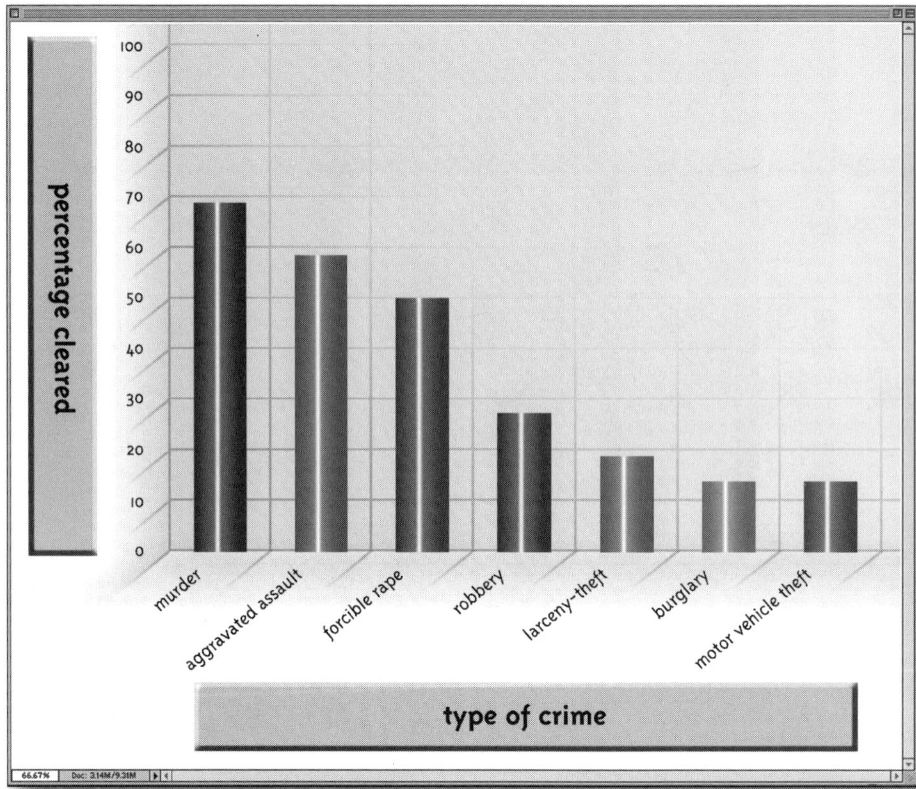

Figure 2-3 Crimes cleared by arrest 1998. *Source:* Federal Bureau of Investigation, *Crime in the United States, 1998* (Washington, D.C.: U.S. Government Printing Office, 1999).

Rape is frequently committed by a man known to the victim—as in the case of **date rape**. Victims may be held captive and subjected to repeated assaults. In the crime of heterosexual rape, any female-regardless of age, appearance, or occupation—is a potential victim. Figure 2-4 shows the rate of reported rape since 1960.

Robbery, sometimes confused with **burglary**, is a personal crime and involves a face-to-face confrontation between victim and perpetrator. Weapons may be used, or strong-armed robbery may occur through intimidation, especially where gangs threaten victims by their sheer number. Purse snatching and pocket-picking are not classified as robbery by the UCR Program, but are included under the category "larceny-theft."

Assaults are of two types: aggravated and simple. For statistical reporting purposes, simple assaults may involve pushing and shoving or even fistfights (although, technically speaking, the correct legal term used to describe such incidents is actually "battery"). **Aggravated assaults** are distinguished from simple assaults by the fact that they either include the use of a weapon, or the assault victim requires medical assistance. When deadly weapons are employed, even though no injury may result, aggravated assaults may be chargeable as attempted murder. Hence, because of their potentially serious consequences, the UCR Program scores some cases of attempted assault as aggravated assaults. Most aggravated assaults are committed with blunt objects or objects near at hand, while hands, feet, and fists are also commonly used. Less frequent are knives and firearms, as Figure 2-5 shows.

Although it may involve personal and even violent confrontations, **burglary** is primarily a property crime. Burglars are interested in financial gain and usually fence (that is, illegally sell) stolen items in order to recover a fraction of their cash value. The UCR Program employs three classifications of burglary: 1) forcible entry, 2) unlawful entry where no force is used, and 3) attempted forcible entry. In most jurisdictions, force need not be employed for a crime to be classified as burglary. Unlocked doors and open windows are invitations to burglars, and the crime of burglary consists not so much of a forcible entry as it does in the intent of the offender to trespass and steal.

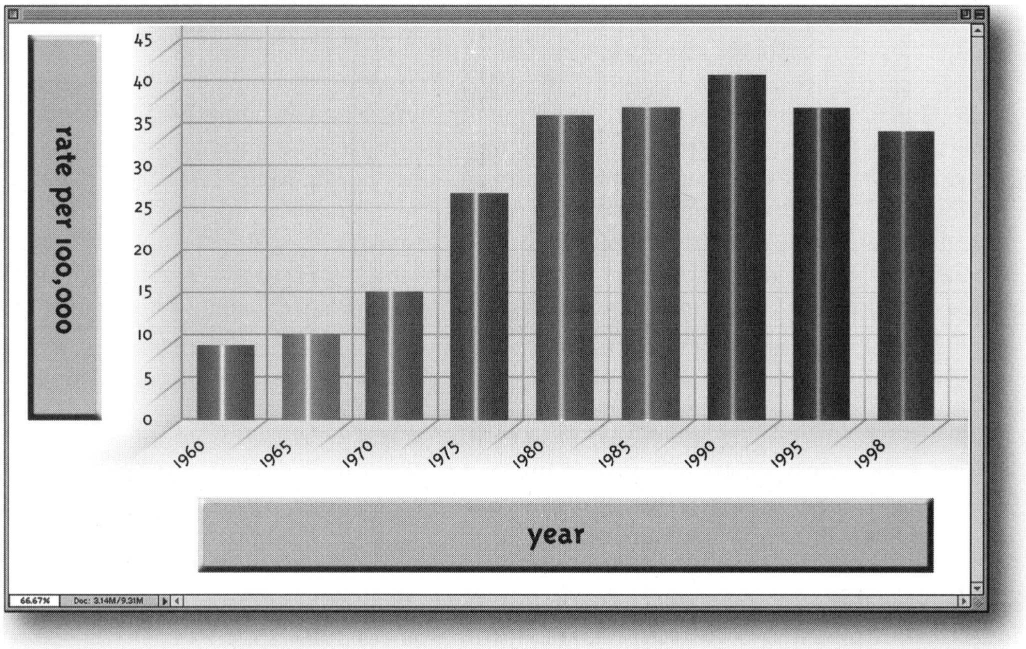

Figure 2-4 Rate of reported rapes, 1960—1998 *Source:* Federal Bureau of Investigation, *Crime in the United States* (Washington, D.C.: U.S. Government Printing Office, various years).

Larceny is another name for theft. Some states distinguish between simple larceny and grand larceny. Grand larceny is usually defined as theft of valuables in excess of a certain set dollar amount, such as $200. Larceny, as defined by the UCR Program, includes thefts of any amount. The reports specifically list the following offenses as types of larceny (listed here in order of declining frequency): 1) thefts from motor vehicles, 2) shoplifting, 3) thefts of motor vehicle parts and accessories, 4) thefts from buildings, 5) bicycle thefts, 6) pocket-picking, 7) purse snatching, and 8) thefts from coin-operated machines

Thefts of farm animals (known as rustling) and thefts of most types of farm machinery also fall into the larceny category. In fact, larceny is such a broad category that it serves as a kind of "catchall" in the UCR, and reported thefts can involve a wide diversity of materials with values that range anywhere from pocket change to the stealing of a $100 million aircraft.

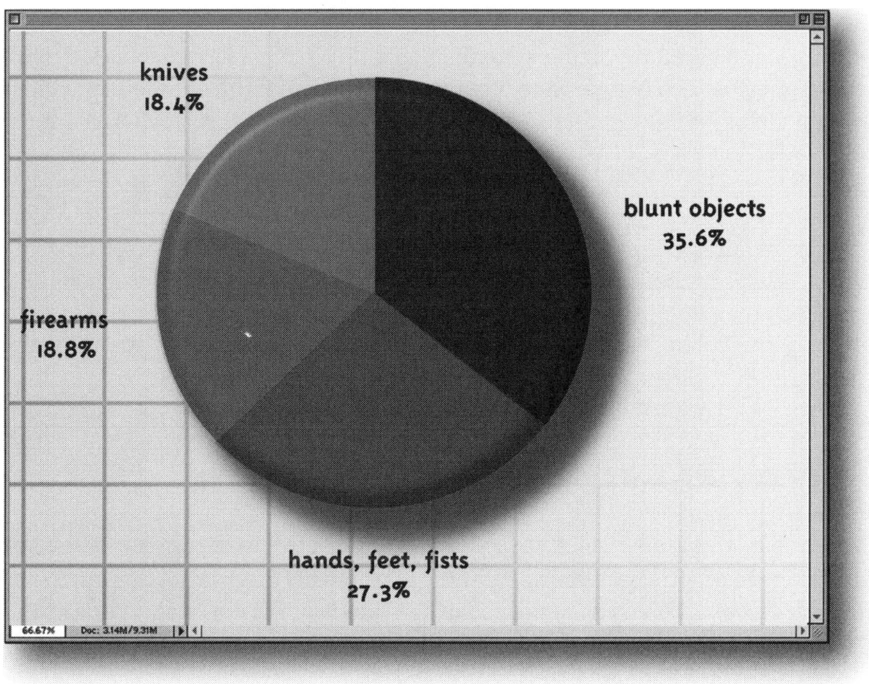

Figure 2-5 Weapons used in aggravated assaults, 1998 *Source:* Federal Bureau of Investigation, *Crime in the United States, 1998* (Washington, D.C.: U.S. Government Printing Office, 1999).

Specifically excluded from the count of larceny for reporting purposes are crimes of embezzlement, "con" games, forgery, and worthless checks.

Motor vehicle theft is a crime in which most occurrences are reported to law enforcement agencies. Insurance companies require police reports before they will reimburse car owners for their losses. For record-keeping purposes, the UCR Program defines motor vehicles as self-propelled vehicles which run on the ground and not on rails. Included in the definition are automobiles, motorcycles, motorscooters, trucks, buses, and snowmobiles. Excluded are trains, airplanes, bulldozers, most farm and construction machinery, ships, boats, and spacecraft—whose theft would be scored as larceny. Motor vehicle theft can turn violent, such as in cases of "carjacking"—a crime in which offenders force the occupants of a car onto the street before stealing the vehicle.

Current **arson** data include only those fires which, through investigation, are determined to have been willfully or maliciously set. Fires of unknown or suspicious origin are excluded from arson statistics. The intentional and unlawful burning of structures (houses, storage buildings, manufacturing facilities, etc.) Is the type of arson most often reported. The arson of vehicles Is the second most common category. Learn more about each of the Part I offenses at *CJNow!* online.

Part II Offenses

The *Uniform Crime Reports* also include information on what the FBI calls Part II offenses. Part II offenses are generally less serious than those that make up the Crime Index and include a number of social order, or so-called "victimless" crimes. The statistics on Part II offenses are for recorded arrests, not crimes reported to the police. The logic inherent in this form of scoring is that most Part II offenses would never come to the attention of the police were it not for arrests. Included in the Part II category are crimes such as simple assault, forgery, counterfeiting, fraud, embezzlement, the receiving of stolen property, vandalism, prostitution, illegal gambling, driving under the Influence, public drunkenness, and disorderly conduct. Part II arrests are counted each time a person is taken into custody. As a result, statistics on Part II offenses do not measure the number of persons arrested, but rather the number of arrests made. Some persons were arrested more than once. Table 2-2 online shows Part 2 offenses along with the number of estimated arrests made in each category.

NIBRS: The New UCR

The *Uniform Crime Reports* are undergoing significant changes in the way in which data are gathered and reported. Whereas the original UCR system was "summary based," the new "enhanced" UCR, called the National Incident-Based Reporting System, or NIBRS, is - as the name implies—an incident-based reporting system. The old (UCR) system depended upon statistical tabulations of crime data which were often little more than frequency counts. Under the new system, many details will be gathered about each criminal incident. Included among them will be information on place of occurrence, weapon used, type and value of property damaged or stolen, the personal characteristics of the offender and the victim, the nature of any relationship between the two, nature of the disposition of the complaint, and so on. The new reporting system replaces the old Part I and Part II offenses with 22 general offenses, including arson, assault, bribery, burglary, counterfeiting, vandalism, narcotic offenses, embezzlement, extortion, fraud, gambling, homicide, kidnapping, larceny, motor vehicle theft, pornography, prostitution, robbery, forcible sex offenses, nonforcible sex offenses, receiving stolen property, and weapons violations. Other offenses on which data will be gathered include bad checks, vagrancy, disorderly conduct, driving under the influence, drunkenness, nonviolent family offenses, liquor law violations, "peeping Tom" activity, runaway, trespass, and a general category of all "other" criminal law violations.

Hate Crimes

A final change in reporting practices followed from the Hate Crime Statistics Act, signed into law by President Bush in April 1990. The act mandates a statistical tally of "hate crimes," and data collection under the law began in January 1991. Hate crimes have been defined by

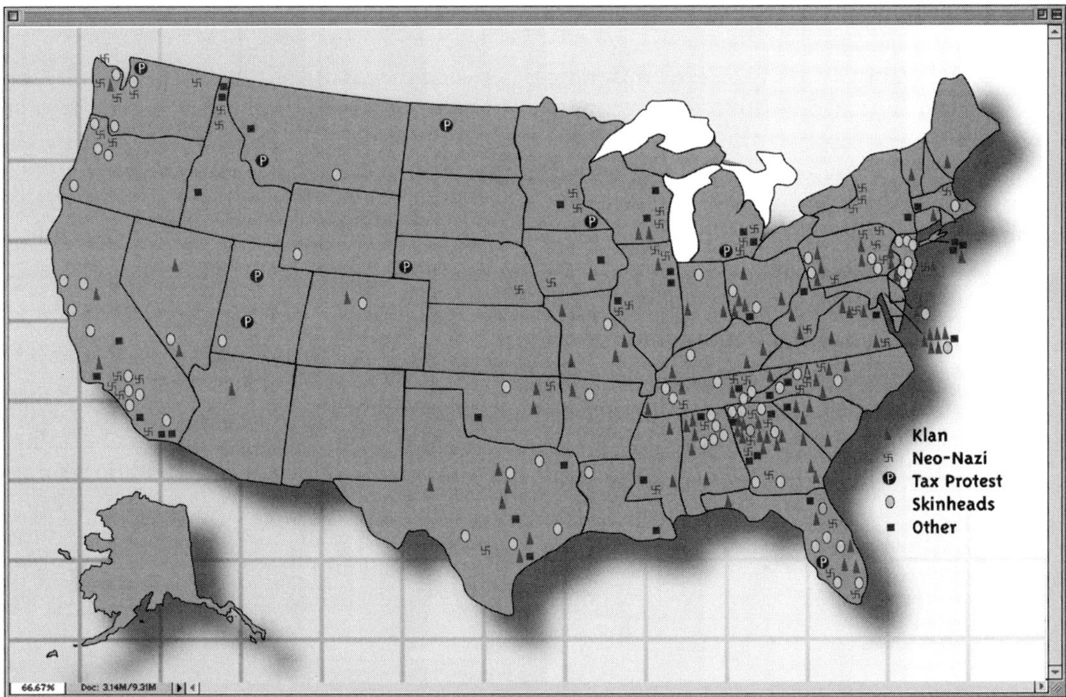

Figure 2-6 White supremacist and survival groups in the United States. *Source:* Intelligence Project, Southern Poverty Law Center. Reprinted with permission.

Congress as offenses "in which the defendant's conduct was motivated by hatred, bias, or prejudice, based on the actual or perceived race, color, religion, national origin, ethnicity, gender, or sexual orientation of another individual or group of individuals."[4] Hate crimes are sometimes called **bias crimes.**

Of considerable concern to many enforcement agencies is the continued growth of separatist groups with their own vision of a future America. Some, like the White Aryan Resistance (WAR), hope for the start of RAHOWA, or racial holy war. Figure 2-6 shows the location of various supremacist and survivalist groups in the United States.

The National Crime Victimization Survey

A second major source of statistical data about crime in the United States is the National Crime Victimization Survey (NCVS), which is based upon victim self-reports rather than on reports made to the police. The NCVS began operation in 1972 and built upon earlier efforts by both the National Opinion Research Center and the President's Commission on Law Enforcement and the Administration of Justice in the late 1960s to uncover what some had been calling the "dark figure" (or unreported offenses) of crime.

NCVS data are gathered by the Bureau of Justice Statistics (BJS) through a cooperative arrangement with the U.S. Census Bureau. NCVS interviewers work with a national sample of more than 50,000 households which are interviewed twice each year. Using definitions similar to those used by the UCR Program, the NCVS includes data on the national incidence of rape, robbery, assault, burglary, personal and household larceny, and motor vehicle theft. Not included are murder, kidnapping, and victimless crimes. The NCVS counts only the most "serious" incident in any series of criminal events perpetrated against the same individual. Both completed and attempted offenses are counted, although only persons 12 years of age and older are included in household surveys. A comparison of NCVS and UCR data can be found in Table 2-3 online.

Comparisons of the UCR and NCVS

Table 2-4 online summarizes the differences between the UCR and the NCVS. As the table shows, both provide estimates of crime in America. But both are limited by the type of crimes they choose to measure, by those they exclude from measurement, and by the methods they use to gather crime data. Crime statistics from the UCR and NCVS are often used in building explanations for criminal behavior. Unfortunately, however, researchers too often forget that statistics which are merely descriptive can be weak in explanatory power.

Emerging Patterns of Criminal Activity

Planned revisions in both the NCVS and the UCR reflect the fact that patterns of criminal activity in the United States are changing. The anticipated growth of a **superpredator** population holds potentially great significance for future crime rates and for the types of crime that will be committed in the future. If a superpredator population truly develops, as some suggest, we can expect to see a dramatic rise in both violent and property crimes by the end of the first decade of the twenty-first century. Street crime will rise once again, and cities will become less safe places in which to live and work.

The Fear of Crime

Although we may read in newspapers or in books that violent street crime is decreasing, we may not fully believe it. In fact we may be just as afraid as ever. As some authors point out,[5] the fear of crime is often out of proportion to the likelihood of criminal victimization. The Bureau of Justice Statistics says that "fear of crime affects many people, including some who have never been victims of crime."[6] Sources of fear are diverse. Some flow from personal experience with victimization, but most people fear crime because of dramatizations of criminal activity on television and in movies and because of frequent newspaper and media reports of crime. Feelings of vulnerability may result from learning that a friend has been victimized or from hearing that a neighbor's home has been burglarized. Table 2-5 online compares the chance of death from homicide with other causes of death for persons in this country aged 14–25.

Women and Crime

Women are victimized far less frequently than are men in every major crime category other than rape. When women are victimized, however, they are more likely than men to be injured.[7] Even though experiencing lower rates of victimization, it is realistic to acknowledge that a larger proportion of women than men make modifications in the way they live because of the threat of crime. Learn more about crimes against women, including data from the National Violence Against Women Survey (NVAWS), at *CJNow!* online.

Crimes committed by women provide another area of study. The relatively small amount of reported female involvement in the FBI's eight major crimes can be seen online in Table 2-6.

The Economic Cost of Crime

The national costs of crime are difficult to measure. The Bureau of Justice Statistics estimates the personal cost of crime (direct dollar losses to individuals, not including criminal justice system costs) at around $17.6 billion per year.[8] Robberies cost the nation about $500 million annually, burglaries nearly $4 billion, and larceny-thefts account for approximately $4 billion in losses per year. Not included in the Bureau's figures are the costs to crime victims of lost work, needed medical care, and the expense of new security measures they may implement.

The commercial costs of crime are substantial as well. Losses from commercial robberies (including bank robberies) and business burglaries have been put at $1.2 billion per year.[9]

The cost to businesses of white-collar crime are not known, but are thought to be substantial. To guard against crimes by employees and members of the public, private businesses spend in excess of $21 billion per year for alarms, surveillance, and private security operations.[10] Learn more about the costs of crime, including costs to the government for the apprehension, prosecution, and disposition of offenders, and crime prevention efforts by the police at *CJNow!* online.

Drugs and Crime

Drug law violations do not figure into crime index calculations. Unlike index crimes, however, they continue to increase, lending support to those who feel that this country is experiencing more crime than traditional index tabulations show. The relentless increase in drug violations largely accounts for the fact that America's prison populations have continued to grow, even when official crime rates (i.e., index offenses) are declining. Figure 2-7 shows the number of persons arrested for drug law violations in the U.S. over the past twenty-five years.

Drugs and other forms of crime are often found together. Drug law violations are themselves criminal, but more and more studies are linking drug abuse to other serious crimes. Many property crimes are committed to sustain "habits," and the numbers of both violent and property crimes committed by drug users have been shown to be directly related to the level at which they use drugs.[11] Chapter 15 online examines the drug-crime link in considerable detail. Suffice it to say here that the link appears strong and shows few signs of abating.

The Elderly and Crime

Relative to other age groups, older offenders rarely appear in the crime statistics. Criminality seems to decline with age, suggesting that a burnout factor applies to criminal behavior as it does to many other areas of life. Still, more older people are committing crimes than ever before, and the population of prisoners age 55 and over has steadily increased. Some authors say these statistics presage the growth of a "geriatric delinquent" population, freed by age and retirement from jobs and responsibilities. Such people, say these authors, may turn to crime as one way of averting boredom and adding a little spice to life.[12] The apparent increase in criminal activity among the elderly may be due to the fact that the older population in this country is growing substantially, with even greater increases expected over the next three decades.

Figure 2-7 Drug arrests in the United States, 1998. *Source:* Federal Bureau of Investigation, *Crime in the United States* (Washington, D.C.: U.S. Government Printing Office, various years).

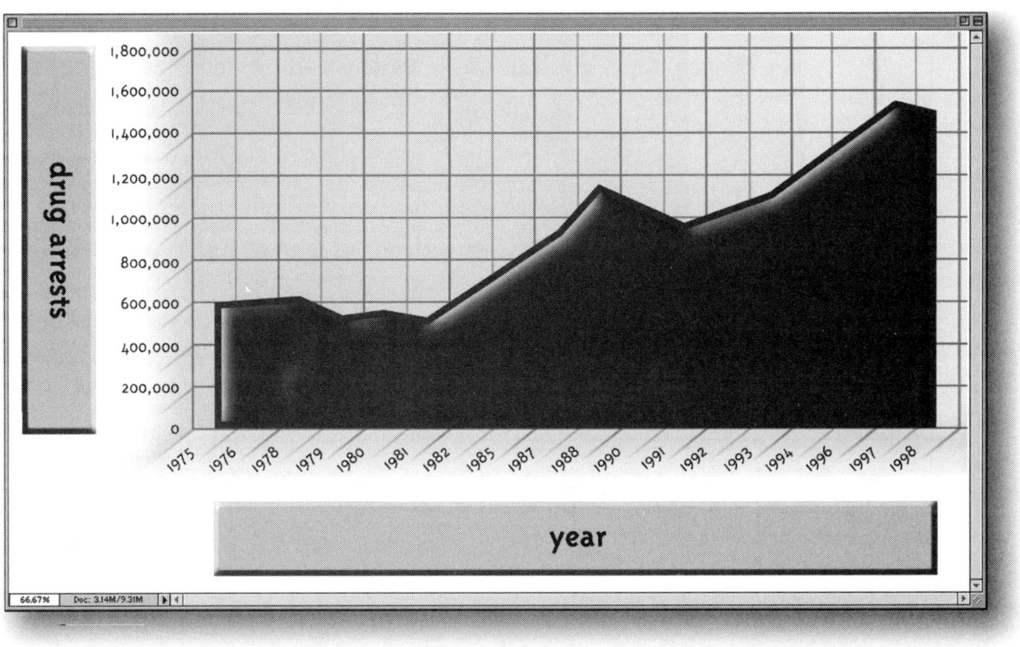

Organized Crime

Organized crime has been defined by the Organized Crime Control Act of 1970 as "the unlawful activities of the members of a highly organized, disciplined association engaged in supplying illegal goods and services, including but not limited to gambling, prostitution, loansharking, narcotics, labor racketeering, and other unlawful activities of members of such organizations."[13] Criminal organizations have existed in America since before the turn of the twentieth century. Contemporary organized crime groups are involved to some degree in just about every aspect of American life, but the manufacture, transportation, and sale of controlled substances has provided an especially lucrative form of illegal enterprise for many of them. A few such groups are thought to be among the largest businesslike enterprises in the world. Learn more about the Cosa Nostra and other organized criminal groups at *CJNow!* online.

What You Should Remember

- Crime statistics provide a comprehensive picture of crime in this country. If used properly they can be a powerful tool for social policy creation.
- All statistics, including crime statistics, are inherently limited by the way in which they are gathered. Statistics can only portray the extent of crime according to the categories they are designed to measure and in terms understood by those whose responses they include.
- Two major national comprehensive crime data-gathering programs are in operation in the United States today: the FBI's *Uniform Crime Reports* (UCR) and the National Institute of Justice's National Crime Victimization Survey (NCVS).
- The UCR and NCVS provide a picture of victim characteristics through self-reports (NCVS) and reports to the police (UCR) and allow for a tabulation of the dollar costs of crime.
- Both the UCR and the NCVS permit historical comparisons in crime rates and allow for some degree of predictability in crime trends.
- Most UCR information is reported as a *rate* of crime. Rates are computed as the number of crimes per some unit of population.
- UCR data are compiled into an annual crime index. The index is arrived at by summing the total of eight major offenses-murder, forcible rape, robbery, aggravated assault, burglary, larceny-theft, motor vehicle theft, and arson, and expressing the result as a crime rate based on population.
- UCR index data are broken down into categories: violent and property. Violent crimes include murder, forcible rape, robbery, and aggravated assault. Property crimes are burglary, larceny, and motor vehicle theft.
- Part I Offenses under the UCR, also called "major crimes," include murder, rape, robbery, aggravated assault, burglary, larceny, motor vehicle theft, and arson.
- Part II Offenses under the UCR includes crime categories used to report arrest data for less serious offenses.
- The term "clearance rate" refers to the proportion of reported crimes which have been "solved."
- The *Uniform Crime Reports* are being gradually replaced with by a new "enhanced" UCR format, called the National Incident-Based Reporting System, or NIBRS.
- NIBRS replaces the old Part I and Part II offenses with 22 general offenses, including arson, assault, bribery, burglary, counterfeiting, vandalism, narcotic offenses, embezzlement, extortion, fraud, gambling, homicide, kidnapping, larceny, motor vehicle theft, pornography, prostitution, robbery, forcible sex offenses, nonforcible sex offenses, receiving stolen property, and weapons violations.

- Of special interest under both the UCR and NIBRS are hate crimes (also known as bias crimes). Hate crimes have been defined by Congress as offenses "in which the defendant's conduct was motivated by hatred, bias, or prejudice, based on the actual or perceived race, color, religion, national origin, ethnicity, gender, or sexual orientation of another individual or group of individuals."
- Although both the UCR and NCVS show that crime has declined in recent years, fear of crime remains high. The heightened fear of crime is most likely due to widespread media coverage of spectacular crimes of random violence, which has led to the belief that no one is safe and that violent personal crime is out of control in this country.
- Women victims of violent crime constitute a special category of victimized persons whose needs have been recognized under the federal Violent Crime Control and Law Enforcement Act of 1994 through a subsection entitled the "Violence Against Women Act" (VAWA).
- Elderly violent crime victims constitute another special category, and are more likely than younger victims to 1) face offenders armed with guns, 2) be victimized by total strangers, 3) be victimized in or near their homes, 4) report their victimization to the police.

LIBRARY EXTRAS!

Library Extras! are suggested readings that are available digitally to readers of this guide. They may be accessed at the *CJNow!* Web site.

Library Extra! 2-1. *Age Patterns of Victims of Serious Violent Crime*, (BJS, September 1997).

Library Extra! 2-2. "Crime's Decline—Why?" *The National Institute of Justice Journal* (NIJ, October 1998).

Library Extra! 2-3. *Criminal Victimization* (BJS, current volume).

Library Extra! 2-4. *Prevalence, Incidence, and Consequences of Violence Against Women: Findings from the National Violence Against Women Survey* (NIJ, November 1998).

Library Extra! 2-5. *Preventing Crime: What Works, What Doesn't, What's Promising* (NIJ, 1998).

Library Extra! 2-6. *Promising Strategies to Reduce Gun Violence* (NIJ, 1999).

Library Extra! 2-7. *Stalking in America: Findings from the National Violence Against Women Survey* (NIJ, April 1998).

Library Extra! 2-8. *Violence by Intimates: Analysis of Data on Crime by Current or Former Spouses, Boyfriends, and Girlfriends* (BJS, March 1998).

ENDNOTES

[1] Federal Bureau of Investigation (FBI), *Uniform Crime Reports for the United States, 1998* (Washington, D.C.: U.S. Government Printing Office, 1999), p. 16.

[2] Most offense definitions in this chapter are derived from those used by the UCR reporting program and are taken from the FBI, *Uniform Crime Reports: Crime in the United States, 1998* (hereafter referred to as the *Uniform Crime Reports*), or from BJS, *Criminal Justice Data Terminology*, 2nd ed. (Washington, D.C.: Bureau of Justice Statistics, 1981).

[3] Federal Bureau of Investigation, *Uniform Crime Reporting Handbook* (Washington, D.C.: FBI, 1984), p. 10.

[4] H.R. 4797, 102d Cong. 2d Sess. (1992).

[5] Georgette Bennett, *Crimewarps: The Future of Crime in America* (Garden City, NY: Anchor/Doubleday, 1987), p. xiv.

[6] Bureau of Justice Statistics, *Report to the Nation on Crime and Justice*, 2nd ed. (Washington, D.C.: U.S. Government Printing Office, 1988), p. 24.

[7] Bureau of Justice Statistics, *Report to the Nation on Crime and Justice*, 2nd ed., p. 25.

[8] Patsy A. Klaus, “The Costs of Crime to Victims,” a Bureau of Justice Statistics Crime Data Brief, 1994.

[9] Bureau of Justice Statistics, *Report to the Nation on Crime and Justice*, 2nd ed.

[10] Ibid., p. 114.

[11] Bernard A. Grooper, *Research in Brief: Probing the Links Between Drugs and Crime* (Washington, D.C.: National Institute of Justice, February 1985).

[12] Bennett, *Crimewarps*, p. 61.

[13] The Organized Crime Control Act of 1970.

Chapter 3

quick view

<< the search for causes >>

Outline

- Why Is There Crime?
- Criminological Theory
- The Classical School
- Biological Theories
- Psychobiological Theories
- Psychological Theories
- Sociological Theories
- Social-Psychological Theories
- Conflict Theories
- The Phenomenological School
- Emergent Theories

What You Should Learn

- The various categories of theoretical approaches used to explain crime that are discussed in the online chapter.
- The basic features of biological theories of crime causation.
- The basic features of psychological explanations for crime.
- The basic features of sociological theories of crime causation.
- The concept of "theory integration" and something about what an integrated theory of crime might encompass.
- The identity of some new and emerging areas of theory development in the area of crime causation.
- The definitions of key terms that appear in boldface throughout this *Quick View* chapter. Definitions can be found online at http://www.cjnowonline.com.

Hear the author introduce this chapter at *CJNow!* online.

Why Is There Crime?

In 1996 John Brennan Crutchley was released after spending ten years in the Florida prison system. Crutchley is the infamous "vampire rapist," so named because he abducted a 19-year-old hitchhiker in 1985, repeatedly raped her, then used an intravenous device to drain nearly half her blood so he could drink it.[1] A neighbor found the nude, bleeding, handcuffed and semiconscious woman after she escaped. She survived, and Crutchley was arrested with the woman's help.

Crimes like Crutchley's are difficult to explain. Fundamental questions about crime causation that have concerned criminologists for years are: "Why do people commit crime? What are the root causes of violence and aggression? Are people basically good, or are they motivated only by self-interest?" More precisely, we might ask, "Why does a *particular person* commit a *distinct crime* on a given occasion and under specific circumstances?"

No discussion of crime and of the criminal justice system would be complete without giving some consideration to the causes of crime and deviance. That is the purpose of this online chapter. Before we begin, however, some brief definitions are in order. Crime, as noted in Chapter 1, is a violation of the criminal law without acceptable legal justification; whereas **deviant behavior** is a violation of social norms specifying appropriate or proper behavior under a particular set of circumstances. It is important to realize that deviant behavior is a broad category that often includes crime.

Many different kinds of theories have been advanced to explain all sorts of rule-violating behavior. Some observers of the contemporary scene, for example, find explanations for modern-day violence and seemingly increased rates of criminal victimization in the now widespread and commonplace episodes of violence in the American media—especially on television, in music, and in film. Experts who study the media estimate that the average American child watches 8,000 murders and 100,000 acts of violence while growing up. At a recent international conference, Suzanne Stutman, president of the Institute for Mental Health Initiatives in Washington, reported that studies consistently show that the extent of exposure to television violence in childhood is a good predictor of future criminal behavior.[2] According to one recent survey, "57% of the public thinks violence in the media is a major factor in real-life violence" of all kinds.[3]

Criminological Theory

Focusing on songwriters, recording companies, and the broadcast media reflects just one way of explaining crime and criminal violence. Many other types of explanations for crime can also be offered, such as genetic abnormalities which may predispose people to crime and violence, or others which look to individual psychological differences or variations in patterns of early socialization. Likewise, social institutions such as the family, schools, and churches can be examined for their role in reducing or enhancing the likelihood of criminality among individuals subject to them.

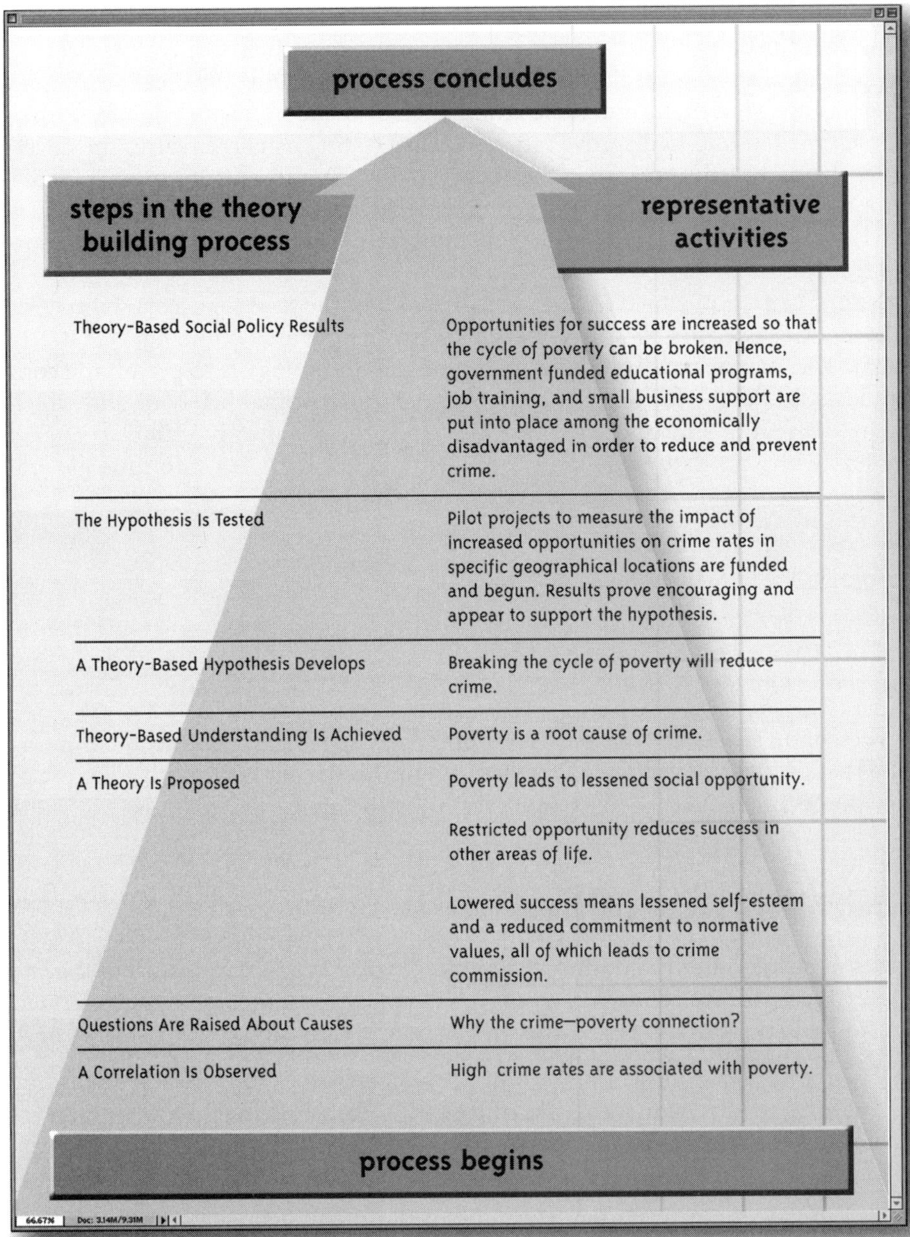

Figure 3-1 Steps in criminal justice theory building and social policy.

There is, however, probably no single cause of crime. Nonetheless, some theories of human behavior help us to understand why certain people engage in acts which society defines as criminal or deviant, while others do not.

A **theory** is a kind of model. Theories posit relationships, often of a causal sort, between events and things under study. So it is not unusual to hear someone suggest that "rap music causes crime." However, while everyone may have his or her own pet theory about crime, about the economy, or about child rearing, the word "theory" takes on a special meaning in the social sciences and in the study of criminal justice. Technically speaking, a complete theory is said to consist of a series of interrelated propositions which attempt to describe, explain, predict, and, ultimately, control some class of events. A theory's explanatory power derives primarily from its inherent logical consistency, and theories are tested by how well they describe and predict reality. In other words, a good theory provides relatively complete understanding of the phenomenon under study, while at the same time carefully made observations support predictions based upon it. A good theory fits the facts, and it stands up to continued scrutiny. Figure 3-1 diagrams the important aspects of theory creation in the social sciences and uses, by way of example, the well-known association between poverty and crime.

Theories, once created, must still be tested to tell whether or not they are true. As a consequence, modern criminology has become increasingly scientific. Generally accepted research designs—coupled with careful data gathering strategies and statistical techniques for data analysis—have yielded considerable confidence in certain explanations for crime, while at the same time tending to disprove others. Theory testing usually involves the development of **hypotheses** based upon what the theory under scrutiny would predict. Sadly, many contemporary theories of deviant and criminal behavior are far from complete, offering only limited ideas rather than complete explanations for the behavior in question. Others are difficult to test.

Theories of crime causation which have met rigorous scientific tests for acceptability provide the intellectual basis needed by policy-makers to create informed crime-control strategies. The ultimate goal of **research** and theory building in criminology is to permit the construction of models that allow for a better understanding of criminal behavior and which enhance the development of strategies intended to address the problem of crime.

The online textbook says that explanations of criminal behavior fall into nine general categories:

- Classical
- Psychobiological
- Sociological
- Conflict
- Emergent
- Biological
- Psychological
- Social-psychological
- Phenomenological

The differences among these approaches are summarized in Table 3-1 online. A tenth category might be that of **interdisciplinary theories**, or approaches that integrate a variety of theoretical viewpoints in an attempt to explain crime and violence.

The Classical School

Classical theories of crime causation dominated criminological thought for much of the late eighteenth and early nineteenth century. A recent rebirth of classical theory has been termed "neoclassical criminology." Most classical theories of crime causation, both old and new, make certain basic assumptions. Among them are:

- Crime is caused by the individual exercise of free will. Human beings are fundamentally rational, and most human behavior is the result of free will coupled with rational choice.
- Pain and pleasure are the two central determinants of human behavior.
- Crime disparages the quality of the bond which exists between individuals and society and is, therefore, an immoral form of behavior.
- Punishment, a necessary evil, is sometimes required to deter law violators and to serve as an example to others who would also violate the law.
- Crime prevention is possible through swift and certain punishment which offsets any gains to be had through criminal behavior.

For more information about classical theories and classical theorists, see Chapter 3 at *CJNow!* online.

Biological Theories

Most early biological theories of crime causation, which built upon inherited or bodily characteristics and features, made certain fundamental assumptions. Among them are:

- The basic determinants of human behavior, including criminal tendencies, are, to a considerable degree, constitutionally or genetically based.

- The basic determinants of human behavior, including criminality, may be passed on from generation to generation. In other words, a penchant for crime may be inherited.
- At least some human behavior is the result of biological propensities inherited from more primitive developmental stages in the evolutionary process. Some human beings may be further along the evolutionary ladder than others, and their behavior may reflect it.

For more Information on biological theories of crime causation and the theorists who developed them, see Chapter 3 at *CJNow!* online.

Psychobiological Theories

In recent years a more contemporary and sophisticated approach to biological theorizing about crime causation has arisen. Contemporary biochemical and physiological perspectives are sometimes termed psychobiology. The psychobiology of crime highlights the role of human DNA, environmental contaminants, nutrition, hormones, physical trauma (especially to the brain), and body chemistry in human cognition, feeling, and behavior. See Chapter 3 online for more information on chromosomes, biochemical imbalances, and heredity and the environment, and their roles in crime causation.

Psychological Theories

Psychological theories of crime causation have claimed a significant place in the criminological literature. Most psychological theories of crime make certain fundamental assumptions. Among them are:

- The individual is the primary unit of analysis.
- Personality is the major motivational element within individuals, since it is the seat of drives and the source of motives.
- Crimes result from inappropriately conditioned behavior or from abnormal, dysfunctional, or inappropriate mental processes within the personality.
- Defective or abnormal mental processes may have a variety of causes, including a diseased mind and inappropriate learning or improper conditioning—often occurring in early childhood.

One special emphasis of most crime-control strategies based upon psychological theories is the attempt to assess personal **dangerousness**, a process which involves psychological testing and other efforts intended to identify personality-based characteristics which may be predictive of interpersonal aggression. Although the ability to accurately predict future dangerousness is of great concern to today's policy makers, definitions of dangerousness are fraught with difficulty. As some authors have pointed out, "dangerousness is not an objective quality like obesity or brown eyes, rather it is an ascribed quality like trustworthiness."[4] Hence, dangerousness is not necessarily a personality trait which is stable or easily identifiable. Even if it were, recent studies[5] of criminal careers seem to show that involvement in crime decreases with age.

Learn more about psychological theories of crime causation, including **behavioral conditioning**, Freudian **psychoanalysis**, **psychopathy**, and the study of psychopathic mental conditions (**psychopathology**), **psychopaths** (also called **sociopaths**), **schizophrenics**, **psychosis** and **psychological profiling** in Chapter 3 online.

Sociological Theories

Sociological theories are largely an American contribution to the study of crime causation. In the 1920s and 1930s, the famous Chicago School of sociology explained criminality as a product of society's impact upon the individual. The structure of prevailing social arrangements, the interaction between individuals and groups, and the social environment were all seen as major determinants of criminal behavior.

Sociological perspectives on crime causation are quite diverse. Most such perspectives, however, build upon certain fundamental assumptions. Among them are:

- Social groups, social institutions, the arrangements of society, and social roles all provide the proper focus for criminological study.
- Group dynamics, group organization, and subgroup relationships form the causal nexus out of which crime develops.
- The structure of society, and the relative degree of social organization or social disorganization, are important factors contributing to the prevalence of criminal behavior.

All sociological perspectives on crime share the foregoing characteristics, but particular theories may give greater or lesser weight to the following aspects of social life:

- The clash of norms and values among variously socialized groups
- Socialization and the process of association between individuals
- The existence of subcultures and varying types of opportunities

Learn more about sociological theories of crime causation, including **social ecology**, **anomie**, **subcultural theory**, and **subcultures of violence** in Chapter 3 online. You may be especially interested in online Table 3-2, which shows various modes of personal adaptation to social conditions.

Social-Psychological Theories

While psychological approaches attempt to uncover aspects of the personality hidden even from the mind in which they reside, and sociological theories look to institutional arrangements in the social world to explain crime, social-psychological approaches to crime causation attempt to explain deviant behavior by relating it to the cultural environment in which the individual matures. Social-psychological theories add to the more structural analysis of sociological theories by including individual behavior and chosen responses to the social world.

Many social-psychological theories highlight the role of social learning. They build upon the premise that behavior—both "good" and "bad"—is learned and suggest that "bad" behavior can be unlearned. Social-psychological theories are probably the most attractive to contemporary policy makers because they demand that responsibility be placed upon the offender for actively participating in rehabilitation efforts and because they are consistent with popular cultural and religious values centered on teaching right from wrong.

Learn more about social-psychological theories and the researchers who promoted them online at *CJNow!* You may be especially interested in online Table 3-3, which explains the principles of **differential association.**

Restraint Theories

Some criminological theories focus less on causes than on constraints. Walter Reckless' (1899-1988) containment theory, for example, assumes that all of us are subject to inducements to crime.[6] Some of us resist these "pushes" toward criminal behavior, whereas others do not. The difference, according to Reckless, can be found in forces that contain behavior.

Another control theorist, Travis Hirschi, emphasizes the bond between individuals and society as the primary operative mechanism in his social control theory.[7] Hirschi identifies four components of that bond: 1) emotional attachments to significant others, 2) a commitment to appropriate lifestyles, 3) involvement or immersion in conventional values, and 4) a belief in the "correctness" of social obligations and the rules of the larger society.

Complementing restraint theory is the neutralization approach of Gresham Sykes and David Matza.[8] Sykes and Matza believed that most people drift into and out of criminal behavior but would not commit crime unless they had available to them techniques of neutralization. Such techniques are actually rationalizations which allow offenders to shed feelings of guilt and any sense of responsibility for their behavior. Learn more about restraint theories, social control, and techniques of neutralization in Chapter 3 online.

Conflict Theories

Basic to the **conflict perspective** is the belief that conflict is a fundamental aspect of social life itself and can never be fully resolved. At best, according to this perspective, formal agencies of social control merely coerce the unempowered or the disenfranchised to comply with the rules established by those in power. From the conflict point of view, laws become a tool of the powerful, useful in keeping others from wresting control over important social institutions. Social order, rather than being the result of any consensus, rests upon the exercise of power through law. The conflict perspective can be described in terms of four key elements:[9]

- Society is composed of diverse social groups, and diversity is based upon distinctions which people hold to be significant, such as gender, sexual orientation, social class, etc.
- Conflict among groups is unavoidable because of differing interests and differing values. Hence, conflict is inherent in social life.
- The fundamental nature of group conflict centers on the exercise of political power. Political power is the key to the accumulation of wealth and to other forms of power.
- Law is a tool of power and furthers the interests of those powerful enough to make it.

Radical Criminology

Radical criminology is a product of the 1960s and 1970s and, like so many other perspectives that developed around that time, places the blame for criminality and deviant behavior squarely upon officially sanctioned cultural and economic arrangements. Radical criminology recognizes that law itself is a tool of the powerful. The focus of radical criminology, however, is capitalism and the evils which capitalism is believed to entail. Radical criminologists, building upon the writings of Karl Marx, believe that the uneven distribution of wealth and power in society is the primary cause of criminal behavior, especially among those who were disenfranchised—or left out of the "American dream." Poverty and discrimination are seen to lead to frustration and pent-up hostilities that express themselves in murder, rape, theft, and other crimes. American radical criminology built upon the ideals of the 1960s and charged that the "establishment," controlled by the upper classes, perverted justice through the unequal application of judicial sanctions. **Peacemaking criminology**, an offshoot from the conflict perspective, holds that crime-control agencies and the citizens they serve should work together to alleviate social problems and human suffering and thus reduce crime. Learn more about radical criminology, conflict theory, and peacemaking criminology in Chapter 3 online.

The Phenomenological School

Phenomenological criminology is a perspective on crime causation that holds that the significance of criminal behavior varies depending upon one's point of view and is ultimately knowable only to those who participate in the crime (either as offender, victim, investigator, and so on). Central to this school of thought are the principles that:

- The significance of any behavior depends upon a social consensus about what that behavior "means."
- "Crime" is the product of an active process of interpretation and social definition.
- Continued criminal activity may be more a consequence of limited opportunities for acceptable behavior which are imposed upon individuals defined as "criminal" than it is a product of choice.

Learn more about phenomenological criminology, and its modern incarnation in **constitutive criminology** in Chapter 3 online.

Labeling Theory

Labeling theory, for example, became fashionable in the 1960s. Its popularity, however, may have been due more to the cultural environment into which it was introduced rather than to any inherent quality of the theory itself. The theory derives largely from a 1963 book by Howard Becker, entitled *Outsiders*. Becker pointed out that "criminality" is not a quality inherent in an act or in a person. Crime, said Becker, results from a social definition, through law, of unacceptable behavior. That definition arises through **moral enterprise**, by which groups on both sides of an issue debate and, eventually, legislate their notion of what is moral and what is not. Becker wrote, "the central fact about deviance [is that] it is created by society . . . . [S]ocial groups," he said, "create deviance by making the rules whose infraction constitutes deviance."[10] The criminal label, however, produces consequences for labeled individuals which may necessitate continued criminality and lead to what is called **secondary deviance**. Learn more about labeling theory in Chapter 3 online.

Emergent Theories

A number of new and exciting theories of crime and criminology hold promise for the future. Learn more about these perspectives, including **feminist criminology**, **postmodern criminology**, and **deconstructionist theories**, in Chapter 3 online.

What You Should Remember

- The online chapter describes theoretical explanations for crime. Most of the perspectives it discusses are grounded in biology, psychology, or sociology.
- Biological theories posit a genetic or a physiological basis for deviant and criminal behavior. The notion of a "weak" gene, which might predispose certain individuals toward criminal activity, has recently been expanded to include the impact of environmental contaminants, poor nutrition, and food additives on behavior. Studies of fraternal twins and chromosome structure have helped to lead biological theories into the modern day.
- Psychological explanations of crime are individualistic. Some psychoanalytical theories see offenders as sick; others claim merely that criminal behavior is a type of conditioned response. The stimulus-response model depicts criminal behavior as the consequence of a conditioning process which extends over the entire lifespan of an individual.
- Sociological theories hold that the individual is a product of the environment and constitute today's perspective of choice. These theories emphasize the role of social structure, inequality, and socialization in generating criminality.
- An integrated perspective, which recognizes that human behavior results from a mix of biology, mental processes, and acquired traits, holds much future promise. As a consequence, our understanding of crime causation seems headed toward the day when a "unified theory" of conduct will draw upon many types of explanations in order to interpret the whole range of human behavior, including crime.

LIBRARY EXTRAS!

Library Extras! are suggested readings that are available digitally to readers of this guide. They may be accessed at the *CJNow!* Web site.

Library Extra! 3-1. *Crime Prevention Through Environmental Design* (NIJ).

Library Extra! 3-2. *Critical Criminal Justice Issues: Task Force Reports from the American Society of Criminology* (NIJ, 1997).

Library Extra! 3-3. *Mapping Out Crime: Providing 21st Century Tools For Safe Communities* (USDOJ, July 1999).

Library Extra! 3-4. *Physical Environment and Crime* (NIJ, 1996).

Library Extra! 3-5. *Project on Human Development in Chicago Neighborhoods* (NIJ, 1997).

Library Extra! 3-6. *The Reintegrative Shaming Experiments* (Australian Institute of Criminology, 1997).

ENDNOTES

[1] Deborah Sharp, "'Vampire Rapist' Case Points Anew to Dilemma," *USA Today*, August 8, 1996, p. 3A.

[2] This and other statistics in these opening paragraphs come from Jonathan Wright, "Media Are Mixed Blessing, Criminologists Say," Reuters wire services, May 2, 1995.

[3] *U.S. News*/UCLA Survey on the Media and Violence, reported in "Hollywood: Right Face," *U.S. News and World Report*, May 15, 1995, p. 71.

[4] Jill Peay, "Dangerousness—Ascription or Description," in M. P. Feldman, ed., *Developments in the Study of Criminal Behavior*, Vol. Two: *Violence* (New York: John Wiley, 1982), p. 211, citing N. Walker, "Dangerous People," *International Journal of Law and Psychiatry*, Vol. 1 (1978), pp. 37-50.

[5] See, for example, Michael Gottfredson and Travis Hirschi, *A General Theory of Crime* (Stanford, CA: Stanford University Press, 1990), and Travis Hirschi and Michael Gottfredson, "Age and the Explanation of Crime," *American Journal of Sociology*, Vol. 89 (1983), pp. 552-584.

[6] Walter C. Reckless, *The Crime Problem*, 4th ed. (New York: Appleton-Century-Crofts, 1961).

[7] Travis Hirschi, *Causes of Delinquency* (Berkeley: University of California Press, 1969).

[8] Gresham Sykes and David Matza, "Techniques of Neutralization: A Theory of Delinquency," *American Sociological Review*, Vol. 22 (1957), pp. 664-670.

[9] Adapted from Raymond Michalowski, "Perspectives and Paradigm: Structuring Criminological Thought," in Robert F. Meier, ed., *Theory in Criminology* (Beverly Hills, CA: Sage, 1977).

[10] Howard Becker, *Outsiders: Studies in the Sociology of Deviance* (New York: The Free Press, 1963), pp. 8-9.

Chapter 4

quick view

<< criminal law >>

Outline

- Sources of Modern Criminal Law
- The Development of Law
- The Rule of Law
- Purposes of the Law
- Types of Law
- General Categories of Crime
- General Features of Crime
- Elements of a Specific Criminal Offense
- Types of Defenses to a Criminal Charge

What You Should Learn

- The history, nature, and purposes of the criminal law.
- The concept of natural law, and the differences between *mala in se* and *mala prohibita* offenses.
- The nature of the rule of law and its purpose in Western democratic societies.
- Various categories or types of law, and the purpose of each.
- Five categories of criminal law violations.
- The eight general features of crime.
- The concept of "*corpus delicti*."
- The four broad categories of defenses to crime that our legal system recognizes.
- The names of at least five new and emerging innovative defenses.
- The definitions of key terms that appear in boldface throughout this *Quick View* chapter. Definitions can be found online at http://www.cjnowonline.com.

Hear the author introduce this chapter at *CJNow!* online.

Sources of Modern Criminal Law

Twenty years ago, as South American jungles were being cleared to make way for farmers and other settlers, a group of mercenaries brutally attacked and wiped out a small tribe of local Indians. About two dozen native men, women, and children were either hacked to death with machetes or shot. The Indians had refused to give up their land and would not move. At their arrest the killers uttered something that, to our ears, sounds frightening: "How can you arrest us?" they said. "We didn't know it was illegal to kill Indians!"

These men killed many people. But, they claimed, they were ignorant of the fact that the law forbade such a thing. In this case, these killers didn't consider their victims "human." It may seem obvious to us that what they had done was commit murder, but to them it was something else. Nevertheless, their ignorance of the law was rejected as a defense at their trial, and they were convicted of murder. All received lengthy prison sentences.

The men in this story were hardly literate, with almost no formal education. They knew very little about the law and, apparently, even less about basic moral principles. We, on the other hand, living in a modern society with highly developed means of communication, much formal schooling, and a large workforce of professionals skilled in interpreting the law, usually know what the law *says*. But do we know what the law really *is*? The job of this *Quick View* chapter is to discuss the law both as a product of rule creation and as a guide for behavior. We will also examine criminal law in some detail, as well as discuss defenses commonly used by defendants charged with violations of the criminal law.

The Nature of Law

Practically speaking, **laws** regulate relationships among people and also among parties (such as agencies of government and individuals). Most of us would probably agree that the law is whatever legislators, through the exercise of their politically sanctioned wisdom, tell us it is. If we hold to that belief, we would expect to be able to find the law unambiguously specified in a set of books or codes. As we shall see, however, such is not always the case.

The laws of our nation, or of a state, are found in **statutory provisions** and constitutional enactments, as well as in hundreds of years of rulings by courts at all levels. According to the authoritative *Black's Law Dictionary*, the word *law* "generally contemplates both statutory and **case law**."[1] If "the law" could be found entirely ensconced in written legal codes, it would be plain to nearly everyone, and we would need far fewer lawyers than we find practicing today. But some laws (in the sense of precedents established by courts) do not exist "on the books," and even those that do are open to interpretation.

The Development of Law

Modern law is the result of a long evolution of legal principles (see Table 4-1 online). A complete and accurate understanding of today's criminal law can only be had by someone who is informed as to both its history and its philosophical foundation.

The U.S. Constitution is one of the most significant and enduring wellsprings of our modern criminal law. The Constitution was created through a long process of debate by the federal Constitutional Convention meeting in Philadelphia in 1787. The Constitution is the final authority in all questions pertaining to the rights of individuals, the power of the federal government and the states to create laws and prosecute offenders, and the limits of punishments which can be imposed for law violations.

Although the Constitution does not itself contain many specific prohibitions on behavior, it is the final authority in deciding whether new and existing laws are acceptable according to the ideals upon which our country is founded. Historically, under the principle of due process, embodied in the Fifth, Sixth, and Fourteenth Amendments, it has also served to guide justices in gauging the merits of citizens' claims concerning the handling of their cases by the agencies of justice.

Natural law, another wellspring of modern criminal law, comes from outside the social group and is thought to be knowable through some form of revelation, intuition, reason, or prophecy. Natural law lends credence to the belief that certain actions are wrong in themselves. These behaviors are called ***mala in se***, a Latin term which generally includes crimes against humanity (such as the planned extermination of much of the Jewish population in parts of Nazi-controlled Europe during World War II) and serious personal crimes, including murder, rape, assault, arson, and other crimes of violence. Crimes that fall outside of the "natural" category are called ***mala prohibita***, meaning that they are wrong only because they are prohibited by the law (*malum prohibitum* is the term that refers to one such crime). Poaching on the king's land is an example of what was a *mala prohibita* crime under English common law. Most crimes which fall under the heading of "morals offenses" today might be called *mala prohibita*. Such offenses include prostitution, gambling, and illicit drug use.

Visit *CJNow!* online to learn more about some of the historical sources of contemporary law including the Code of Hammurabi, early Roman law, English common law, the Magna Carta, natural law, and the U.S. Constitution.

The Rule of Law

The social, economic, and political stability of any society depends largely upon the development and institutionalization of a predictable system of laws. Western democratic societies adhere to the **rule of law**, which is sometimes also referred to as "the supremacy of law."

The rule of law concept centers around the belief that an orderly society must be governed by established principles and known codes that are applied uniformly and fairly to all of its members. Under the rule of law no one is above the law, and those who enforce the law must abide by it.

The rule of law has been called "the greatest political achievement of our culture." Without it few other human achievements—especially those which require the efforts of a large number of people working together in coordinated fashion—would be possible.

President John F. Kennedy eloquently explained the rule of law, saying: "Americans are free to disagree with the law, but not to disobey it; for a government of laws and not of men, no man, however prominent and powerful, no mob, however unruly or boisterous, is entitled to defy a court of law." To learn more about the rule of law visit *CJNow!* online.

Purposes of the Law

Laws channel human behavior while they simultaneously constrain it, and they empower individuals while making the behavior of others predictable. This first, and most significant, purpose of the law can be simply stated: Laws support social order.

Laws also serve a variety of other purposes. They ensure that the philosophical, moral, and economic perspectives of their creators are protected and made credible. They maintain values and uphold established patterns of social privilege. They sustain existing power relationships, and, finally, they support a system for the punishment and rehabilitation of offenders. Modifications of the law, when gradually induced, promote orderly change in the rest of society.

Once law has been created it is generally slow to change because it is built upon years of tradition. The law can be thought of as a force which supports social order but which is opposed to rapid social change. When law facilitates change, that change usually proceeds in an orderly and deliberate fashion. Revolutions, on the other hand, produce near-instantaneous legal changes, but bring with them massive social disorder. One of the greatest legal scholars of the twentieth century, **Roscoe Pound** (1870–1964), described law as a useful tool for intentional social engineering.[2] The law can be used as a tool, Pound said, to meet the demands of men and women living together in society. Intentional changes in the law, said Pound, can result in predictable and preplanned changes in the structure and functioning of society. Pound distilled his ideas into a set of **jural postulates**. Such postulates, claimed Pound, form the basis of all law because they reflect shared needs. His ideas formed a kind of **jurisprudence**, or philosophy of law.[3] Visit *CJNow!* online to learn more about Roscoe Pound's jural postulates.

Opposed to Pound's theory of consensus is another view which sees the law as a tool of powerful individuals and groups acting in their own interests—and often in conflict with one another. Known as conflict theory, this perspective has its roots in the writings of **Karl Marx**, who explained all of social history as the result of an ongoing conflict between the "haves" and the "have-nots."

Types of Law

"Criminal" and "civil" law are the best-known types of modern law. However, scholars and philosophers have drawn numerous distinctions between categories of the law that rest upon their source, intent, and application. Laws in modern societies can be usefully described in terms of the following groups:

- Criminal law or penal law
- Civil law or tort law
- Administrative law
- Case law or the law of precedent
- Procedural law

This typology is helpful in understanding and thinking about the law, and you can learn more about each type of law at *CJNow!* online.

General Categories Of Crime

Violations of the criminal law can be of many different types and vary in severity. Five categories of violation are especially important, and details about each are available at the *CJNow!* Web site. Those five categories are:

- Felonies
- Misdemeanors
- Offenses
- Treason
- Inchoate offenses

Felonies are serious crimes. The felony category includes crimes such as murder, rape, aggravated assault, robbery, burglary, arson, and so on. **Misdemeanors** are relatively minor crimes, consisting of offenses such as petty theft (the theft of items of little worth), simple assault (in which the victim suffers no serious injury and in which none was intended), breaking and entering, the possession of burglary tools, disorderly conduct, disturbing the peace, filing a false crime report, and writing bad checks (although the amount for which the check is written may determine the classification of this offense). In general, misdemeanors can be thought of as any crime punishable by a year or less in prison. The term **offense**, when used to describe a type of violation of the criminal law, refers to minor violations of the law which are less serious than misdemeanors. When the term is used in that sense, it refers to such things as jaywalking, spitting on the sidewalk, littering, and certain traffic violations, including the failure to wear a seat belt. Another word used to describe such minor law violations is **infraction**.

Treason, our fourth category, has been defined as "the act of a U.S. citizen's helping a foreign government to overthrow, make war against, or seriously injure the United States."[4] Treason is also a crime under the laws of most states. Hence, treason can be more generally defined as the attempt to overthrow the government of the society of which one is a member. **Espionage**, an offense akin to treason, refers to the "gathering, transmitting, or losing"[5] of information related to the national defense in such a manner that the information becomes available to enemies of the United States and may be used to their advantage. The final category, **inchoate offense**, are those which have not yet been fully carried out. Conspiracies are an example. When a person conspires to commit a crime, any action undertaken in furtherance of the conspiracy is generally regarded as a sufficient basis for arrest and prosecution. Learn more at *CJNow!* online.

General Features of Crime

From the perspective of Western jurisprudence, all crimes can be said to share certain features, and the notion of crime itself can be said to rest upon such general principles. Taken together, these features, which are described in detail at the *CJNow!* Web site, comprise the legal essence of the concept of crime. Conventional legal wisdom holds that the essence of crime consists of three conjoined elements: 1) the criminal act (which, in legal parlance is termed the ***actus reus***), 2) a culpable mental state known as a "guilty mind" (***mens rea***), and 3) a **concurrence** of the two. Hence, as we shall see in the following few pages, the essence of criminal conduct consists of a concurrence of a criminal act with a culpable mental state.

A special category of crimes, called **strict liability** offenses, requires no culpable mental state and presents a significant exception to the principle that all crimes require a conjunction of *actus reus* and *mens rea*. Strict liability offenses (also called "absolute liability offenses") make it a crime simply to *do* something, even if the offender has no intention of violating the law. Strict liability is philosophically based upon the presumption that causing harm is in itself blameworthy, regardless of the actor's intent. Statutory rape provides an example of the concept of strict liability. The crime of statutory rape generally occurs between two consenting individuals and requires only that the offender have sexual intercourse with a person under the age of legal consent. Statutes describing the crime routinely avoid any mention of a culpable mental state. In many jurisdictions it matters little in the crime of statutory rape that the "perpetrator" knew the exact age of the "victim" or that the "victim" lied about his or her age or may have given consent, since such laws are "an attempt to prevent the sexual exploitation of persons deemed legally incapable of giving consent."[6]

Some scholars contend that these three features of crime—*actus reus, mens rea,* and concurrence—are sufficient to constitute the essence of the legal concept of crime. Other scholars, however, see modern Western law as more complex. They argue that recognition of five additional principles is necessary to fully appreciate contemporary understandings of crime. These five principles are: 1) **causation**, 2) a resulting **harm**, 3) the principle of **legality**, 4) the principle of **punishment**, and 5) necessary **attendant circumstances**. Detailed descriptions of each principle are available at the *CJNow!* online site.

Elements of a Specific Criminal Offense

The principles that constitute the *general* notion of crime differ from those particular statutory **elements** that describe a *specific* crime. Written laws specify exactly what conditions are necessary for a person to be charged in a given instance of criminal activity, and they do so for every particular offense. Hence, elements of a crime are specific legal aspects of a criminal offense which must be proven by the prosecution in order to obtain a conviction. The crime of first-degree murder, for example, in almost every jurisdiction in the United States involves four quite distinct elements:

1. An unlawful killing
2. Of a human being
3. Intentionally
4. With planning (or "malice aforethought")

The elements of any specific crime are the statutory minimum without which that crime cannot be said to have occurred. In any case that goes to trial, the task of the prosecution is to prove that all the elements were indeed present and that the accused was ultimately responsible for producing them. Since statutes differ between jurisdictions, the specific elements of a particular crime, such as murder, may vary. In order to convict a defendant of a particular crime, prosecutors must prove to a judge or jury that all the required statutory elements are present. If even one element of an offense cannot be established beyond a reasonable doubt, criminal liability will not have been demonstrated, and the defendant will be found not guilty.

The *Corpus Delicti* of a Crime

The term ***corpus delicti*** literally means "body of crime." The term is often confused with the statutory elements of a crime. Sometimes the concept is mistakenly thought to mean the body of a murder victim or some other physical result of criminal activity. It actually means something quite different. Simply put, the *corpus delicti* of a crime is the fact of its having been actually committed.

One way to understand the concept of *corpus delicti* is to realize that a person cannot be tried for a crime unless it can first be shown that the offense has, in fact, occurred. In other words, to establish the *corpus delicti* of a crime, the state has to demonstrate that a criminal law has been violated and that someone violated it. Hence, there are only two aspects to the *corpus delicti* of an offense: 1) that a certain result has been produced and 2) that a person is criminally responsible for its production. As one court said, "*[c]orpus delicti* consists of a showing of 1) the occurrence of the specific kind of injury and 2) someone's criminal act as the cause of the injury."[7] So, for example, the crime of larceny requires proof that the property of another has been stolen—that is, unlawfully taken by someone whose intent it was to permanently deprive the owner of its possession.[8] Hence, evidence offered to prove the *corpus delicti* in a trial for larceny is insufficient where the evidence fails to prove that any property has been stolen or where property found in a defendant's possession cannot be identified as having been stolen. Similarly, "[i]n an arson case, the *corpus delicti* consists of: 1) a burned building or other property, and 2) some criminal agency which caused the burning . . . In other words, the *corpus delicti* includes not only the fact of burning, but it must also appear that the burning was by the willful act of some person, and not as a result of a natural or accidental cause . . . ."[9]

The identity of the perpetrator is not an element of the *corpus delicti* of an offense. Hence, the fact that a crime has occurred can be established without having any idea who committed it or even why it was committed. For an expanded discussion of the elements of a crime and of the concept of *corpus delicti*, visit *CJNow!* online.

Types of Defenses to a Criminal Charge

When a person is charged with a crime, he or she typically presents some defense. A **defense** consists of evidence and arguments offered by a defendant and his or her attorneys to show why that person should not be held liable for a criminal charge. Our legal system generally recognizes four broad categories of defenses: 1) **alibi**, 2) **justifications**, 3) **excuses**, and 4) **procedural defenses**. An alibi, if shown to be valid, means that the defendant could not have committed the crime in question because he or she was somewhere else (and generally with someone else) at the time of the crime. When a defendant offers a **justification** as a defense, he or she admits committing the act in question, but claims that it was necessary in order to avoid some greater evil. A defendant who offers an **excuse** as a defense, on the other hand, claims that some personal condition or circumstance at the time of the act was such that he or she should not be held accountable under the criminal law. Procedural defenses make the claim that the defendant was in some significant way discriminated against in the justice process or that some important aspect of official procedure was not properly followed in the investigation or prosecution of the crime charged. Finally, a number of innovative defense strategies have emerged in recent years and will be discussed as a fifth category—although, technically speaking, each of the innovative defenses we shall discuss could be classified as a justification or as an excuse. Table 4-2, which can be found online, lists the types of defenses that fall into our five categories. Each is discussed in detail online.

Alibi is different from all of the other defenses because it is based upon the premise that the defendant is truly innocent.[10] The defense of alibi denies that the defendant committed the act in question. All of the other defenses grant that the defendant committed the act, but they deny that he or she should be held criminally responsible. While justifications and excuses may produce findings of "not guilty," the defense of alibi claims outright innocence.

As defenses, justifications claim a kind of moral high ground. Justifications may be offered by people who find themselves facing a choice between a "lesser of two evils." Generally speaking, conduct which a person believes is necessary in order to avoid a harm or evil to him- or herself or to avoid harm to another is justifiable if the harm or evil to be avoided is greater than that which the law defining the offense seeks to avoid. So, for example, a fireman might set a controlled fire in order to create a firebreak to head off a conflagration threatening a community. While intentionally setting a fire may constitute arson, doing so in order to save a town may be justifiable behavior in the eyes of the community and in the eyes of the law. Included under the broad category of "justifications" are 1.) self-defense, 2.) the defense of others, 3.) defense of home and property, 4.) necessity, .5) consent, and 6.) resisting unlawful arrest.

An excuse, in contrast to a justification, does not claim that the conduct in question is justified by the situation nor that it is moral. An excuse claims, rather, that the actor who engaged in the unlawful behavior was, at the time, not legally responsible for his or her actions and should not be held accountable under the law. So, for example, a person who assaults a police officer thinking that the officer is really a disguised "space alien" who has come to abduct him may be found "not guilty" of the charge of assault and battery by reason of insanity. Actions for which excuses are offered do not morally outweigh the wrong committed, but criminal liability may still be negated on the basis of some personal disability of the actor or because of some special circumstances that characterize the situation. Excuses recognized by the law include: 1) duress, 2) age, 3) mistake, 4) involuntary intoxication, 5) unconsciousness, 6) provocation, 7) insanity, and 8) diminished responsibility.

It is important to realize that, for purposes of the criminal law, insanity is a legal definition and not a psychiatric one. Legal definitions of insanity often have very little to do with psychological or psychiatric understandings of mental illness. Legal insanity is a concept developed over time to meet the needs of the judicial system in assigning guilt or innocence to particular defendants. It is not primarily concerned with understanding the origins of mental pathology or with its treatment, as is the idea of mental illness in psychiatry. As a consequence, medical conceptions of mental illness do not always fit well into the legal categories created by courts and legislators to deal with the phenomenon. The differences between psychiatric and legal conceptualizations of insanity often lead to disagreements among expert witnesses who, in criminal court, may appear to provide conflicting testimony as to the sanity of a defendant. Insanity defenses in use today include the the **M'Naghten rule**, the **irresistible impulse test**, the **Durham rule**, the **Brawner rule** and the **substantial capacity test**. **Guilty but insane**, **temporary insanity**, and **diminished capacity** are special issues related to the concept of legal insanity. Learn more about each of these concepts at *Criminal Justice Today* online.

Procedural defenses, or those which constitute the fourth major defense category, make the claim that defendants were in some manner discriminated against in the justice process or that some important aspect of official procedure was not properly followed and that, as a result, they should be released from any criminal liability. Procedural defenses include 1) **entrapment**, 2) **double jeopardy**, 3) ***collateral estoppel***, 4) **selective prosecution**, 5) **denial of speedy trial**, 6) **prosecutorial misconduct**, and 7) **police fraud.**

A final, and somewhat different, defense category that of innovative defenses, contains unique defense strategies that can be technically subsumed under the broader categories of justifications or excuses. Innovative defenses deserve separate consideration, however, because each is virtually new and relatively untried. The unique and emerging character of these novel defenses, however, makes noting them worthwhile. Innovative defenses include: 1) the **abuse defense**, which encompasses Battered Women's Syndrome (BWS), 2) **premenstrual stress syndrome** (PMS), 3) other biological defenses, 4) **black rage**, and 5) **urban survival syndrome.** For further discussion of each of the defenses identified here visit *CJNow!* online.

What You Should Remember

- Modern law is the result of a long evolution of legal principles. Laws regulate relationships among people and among parties. The laws of our nation, or of a state, are found in statutory provisions and constitutional enactments, as well as in hundreds of years of rulings by courts at all levels.
- Natural law comes from outside the social group and is thought to be knowable through some form of revelation, intuition, reason, or prophecy. Actions considered to be wrong in themselves are called *mala in se*. Crimes that fall outside of the "natural" category are called *mala prohibita*, meaning that they are wrong only because they are prohibited by the law
- The rule of law concept centers around the belief that an orderly society must be governed by established principles and known codes which are applied uniformly and fairly to all of its members. Under the rule of law no one is above the law, and those who enforce the law must abide by it.
- The different categories or types of law are: 1) criminal or penal law, 2) civil or tort law, 3) administrative law, 4) case law or the law of precedent, and 5) procedural law.
- The five categories of violations of the criminal law are: 1) felonies, 2) misdemeanors, 3) offenses, 4) treason, and 5) inchoate offenses.
- The eight general features of crime are: 1) the criminal act (*actus reus*), 2) a guilty mind (*mens rea*), 3) a concurrence of *actus reus* and *mens rea*, 4) causation, 5) harm, 6) legality, 7) punishment, and 8) attendant circumstances.
- *Corpus delicti* means "body of crime." The *corpus delicti* of a crime is the fact of its having been actually committed.
- The four broad categories of defenses to crime that our legal system recognizes are: 1) alibi, 2) justifications, 3) excuses, and 4) procedural defenses.
- Innovative offenses, while technically classifiable under justifications or excuses, are unique because they are virtually new and untried. Innovative defenses include: 1) the abuse defense, which encompasses Battered Women's Syndrome (BWS), 2) premenstrual stress syndrome (PMS), 3) other biological defenses, 4) black rage, and 5) urban survival syndrome.

LIBRARY EXTRAS!

Library Extras! are suggested readings that are available digitally to readers of this guide. They may be accessed at the *CJNow!* Web site.

Library Extra! 4-1. The *Cox Report* on Chinese spying (U.S. Congress, 1999).

Library Extra! 4-2. *The National Institute of Justice Journal* (current issue).

Library Extra! 4-3. *The National Institute of Justice Journal* (prior issue).

Library Extra! 4-4. *Tort Cases in Large Counties* (BJS, 1995).

ENDNOTES

[1] Henry Campbell Black, Joseph R. Nolan, and Jacqueline M. Nolan-Haley, *Black's Law Dictionary*, 6th ed. (St. Paul, MN: West, 1990), p. 884.

[2] Roscoe Pound, *Social Control Through the Law* (Hamden, CT: Archon, 1968), pp. 64–65.

[3] See William Chambliss and Robert Seidman, *Law, Order, and Power* (Reading, MA: Addison-Wesley, 1971), pp. 141–142, 154.

[4] Daniel Oran, *Oran's Dictionary of the Law* (St. Paul, MN: West, 1983).

[5] Black, Nolan, and Nolan-Harley, *Black's Law Dictionary*, 6th ed.

[6] *State* v. *Stiffler*, 763 P.2d. 308 (Idaho App. 1988).

[7] *Willoughby* v. *State* (1990), Ind., 552 N.E.2d 462, 466.

[8] See *Maughs* v. *Commonwealth*, 181 Va. 117, 120, 23 S.E.2d 784, 786 (1943).

[9] See *State* v. *Stephenson*, Opinion No. 24403 (South Carolina, 1996), and *State* v. *Blocker*, 205 S.C. 303, 31 S.E.2d 908 (1944).

[10] Patrick L. McCloskey and Ronald L. Schoenberg, *Criminal Law Deskbook* (New York: Matthew Bender, 1988), Section 20.03[13].

Part 2

<< policing >>

Chapter 5

POLICING: HISTORY AND STRUCTURE

Chapter 6

POLICE MANAGEMENT

Chapter 7

POLICING: LEGAL ASPECTS

Chapter 5

quick view

<< policing: history and structure >>

Outline

- Historical Development of the Police
- American Law Enforcement Today: From the Federal to the Local Level
- Private Protective Services

What You Should Learn

- The basic purposes of policing in democratic societies.
- An overview of the historical development of the police in this country, including the impact of the Prohibition era on American policing.
- The nature, history, and purpose of the Law Enforcement Assistance Administration (LEAA) and its impact on American policing.

- The nature of the Kansas City police experiments, and the significance they hold for law enforcement practice today.
- The three major levels of public law enforcement in the United States today.
- The identity of a fourth, but non-public, level of law enforcement activity in the United States, and the significance it may hold for the future.
- The relationship of the private security industry in this country to public policing, and the predictions the online chapter makes about the future of private security.
- The definitions of key terms that appear in boldface throughout this *Quick View* chapter. Definitions can be found online at http://www.cjnowonline.com.

Hear the author introduce this chapter at *CJNow!* online.

Historical Development of the Police

Police tactics and strategy have changed substantially since historical times, and many different kinds of police agencies—some of them highly specialized—function within the modern criminal justice system. Even so, the basic purposes of policing in democratic societies remain the same: 1) to prevent and investigate crimes, 2) to apprehend offenders, 3) to help ensure domestic peace and tranquillity, and 4) to enforce and support the laws (especially the criminal laws) of the society of which the police are a part.

The New Police

In 1829 Sir Robert Peel, who was later to become prime minister of England, formed what many have hailed as the world's first modern police force. Passage of the Metropolitan Police Act that same year allocated the resources for Peel's force of 1,000 uniformed, hand-picked men. The London Metropolitan Police, also known simply as the "new police," soon became a model for police forces around the world. The Metropolitan Police were quickly dubbed "**Bobbies**," after their founder. London's Bobbies were organized around two principles: the belief that it was possible to discourage crime and the practice of preventive patrol.

Policing America's Early Cities

Peel's new police were closely studied by American leaders. In 1844 New York's separate day and night forces were combined into the New York City Police Department. Boston followed suit in 1855 with a similar merging of forces. Further advances in American policing, however, were precluded by the Civil War. Southern cities captured in the war found themselves under martial law and subject to policing by the military.

During the early 1900s, automobiles, telephones, and radios all had their impact on the American police. Teddy Roosevelt, 26th president of the United States, pioneered his career by serving as a police commissioner in New York City from 1895 to 1897. While there, he promoted use of a call box system of telephones, which allowed citizens to report crimes rapidly and made it possible for officers to call quickly for assistance. As president, Roosevelt later helped to organize the FBI, which was then called the Bureau of Investigation. The FBI became a national investigative service designed to quickly identify and apprehend offenders charged with a growing list of federal offenses.

Prohibition and Police Corruption

A dark period began for American law enforcement agencies in 1920 with passage of a constitutional prohibition against all forms of alcoholic beverages. Until prohibition was repealed in 1933, most parts of the country were rife with criminal activity—much of it supporting the trade in bootlegged liquor. Massive wealth in the hands of law violators greatly increased the potential for corruption among police officials, some of whom were "paid off" to support bootlegging operations. In 1931 the **Wickersham Commission**, officially called the National Commission on Law Observance and Enforcement, recognized that prohibition was unenforceable and reported that it carried a great potential for police corruption.[1]

The Last Half-Century

The 1960s and 1970s were a period which saw intense public and professional scrutiny of police operations, from day-to-day enforcement decisions to administrative organization and police community relations. In 1967 the President's Commission on Law Enforcement and the Administration of Justice issued its report, *The Challenge of Crime in a Free Society*,[2] which found that the police were often interpersonally isolated from the communities they served. In 1973 the National Advisory Commission on Criminal Justice Standards and Goals[3] issued a comprehensive report detailing strategies for attacking and preventing crime and for increasing the quality of law enforcement efforts at all levels. Included in the report was a call for greater participation in police work by women and ethnic minorities and the recommendation that a college degree should become a basic prerequisite for police employment by the 1980s.

Scientific Police Management

In 1969 the Law Enforcement Assistance Administration (**LEAA**) was formed to assist police forces across the nation in acquiring the latest in technology and enforcement methods. LEAA-sponsored research during the period 1969–1982 has left a wealth of scientific findings of relevance to police administration and, more importantly, has established a tradition of program evaluation within police management circles. This tradition is known as **scientific police management**. In 1973 LEAA established the **Exemplary Projects Program** designed to recognize outstanding innovative efforts to combat crime and provide assistance to crime victims, so that such initiatives might serve as models for the nation. Although LEAA funding ended long ago, federal support for criminal justice research and evaluation continues today under the National Institute of Justice (NIJ) and the Bureau of Justice Statistics (BJS), both parts of the Office of Justice Assistance, Research, and Statistics (OJARS).

The Kansas City Experiment

The most famous application of social research principles to police management was the Kansas City Preventive Patrol Experiment,[4] the results of which were published in 1974. Records of "preventable crimes," those toward which the activities of patrol were oriented—like burglary, robbery, auto theft, larceny, and vandalism—showed no significant differences in rate of occurrence between experimental beats in which standard patrol practices were used and in those where the police did not patrol. Similarly, citizens didn't seem to notice the change in patrol patterns in the areas where patrol frequency had been changed. Surveys conducted at the conclusion of the experiment also showed no difference among citizens in the experimental areas as to their fear of crime before and after the study. A second Kansas City study focused on police response time.[5] It found that even consistently fast police response to citizen reports of crime had little effect on either citizen satisfaction with the police or on the arrest of suspects. The Kansas City study, along with other scientific studies of special significance to law enforcement, are summarized in Table 5-1 online.

Following the Kansas City studies **directed patrol** activities developed. One form of directed patrol varies the number of officers involved in patrolling according to time of day or on the basis of frequency of reported crimes within areas. The idea behind directed patrol is to put the most officers where and when crime is most prevalent.

American Law Enforcement Today: From the Federal to the Local Level

The organization of American law enforcement has been called the most complex in the world. Three major legislative and judicial jurisdictions exist in the United States—federal, state, and local—and each has created a variety of police agencies to enforce its laws. Unfortunately, there has been little uniformity among jurisdictions as to the naming, function, or authority of enforcement agencies.

Federal Law Enforcement Agencies

There are 21 separate federal law enforcement agencies distributed among eight U.S. government departments. In addition to the enforcement agencies listed in Table 5-2 online, dozens of other federal government offices are involved in enforcement activities through inspections, regulation, and control activities.

State-Level Agencies

Most state police agencies were created in the late 1800s or early 1900s to meet specific needs brought about by state-level legislation. The Texas Rangers, for example, an organization that was created in 1835 (before Texas gained statehood), functioned as a military organization responsible for patrolling the Republic's borders. Apprehension of Mexican cattle rustlers was one of its main concerns.[6] Massachusetts, targeting vice control, was the second state to create a law enforcement agency. The Pennsylvania Constabulary, known today as the Pennsylvania State Police, has been called the "first modern state police agency."[7] Today, a wide diversity of policing agencies exist at the state level. Table 5-3 online provides a list of typical state-sponsored law enforcement agencies.

Local Agencies

The term *local police* encompasses agencies of wide variety. Municipal departments, rural sheriff's departments, and specialized groups such as campus police and transit police can all be grouped under the "local" rubric. Local police agencies employ approximately 922,000 persons (423,000 of them are sworn) throughout the U.S. today.[8] Large municipal departments are highly visible because of their huge size, vast budgetary allotments, and innovative programs. The nation's largest law enforcement agency, the New York City Police Department, has about 44,000 full-time employees, including 36,813 full-time sworn officers.[9] Far greater in number, however, are local small-town and county sheriff's departments. There are approximately 13,580 municipal police departments, and 3,100 sheriff's departments in the United States.[10] A list of police agencies variously found at the local level is shown in Table 5-4 online.

Private Protective Services

Private police constitute a fourth level of enforcement activity in the United States today. Public police are employed by the government and enforce public laws. Private security personnel work for corporate employers and secure private interests. According to the Hallcrest Report II,[11] a major government-sponsored analysis of the private security industry, more people are employed in private security than in all local, state, and federal police agencies combined. Table 5-5 online lists the ten largest private security agencies in business today, along with some of the types of services they offer.

What You Should Remember

- The basic purposes of policing in democratic societies are: 1) to prevent and investigate crimes, 2) to apprehend offenders, 3) to help ensure domestic peace and tranquility, and 4) to enforce and support the laws (especially the criminal laws) of the society of which the police are a part.
- The style of policing characteristic of contemporary American society had its start in 1829, with Sir Robert Peel's Metropolitan Police in London, England. Peel's police wore uniforms and patrolled beats. The Prohibition era in America led to increased corruption among police departments nationwide, a fact recognized by the 1931 Wickersham Commission report.

- The Law Enforcement Assistance Administration (LEAA) had a significant impact on American policing during the 1970s with its emphasis on scientific studies of the police and its contribution to the development of principles of scientific police management.
- The Kansas City police experiments questioned traditional ideas about police patrol and calls for service, leading to innovations in both areas.
- Three levels of public law enforcement can be found today in local, state, and national law enforcement organizations.
- Private police constitute a fourth level of enforcement activity in the United States today. The number of private police employees is growing rapidly throughout the country and will soon substantially exceed the number of officers employed in the public sector.
- Private security personnel work for corporate employers and protect private interests. Private security is now undergoing many of the changes which have already occurred in other law enforcement areas. Heightened training requirements, legislative regulation, court-mandated changes, and college-level educational programs in private security are all leading to increased professionalism within the security profession.
- Recognizing the pervasiveness of today's private security operations, many municipal departments have begun concerted efforts to involve security organizations in their crime detection and prevention efforts.

LIBRARY EXTRAS!

Library Extras! are suggested readings that are available digitally to readers of this guide. They may be accessed at the *CJNow!* Web site.

Library Extra! 5-1. *Attitudes Toward Crime, the Police, and the Law: Individual and Neighborhood Differences* (NIJ, June 1999).

Library Extra! 5-2. *Census of State and Local Law Enforcement Agencies* (BJS, current volume).

Library Extra! 5-3. *Federal Law Enforcement Officers* (BJS, current volume).

Library Extra! 5-4. *The Kansas City Gun Experiment* (NIJ, 1995).

Library Extra! 5-5. *Law Enforcement Management and Administrative Statistics*, (BJS, current volume).

Library Extra! 5-6. *National Evaluation of Weed and Seed: Cross-Site Analysis* (NIJ, 1999).

ENDNOTES

[1] National Commission on Law Observance and Enforcement, *Wickersham Commission Reports*, 14 vols. (Washington, D.C.: U.S. Government Printing Office, 1931).

[2] President's Commission on Law Enforcement and Administration of Justice, *The Challenge of Crime in a Free Society* (Washington, D.C.: U.S. Government Printing Office, 1967).

[3] The National Advisory Commission on Criminal Justice Standards and Goals, *A National Strategy to Reduce Crime* (Washington, D.C.: U.S. Government Printing Office, 1973).

[4] George L. Kelling et al., *The Kansas City Patrol Experiment* (Washington, D.C.: The Police Foundation, 1974).

[5] William Bieck and David Kessler, *Response Time Analysis* (Kansas City, MO: Board of Police Commissioners, 1977). See also J. Thomas McEwen et al., *Evaluation of the Differential Police Response Field Test: Executive Summary* (Alexandria, VA: Research Management Associates, 1984), and Lawrence Sherman, "Policing Communities: What Works?" in Michael Tonry and Norval Morris, eds., *Crime and Justice: An Annual Review of Research*, Vol. 8 (Chicago: University of Chicago Press, 1986).

[6] Henry M. Wrobleski and Karen M. Hess, *Introduction to Law Enforcement and Criminal Justice*, 4th ed. (St. Paul, MN: West, 1993), p. 34.

[7] Ibid., p. 35.

[8] Brian A. Reaves and Andrew L. Goldberg, *Census of State and Local Law Enforcement Agencies, 1996* (Washington, D.C.: BJS, 1998).

[9] Reaves and Goldberg, *Census of State and Local Law Enforcement Agencies*, 1996.

[10] Ibid.

[11] William C. Cunningham, John J. Strauchs, and Clifford W. Van Meter, *The Hallcrest Report II: Private Security Trends 1970–2000* (McLean, VA: Hallcrest Systems, 1990).

Chapter 6

quick view

<< police management >>

Outline

- Contemporary Policing: The Administrative Perspective
- Contemporary Policing: The Individual Officer
- Contemporary Policing: Issues and Challenges
- Professionalism and Ethics

What You Should Learn

- The three styles of policing that can be found in the United States today and the major differences in these approaches.
- The many factors that influence police use of discretion in individual situations.
- The different types and degrees of police corruption.

- The nature of civil liability issues in policing.
- The nature of ongoing efforts to professionalize the police in the United States today.
- The definitions of key terms that appear in boldface throughout this *Quick View* chapter. Definitions can be found online at http://www.cjnowonline.com.

Contemporary Policing: The Administrative Perspective

Hear the author introduce this chapter at *CJNow!* online.

A few years ago, a Stanislaus County police SWAT team wearing ski masks and acting on a tip that an illegal methamphetamine lab was in operation, kicked down the doors of the Oakdale, California, home of Marian and William Hauselmann.[1] Once inside they handcuffed Mrs. Hauselmann, put a pillowcase over her head, and wrestled her to the floor. Her 64-year-old husband, who suffers from a heart condition, was shouted into silence. His face was cut and officers stepped on his back after throwing him down. No illegal drugs were found. Police soon realized that they had been misled by their informant and apologized to the Hauselmanns. Then they borrowed a knife from the couple's kitchen to cut the plastic handcuffs from their wrists. The county sheriff offered to pay for the broken doors. Following the incident the Hauselmanns reported being unable to sleep.

The Hauselmann case highlights the potentially disastrous consequences of improper police action. Effective **police management**, through which laws are enforced while the rights of suspects and of innocent people are protected, may be the single most important emerging issue facing the criminal justice system in the twenty-first century.

Police management refers to the administrative activities of controlling, directing, and coordinating police personnel, resources, and activities in the service of crime prevention, the apprehension of criminals, the recovery of stolen property, and the performance of a variety of regulatory and helping services.[2] Police managers include any "sworn" law enforcement personnel with administrative authority, from the rank of sergeant to captain, chief or sheriff, and civilian personnel such as police commissioners, attorneys general, state secretaries of crime control, public safety directors, and so on.

Styles of Policing

James Q. Wilson, one of the foremost analysts of crime and justice in America, has identified three policing styles.[3] Simply put, a style of policing describes how a particular police agency sees its purpose and the methods and techniques it undertakes to fulfill that purpose. Wilson's three types of policing—which he did not identify with a particular historical era—are: 1) the watchman, 2) the legalistic style, and 3) the service style. These three styles, taken together, characterize nearly all municipal law enforcement agencies now operating in this country—although some departments are a mixture of two or more styles.

Police departments marked by the watchman style of policing are primarily concerned with achieving the goal of "order maintenance." They see their job as one of controlling illegal and disruptive behavior. Departments operating under the legalistic model are committed to enforcing the "letter of the law." Departments that stress the goal of service reflect the felt needs of the community. In service-oriented departments, the police see themselves more as helpers than as embattled participants in a war against crime.

Historically, American police work has involved a fair amount of order maintenance activity. As times changed, so too have American communities. It is probably fair to say that the style of policing which characterizes a community today tends to flow from the lifestyles of those who live in it.

Police-Community Relations

As social disorganization increased across America in the 1960s, police departments sought ways to understand and deal better with the problems they faced. Significant outgrowths of this effort were police-community relations (PCR) programs. PCR represents a movement away from an exclusive police emphasis on the apprehension of law violators and toward increasing the level of positive police-citizen interaction.

In recent years the police-community relations concept has undergone a substantial shift in emphasis. In contemporary America three generic kinds of "corporate strategies" guide American policing.[4] They are: 1) **strategic policing**, 2) **problem-solving policing**, and 3) **community policing**. Table 6-1 online highlights the differences between traditional and community policing. See *CJNow!* online for detailed descriptions of each strategy identified here.

Contemporary Policing: The Individual Officer

Regardless of the "official" policing style espoused by a department, individual officers retain considerable **discretion** in what they do. Police discretion refers to the exercise of choice by law enforcement officers in the decision to investigate or apprehend, the disposition of suspects, the carrying out of official duties, and in the application of sanctions. Various studies of police discretion tell us that a number of factors influence the discretionary decisions of individual officers. Learn more about these factors at *CJNow!* online.

Contemporary Policing: Issues and Challenges

A number of issues hold special interest for today's police administrators and officers. The online chapter covers issues such as police personality, **police subculture**, police corruption (including techniques to combat corruption), violence in the line of duty, the dangers of police work, police stress, the risk of contracting disease and infected evidence. Some concerns, such as police stress, danger, and the use of deadly force, derive from the very nature of police work. Others have arisen over the years due to commonplace practice, characteristic police values, and public expectations surrounding the enforcement of laws. Included here are such negatives as the potential for corruption, as well as positive efforts which focus on ethics and recruitment

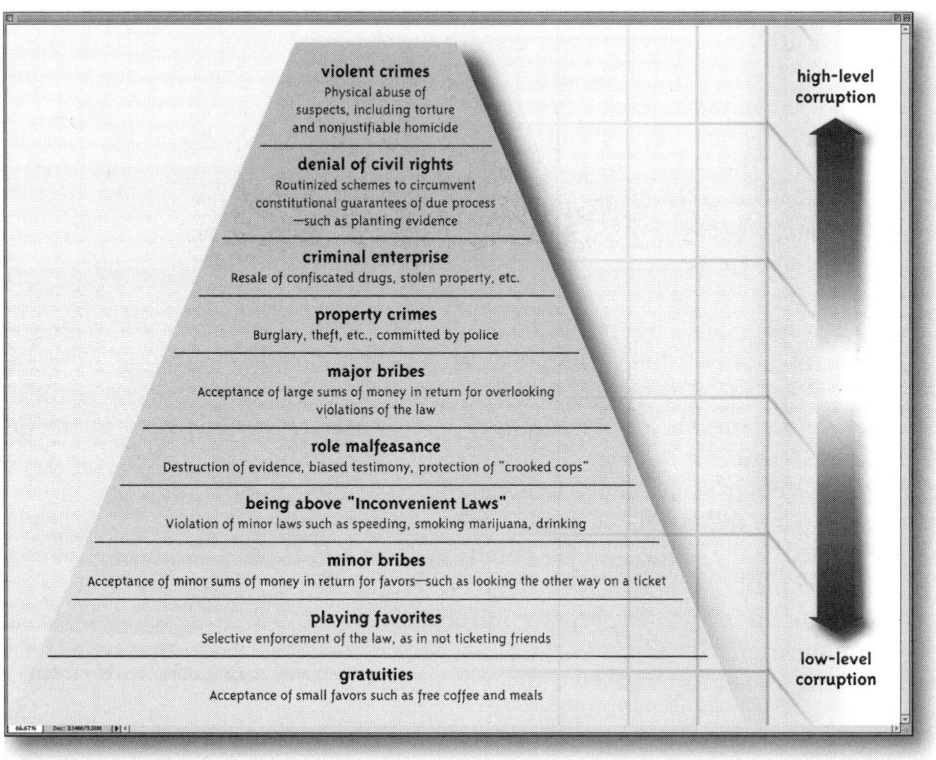

Figure 6-1 Types of police deviance by category and example.

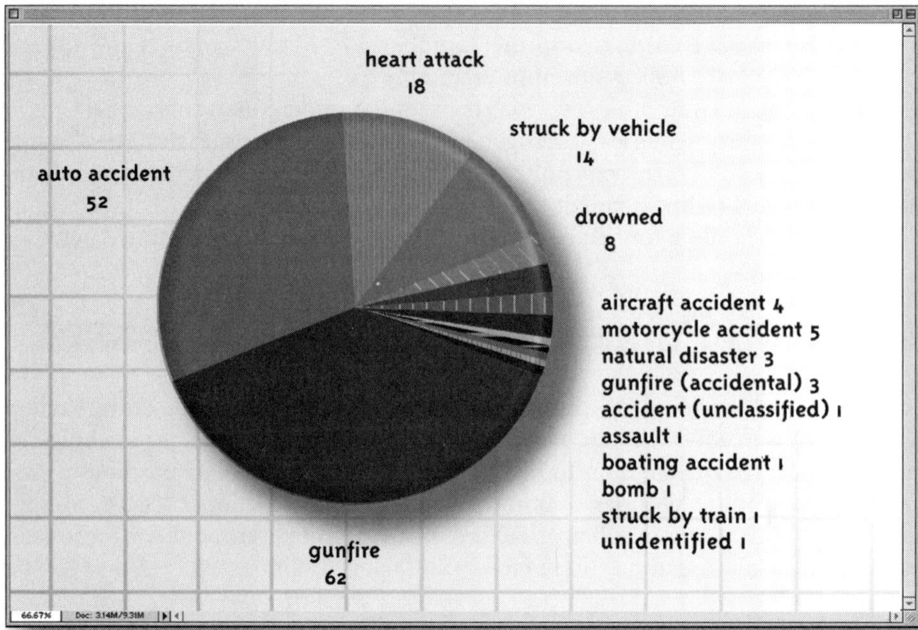

Figure 6-2 Law inforcement officers killed in the line of duty—number by type of incident, 1998. *Source:* Officer Down Memorial Page on the World Wide Web, http://www.odmp.org.

strategies to increase professionalism. Examples of police deviance are shown in Figure 6-1, and an overview of the police personality is provided by Table 6-2 online. Figure 6-2 shows the number of officers killed in the line of duty by circumstances in 1998. Defenses against exposure to infectious substances are listed in Table 6-3 online.

Police Civil Liability

Civil liability is an important special issue facing police managers today. Police civil liability stems from negligent actions by officers, lack of training, inadequate standards, and on-the-spot decisions that may result in harm to innocent bystanders (as may happen in high-speed pursuits). When an officer makes an arrest without just cause, or simply impedes an individual's right to leave the scene without good reason, he or she may also be liable for the charge of false arrest.

Civil suits brought against law enforcement personnel are of two types: state or federal. Suits brought in state courts have generally been the most common form of civil litigation involving police officers. In recent years, however, an increasing number of suits are being brought in federal courts on the basis of the legal rationale that the civil rights of the plaintiff, as guaranteed by federal law, have been denied. The use of deadly force by police officers is one area of potential civil liability which has received considerable attention in recent years. Law enforcement supervisors may find themselves the object of lawsuits by virtue of the fact that they are responsible for the actions of their officers. Alternatively, departments may protect themselves to some degree through regulations limiting the authority of their personnel. Major sources of police civil liability are listed in Table 6-4 online.

Federal suits are often called **1983 lawsuits** because they are based upon Section 1983 of Title 42 of the United States Code—an act passed by Congress in 1871 to ensure the civil rights of men and women of all races. That act requires due process of law before any person can be deprived of life, liberty, or property and specifically provides redress for the denial of these constitutional rights by officials acting under color of state law. Another type of liability action, this one directed specifically at federal officials or enforcement agents, is called a **Bivens suit**. Bivens actions may be addressed against individuals, but not against the United States or its agencies.[5]

Professionalism and Ethics

Police administrators have responded in a variety of ways to issues of danger, liability, and the potential for corruption. Among the most significant responses have been calls for increased professionalism at all levels of policing. A profession is characterized by a body of specialized knowledge, acquired through extensive education,[6] and by a well-considered set of internal standards and ethical guidelines which hold members of the profession accountable to one another and to society. Contemporary policing evidences many of the attributes of a profession. Specialized knowledge in policing—typically communicated through academy classes and on-the-job training—includes a close familiarity with criminal law, laws of procedure, constitutional guarantees and relevant Supreme Court decisions, a working knowledge of weapons and hand-to-hand tactics, driving skills and vehicle maintenance, and a knowledge of radio communications, report-writing abilities, interviewing techniques, and media and human-relations skills.

Ethnic and Racial Minorities and Women

In 1967 the National Advisory Commission on Civil Disorders conducted a survey of supervisory personnel in police departments.[7] They found a marked disparity between the number of black and white officers in leadership positions. One of every 26 black police officers had been promoted to the rank of sergeant, whereas the ratio among whites was 1 in 12. Only 1 of every 114 black officers had become a lieutenant, while among whites the ratio was 1 out of 26. At the level of captain the disparity was even greater—1 out of every 235 black officers had achieved the rank of captain, whereas 1 of every 53 whites had climbed to that rank.

Although today the situation is much improved, minorities are still somewhat underrepresented in police ranks. According to a 1998 report by the Bureau of Justice Statistics,[8] blacks comprise 11.3% of sworn officers, whereas other ethnic minorities constitute 7.7% of sworn personnel (see Figure 6-3). Although ethnic minorities have moved into policing in substantial numbers, females are still significantly underrepresented.

Figure 6-3 Ethnic minorities as a proportion of local law enforcement officers and as a proportion of the U.S. population. *Source:* Adapted from Kathleen Maguire and Ann L. Pastore, *Sourcebook of Criminal Justice Statistics, 1998* (Washington, D.C.: Bureau of Justice Statistics, 1999).

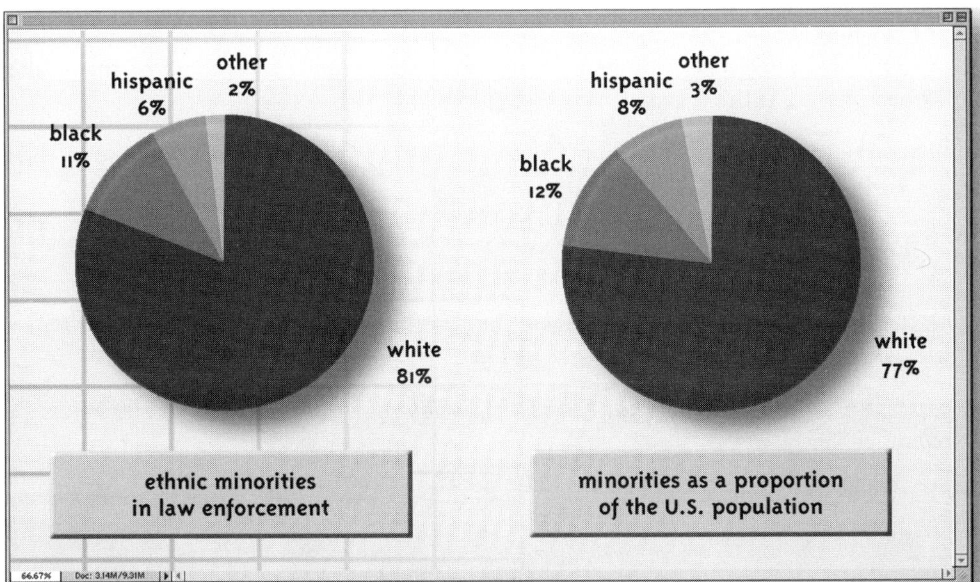

What You Should Remember

- The three types of policing styles are the watchman style (found in departments that are most concerned with order maintenance), the legalistic style (under which departments emphasize enforcing the letter of the law), and the service style (where department are more concerned with providing assistance to citizens).
- The online chapter discusses many factors that might influence the use of discretion by police officers, including the background of the officer, characteristics of the suspect, community interests, and pressures from the victim.
- Occupational deviance and abuse of authority are two types of police corruption. Occupational deviance is motivated by the desire for personal benefit, whereas abuse of authority occurs most often in order to further the organizational goals of law enforcement. The Knapp Commission, discussed in the online chapter, distinguished between two types of corrupt officers: grass eaters and meat eaters. "Grass eating" is the most common form of police deviance and involves mostly small bribes or the acceptance of minor services. "Meat eating" is a much more serious form of corruption, and involves the active seeking of illicit money-making opportunities by officers.
- Police officers, their supervisors, and their departments are liable under civil law for failures in judgment, negligence, and (sometimes) the unintentional harm they may cause to innocent citizens. The most common sources of lawsuits against the police involve assault, battery, false imprisonment, and malicious prosecution. Civil suits against law enforcement personnel may be brought on either the state or federal level. They may be based upon Section 1983 of Title 42 of the United States Code, or may consist of a *Bivens* action—a specific form of federal lawsuit.
- Efforts to professionalize the police include training, certification, accreditation, improved recruitment and selection practices, and an emphasis on ethics and ethical behavior.

LIBRARY EXTRAS!

Library Extras! are suggested readings that are available digitally to readers of this guide. They may be accessed at the *CJNow!* Web site.

Library Extra! 6-1. *Americans' Views on Crime and Law Enforcement: Survey Findings* (NIJ, 1997).

Library Extra! 6-2. *Community Policing in Action: Lessons from an Observational Study* (NIJ, 1998).

Library Extra! 6-3. "Community Policing: Chicago's Experience," *The National Institute of Justice Journal* (NIJ, April 1999).

Library Extra! 6-4. *Measuring What Matters: Developing Measures of What the Police Do* (NIJ, November 1997).

Library Extra! 6-5. "Noble Cause Corruption and the Police Ethic," *FBI Law Enforcement Bulletin* (August, 1999).

Library Extra! 6-6. *Understanding the Use of Force by and Against the Police* (NIJ, 1996).

ENDNOTES

[1] "Bust 180 Degrees Wrong," *USA Today*, December 1, 1992, p. 3A.

[2] The elements of this definition draw upon the now-classic work by O.W. Wilson, *Police Administration* (New York: McGraw-Hill, 1950), pp. 2-3.

[3] James Q. Wilson, *Varieties of Police Behavior: The Management of Law and Order in Eight Communities* (Cambridge, MA: Harvard University Press, 1968).

[4] Mark H. Moore and Robert C. Trojanowicz, "Corporate Strategies for Policing," *Perspectives on Policing*, No. 6 (Washington, D.C.: National Institute of Justice, November 1988).

[5] See *F.D.I.C.* v. *Meyer*, 510 U.S. 471 (1994), in which the U.S. Supreme Court reiterated its ruling under *Bivens,* stating that only government employees and not government agencies can be sued.

[6] As quoted by Michael Siegfried, "Notes on the Professionalization of Private Security," *The Justice Professional* (Spring 1989).

[7] Report of the National Advisory Commission on Civil Disorders, (New York: E.F. Dutton and Company, 1968), p. 332.

[8] Brian A. Reaves, *Local Police Departments, 1993* (Washington, D.C.: Bureau of Justice Statistics, April 1996).

Chapter 7

quick view

<< policing: legal aspects >>

Outline

- The Abuse of Police Power
- Individual Rights
- Search and Seizure
- Arrest
- The Intelligence Function

What You Should Learn

- How the Bill of Rights and democratically inspired legal restraints upon the police help to ensure personal freedoms in our society, and how they prevent the development of a police state in America.

- The nature of due process, and the specific Constitutional Amendments upon which due process guarantees are based.
- The importance of the exclusionary rule and the fruit of the poisoned tree doctrine.
- Differences among the Warren, Burger, and Rehnquist Courts.
- The chapter's definition of arrest, and how popular depictions of arrest by the police may not be consistent with legal understandings of the term.
- The circumstances under which police officers may search vehicles, and the extent to which such searches are permissible.
- How the need to ensure public safety may justify suspicionless searches.
- The *Miranda* warnings and details about recent U.S. Supreme Court cases that have impacted *Miranda* warning requirements.
- The definitions of key terms that appear in boldface throughout this *Quick View* chapter. Definitions can be found online at http://www.cjnowonline.com.

Hear the author introduce this chapter at *CJNow!* online.

The Abuse of Police Power

The online chapter shows how the police, like everyone else, are not above the law. It describes the legal environment surrounding police activities—from search and seizure through arrest and the interrogation of suspects. The chapter teaches that it is democratically inspired legal restraints upon the police that help to ensure individual freedoms in our society, and that prevent the development of a "police state" in America. Like anything else, however, the rules by which the police are expected to operate are in constant flux, and their continuing development forms the meat of the online chapter.

A Changing Legal Climate

The Constitution of the United States—especially the **Bill of Rights**—is designed to protect citizens against abuses of police power (see Table 7-1 online). However, the legal environment surrounding the police in modern America is much more complex than it was just 40 years ago. Up until that time, the Bill of Rights was largely given only lip service in criminal justice proceedings.

It was during the 1960s that the U.S. Supreme Court, under the direction of Chief Justice Earl Warren, accelerated the process of guaranteeing individual rights in the face of criminal prosecution. Warren court rulings bound the police to strict procedural requirements in the areas of investigation, arrest, and interrogation. Later rulings scrutinized trial court procedure and enforced humanitarian standards in sentencing and punishment. The Warren court also seized upon the Fourteenth Amendment and made it a basis for judicial mandates requiring that both state and federal criminal justice agencies adhere to the Court's interpretation of the Constitution. The apex of the individual rights emphasis in Supreme Court decisions was reached in the 1966 case of *Miranda* v. *Arizona*,[1] which established the famous requirement of a police "rights advisement" of suspects.

Supreme Court decisions of the last two decades—the product of a new conservative Court philosophy—have begun what some call a "reversal" of Warren-era advances in the area of individual rights. By creating exceptions to some of the Warren court's rules and restraints, and in allowing for the emergency questioning of suspects before they are read their rights, a changed Supreme Court has recognized the realities attending day-to-day police work and the need to ensure public safety.

Individual Rights

It is common to hear arrestees today say: "You can't do that! I know my rights!" Rights are concerned with procedure—that is, with how police and other actors in the criminal justice system handle each part of the process of dealing with suspects. Rights violations have often become the basis for the dismissal of charges, acquittal of defendants, or the release of convicted offenders after an appeal to a higher court. The full online version of this chapter contains material that describes famous court cases that are important because they clarified constitutional guarantees concerning individual rights within the criminal justice arena.

Due Process Requirements

Due process is a requirement of the Fifth, Sixth, and Fourteenth Amendments to the U.S. Constitution; it mandates that justice-system officials respect the rights of accused individuals throughout the criminal justice process. Most due process requirements of relevance to the police pertain to three major areas: 1) evidence and investigation (often called "search and seizure"), 2) arrest, and 3) interrogation. Each of these areas has been addressed by a plethora of landmark U.S. Supreme Court decisions. **Landmark cases** are recognizable by the fact that they produce substantial changes in both the understanding of the requirements of due process and in the practical day-to-day operations of the justice system.

Search and Seizure

The U.S. Constitution declares that people must be secure in their homes and in their persons against unreasonable searches and seizures. This right is asserted by the Fourth Amendment, which reads: "The right of the people to be secure in their persons, houses, papers, and effects, against unreasonable searches and seizures shall not be violated, and no warrants shall issue but upon probable cause, supported by oath or affirmation, and particularly describing the place to be searched, and the persons or things to be seized." It is the interpretation of this phrase over time by the U.S. Supreme Court that has given it the impact it has on the justice system today.

Of special importance in the area of search and seizure are the **exclusionary rule**, which says that evidence illegally seized by the police cannot be used in a criminal trial, and the **fruit of the poisoned tree doctrine**, which says that evidence which *derives* from an illegal seizure cannot be used at trial.

The Warren Court Era (1953–969)

Although the exclusionary rule became an overriding consideration in federal law enforcement from the time that it was first defined by the Supreme Court in 1914, it was not until 1961 that the Warren court, under Chief Justice Earl Warren, made the exclusionary rule applicable to criminal prosecutions at the state level.[2] Another important Warren-era case, that of *Chimel* v. *California* (1969)[3], involved both arrest and search activities by local law enforcement officers. Legal implications of *Chimel* v. *California* are summarized in Table 7-2 online.

The Burger (1969–1986) and Rehnquist (1986–Present) Courts

Throughout the late 1980s, the U.S. Supreme Court mirrored the nation's growing conservative tenor by distancing itself from certain earlier decisions of the Warren court. The underlying theme of the new Court, the Burger court (which held sway from 1969 until 1986), was its adherence to the principle that criminal defendants, in claiming violations of their due process rights, need to bear the bulk of responsibility in showing that police went beyond the law in the performance of their duties. That trend continues into the present day under the Rehnquist Court (1986–present), led by Chief Justice William H. Rehnquist.

The Burger court, led by Chief Justice Warren E. Burger, began a "chipping away" at the strict application of the exclusionary rule established by the Warren Court. In 1984, for example, the Court recognized what has come to be called the **good faith exception to the exclusionary rule**. The Court held that: "When law enforcement officers have acted in objective good faith or their transgressions have been minor, the magnitude of the benefit conferred on . . . guilty defendants offends basic concepts of the criminal justice system." This is especially true when officers honestly believe that they have **probable cause** to effect an arrest or to conduct a search. Similarly, under the **plain view doctrine** police officers have the opportunity to begin investigations or confiscate evidence, without the need for a warrant, based upon what they find in plain view and open to public inspection. Finally, certain emergencies may justify a police officer in searching a premise, even without a warrant. Such searches are termed **exigent circumstances** searches. A general listing of established exceptions to the exclusionary rule is provided in Table 7-3 online.

Arrest

Officers seize not only property, but persons as well—a process referred to as "arrest." Most people think of arrest in terms of what they see on popular TV crime shows. The suspect is chased, subdued, and "cuffed" after committing some loathsome act in view of the camera. Some arrests do occur that way. In technical terms, however, an **arrest** occurs whenever a law enforcement officer restricts a person's freedom to leave. There may be no yelling "*You're under arrest!*" no *Miranda* warnings may be offered, and, in fact, the suspect may not even consider himself or herself to be in custody.

The U.S. Supreme Court has established a clear rule that police officers have the right to conduct a search of a person being arrested and to search the area under the immediate control of that person in order to protect themselves from attack. Learn more about Supreme Court decisions that have shaped the law of arrest, including emergency searches of persons and the rights that citizens have to protect themselves and their belongings from unwarranted police inspection, at *CJNow!* online.

Vehicle Searches

Vehicles present a special law enforcement problem. They are highly movable, and, when an arrest of a driver or an occupant occurs, the need to search them may be immediate. In 1925, in the case of *Carroll* v. *U.S.*,[4] the Court ruled that a warrantless search of an automobile or other vehicle is valid if it is based upon a reasonable belief that contraband is present. Generally speaking, where vehicles are concerned, an investigatory stop is permissible under the Fourth Amendment if supported by reasonable suspicion,[5] and a warrantless search of a stopped car is valid if it is based on probable cause.[6] Reasonable suspicion can expand into probable cause when the facts in a given situation so warrant.[7] Probable cause permits a warrantless search of a vehicle under what has been called the **fleeting targets exception** to the exclusionary rule.[8]

Warrantless vehicle searches may extend to any area of the vehicle, and may include sealed containers, the trunk area, and the glove compartment if officers have probable cause to conduct a purposeful search or if officers have been given permission to search the vehicle.[9] Moreover, according to a 1996 U.S. Supreme Court decision,[10] officers may stop a vehicle being driven suspiciously and then search it once probable cause has developed, even though their primary assignment centers on duties other than traffic enforcement *or* "if a reasonable officer would not have stopped the motorist absent some additional law enforcement objective."

While a search incident to arrest may be justifiable in the eyes of the Court, a search incident to citation is not.[11] In 1999,[12] the Court ruled that police officers with probable cause to search a car may inspect passengers' belongings found in the car that are capable of concealing the object of the search.

Suspicionless Searches

In two 1989 decisions the U.S. Supreme Court ruled that there may be instances when the need to ensure public safety provides a **compelling interest** which negates the rights of any individual to privacy, permitting searches even when a person is not suspected of a crime. Likewise, the 1991 Supreme Court case of *Florida* v. *Bostick*,[13] permitted warrantless "sweeps" of intercity buses. In *Bostick*, the Court concluded that police warrantless, suspicionless "sweeps" of buses, "trains, planes, and city streets" are permissible as long as officers 1) ask individual passengers for permission before searching their possessions, 2) do not coerce passengers to consent to a search, and 3) do not convey the message that citizen compliance with the search request is mandatory.

The Intelligence Function

The police role includes the need to gather information through the questioning of both suspects and informants. Even more often, the need for information leads police investigators to question potentially knowledgeable citizens who may have been witnesses or victims. Data gathering is a crucial form of intelligence, without which enforcement agencies would be virtually powerless to plan and effect arrests.

Informants

The successful use of informants in supporting requests for a warrant depends upon the demonstrable reliability of their information. The case of *Aguilar* v. *Texas* (1964)[14] clarified the use of informants and established a two-pronged test to the effect that informant information could establish probable cause if 1) the source of the informant's information is made clear, and 2) the police officer has a reasonable belief that the informant is reliable. Two later cases provided exceptions to the two-pronged test. For additional information on the use of police informants see *CJNow!* online.

Police Interrogation

Interrogation has been defined by the U.S. Supreme Court as any behaviors by the police "that the police should know are reasonably likely to elicit an incriminating response from the suspect." Hence, interrogation may include staged lineups, reverse lineups, positing guilt, minimizing the moral seriousness of crime, and casting blame on the victim or society. It is noteworthy that the Court has also held that "police words or actions normally attendant to arrest and custody do not constitute interrogation,"[15] unless they involve pointed or directed questions. For more information on police interrogation, including physical abuse, psychological manipulation, inherent coercion, and the right to a lawyer at interrogation, see *CJNow!* online.

Suspect Rights: The *Miranda* Decision

In the area of suspect rights, no case is as well known as that of *Miranda* v. *Arizona*, (1966).[16] To ensure that proper advice is given to suspects at the time of their arrest, the now-famous *Miranda* rights are read before any questioning begins. These rights, as they appear on a *Miranda* warning card commonly used by police agencies, include the following admonishments: 1) You have the right to remain silent; 2) Anything you say can and will be used against you in a court of law; 3) You have the right to talk to a lawyer and to have a lawyer present while you are being questioned; 4) If you want a lawyer before or during questioning but cannot afford to hire a lawyer, one will be appointed to represent you at no cost before any questioning; and 5) If you answer questions now without a lawyer here, you still have the right to stop answering questions at any time. See *CJNow!* online for additional information on rights advisements, including recent U.S. Supreme Court cases that have modified the original *Miranda* ruling.

What You Should Remember

- The Bill of Rights requires due process in the handling of criminal defendants, thereby helping to ensure personal freedoms. Legal restraints placed upon the police by due process requirements help protect individual rights and prevent the development of a police state in America.

- Due process is a requirement of the Fifth, Sixth, and Fourteenth Amendments to the U.S. Constitution which mandates that justice-system officials respect the rights of accused individuals throughout the criminal justice process.
- The exclusionary rule prohibits illegally seized evidence from being used in a criminal trial. The fruit of the poisoned tree doctrines prohibits the use of information developed as a result of illegally seized evidence. Both rules act as controls over police behavior.
- Warren Court rulings bound the police to strict procedural requirements in the areas of investigation, arrest, and interrogation. More recent rulings by the Burger and Rehnquist Courts have begun a reversal of Warren-era advances in the area of individual rights by creating exceptions to some of the Warren court's rules and restraints.
- In contrast to popular depictions, an arrest occurs whenever a law enforcement officer restricts a person's freedom to leave.
- Since vehicles may quickly leave police jurisdiction, the U.S. Supreme Court has held that a warrantless search of an automobile or other vehicle is valid if it is based upon a reasonable belief that contraband is present. Similarly, an investigatory stop of a vehicle is permissible if supported by reasonable suspicion, and a warrantless search of a stopped car is valid if it is based upon probable cause.
- Suspicionless searches of persons, things and places are permissible in instances where the need to ensure public safety provides a compelling interest that negates a person's rights to privacy, even when that person is not suspected of a crime.
- The *Miranda* warnings consist of the following admonishments: 1) You have the right to remain silent; 2) Anything you say can and will be used against you in a court of law; 3) You have the right to talk to a lawyer and to have a lawyer present while you are being questioned; 4) If you want a lawyer before or during questioning but cannot afford to hire a lawyer, one will be appointed to represent you at no cost before any questioning; and 5) If you answer questions now without a lawyer, you still have the right to stop answering questions at any time.

LIBRARY EXTRAS!

Library Extras! are suggested readings that are available digitally to readers of this guide. They may be accessed at the *CJNow!* Web site.

Library Extra! 7-1. *FBI Law Enforcement Bulletin,* May 2000 (Vol. 69, No. 5).

Library Extra! 7-2. *FBI Law Enforcement Bulletin,* April 2000 (Vol. 69, No. 4).

Library Extra! 7-3. *FBI Law Enforcement Bulletin,* March 2000 (Vol. 69, No. 3).

Library Extra! 7-4. *FBI Law Enforcement Bulletin,* February 2000 (Vol. 69, No. 2).

Library Extra! 7-5. *FBI Law Enforcement Bulletin,* January 2000 (Vol. 69, No. 1).

ENDNOTES

[1] *Miranda* v. *Arizona*, 384 U.S. 436 (1966).

[2] *Mapp* v. *Ohio*, 367 U.S. 643 (1961).

[3] *Chimel* v. *California*, 395 U.S. 752 (1969).

[4] *Carroll* v. *U.S.*, 267 U.S. 132 (1925).

[5] *Terry* v. *Ohio*, 392 U.S. 1 (1968).

[6] *California* v. *Acevedo*, 500 U.S. 565 (1991).

[7] *Ornelas* v. *U.S.*, 116 S.Ct. 1657 L.Ed. 2d 911 (1996).

[8] The phrase is usually attributed to the 1991 U.S. Supreme Court case of *California* v. *Acevedo.*

[9] *Florida* v. *Jimeno*, 111 S.Ct. 1801 (1991).

[10] *Whren* v. *U.S.*, 116 S.Ct. 1769, 135 L.Ed. 2d (1996).

[11] *Knowles* v. *Iowa*, No. 97-7597 (1998).

[12] *Wyoming* v. *Houghton*, No. 98-184 (1999).

[13] *Florida* v. *Bostick*, 111 S.Ct. 2382 (1991).

[14] *Aguilar* v. *Texas*, 378 U.S. 108 (1964).

[15] *South Dakota* v. *Neville*, 103 S.Ct. 916 (1983).

[16] *Miranda* v. *Arizona*, 384 U.S. 436 (1966).

Part 3

<< adjudication >>

Chapter 8

THE COURTS

Chapter 9

THE COURTROOM WORK GROUP AND THE CRIMINAL TRIAL

Chapter 10

SENTENCING

Chapter 8

quick view

<< the courts >>

Outline

- American Court History
- Pretrial Activities

What You Should Learn

- The differences between the federal and state court systems.
- The unique characteristics of American court history.
- The steps that are typically taken during pretrial activities.
- The definitions of key terms that appear in boldface throughout this *Quick View* chapter. Definitions can be found online at http://www.cjnowonline.com.

Hear the author introduce this chapter at *CJNow!* online.

American Court History

Two types of courts function within the American criminal justice system: 1) state courts and 2) federal courts. Figure 8-1 outlines the structure of today's **federal court system**, while Figure 8-2 diagrams a typical **state court system**. A state-specific example is shown in Figure 8-3, which diagrams the court system in Florida. The dual court system in the United States today is the result of general agreement among the nation's founders about the need for individual states to retain significant legislative authority and judicial autonomy separate from federal control. The online chapter describes both federal and state court systems in terms of their historical development, **jurisdiction**, and current structure.

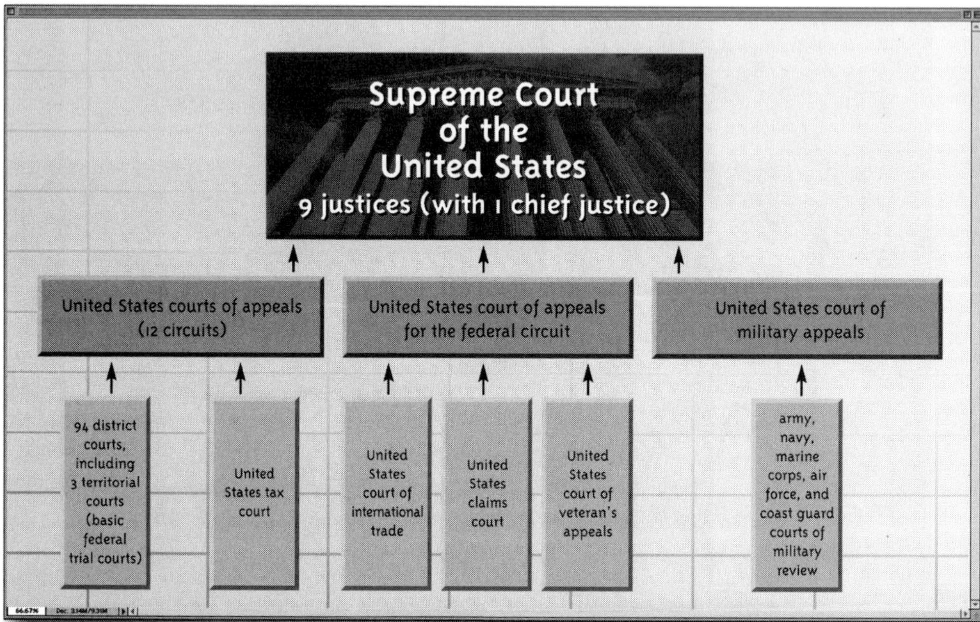

Figure 8-1 The structure of the federal courts.

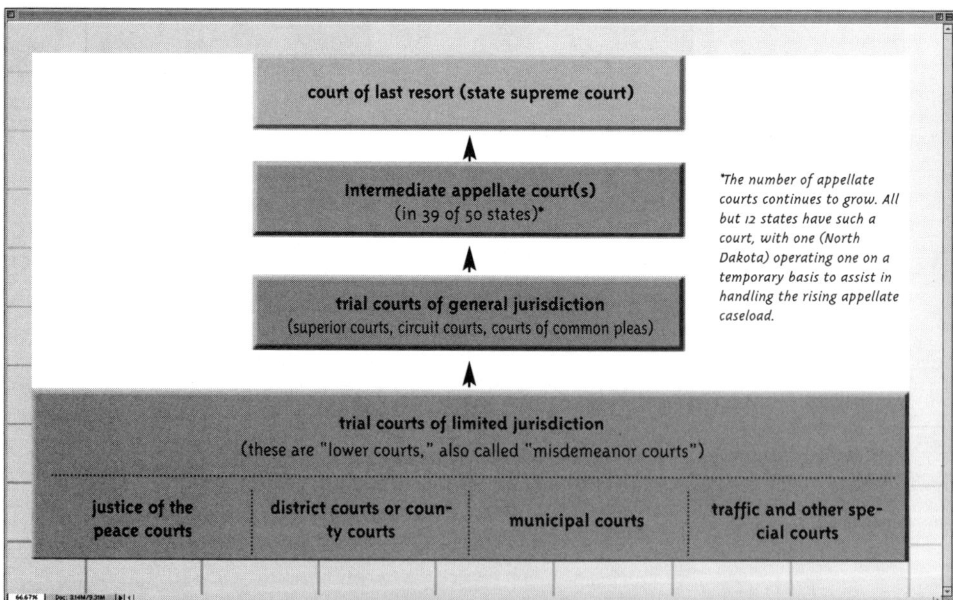

Figure 8-2 The typical state court system.

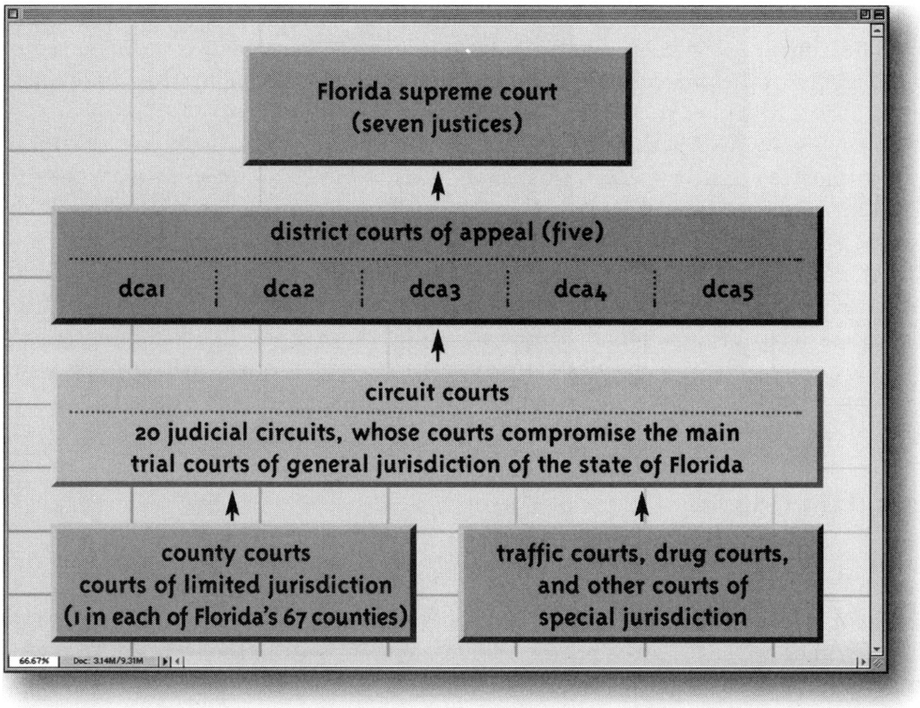

Figure 8-3 The court system of the state of Florida.

State Court Development

Prior to 1776 all American colonies had established fully functioning court systems. Following the American Revolution, colonial courts provided the organizational basis for the growth of fledgling state court systems. Since there had been considerable diversity in the structure of colonial courts, state courts were anything but uniform. Initially, most states made no distinction between **original jurisdiction** and **appellate jurisdiction**. Many had no provisions for appeal. States which did permit appeals often lacked any established appellate courts and sometimes used state legislatures for that purpose.

By the late 1800s a dramatic increase in population, growing urbanization, the settlement of the West, and other far-reaching changes in the American way of life led to a tremendous increase in civil litigation and criminal arrests. Legislatures tried to keep pace with the rising tide of suits. They created a multiplicity of courts at the trial, appellate, and supreme court levels, calling them by a diversity of names and assigning them functions which sometimes bore little resemblance to like-sounding courts in neighboring states. The result was a patchwork quilt of hearing bodies, some only vaguely resembling modern notions of a trial court.

A movement toward simplification of state court structures, led primarily by the American Bar Association and the American Judicature Society, began in the early 1900s. Proponents of state court reform sought to unify redundant courts, which held overlapping jurisdiction. Most reform-minded thinkers suggested a uniform model for states everywhere. The court reform movement is still ongoing today. Although it has made a substantial number of inroads in many states, there are still many differences between and among state court systems. Learn more about American court history at *CJNow!* online.

State Trial Courts

Trial courts are where criminal cases begin. The trial court conducts arraignments, sets bail, takes pleas, and conducts trials. If the defendant is found guilty (or pleads guilty), the trial court imposes sentence. Trial courts of limited or special jurisdiction are also called lower courts. Lower courts are authorized to hear only less serious criminal cases, usually involving misdemeanors, or to hear special types of cases, such as traffic violations, family disputes, small claims, and so on. Courts of limited jurisdiction rarely hold jury trials, depending instead on the hearing judge to make determinations of both fact and law. At the lower-court level a detailed record of the proceedings is not maintained. Case files will only include information on the charge, the plea, the finding of the court, and the sentence.

Trial courts of general jurisdiction, called variously high courts, circuit courts, or superior courts, are authorized to hear any criminal case. In many states they also provide the first appellate level for courts of limited jurisdiction. In most cases, superior courts offer defendants whose cases originated in lower courts the chance for a new trial instead of a review of the record of the earlier hearing. When a new trial is held, it is referred to as **trial *de novo***.

Trial courts of general jurisdiction operate within a fact-finding framework called the adversarial process. That process pits the interests of the state, represented by prosecutors, against the professional skills and abilities of defense attorneys. The adversarial process is not a free-for-all, but is, rather, constrained by procedural rules specified in law and sustained through tradition. Learn more about the adversarial process at *CJNow!* online.

State Appellate Courts

Most states today have an appellate division, consisting of an intermediate appellate court (often called the Court of Appeals) and a high-level appellate court (generally termed the state supreme court). High-level appellate courts are referred to as courts of last resort, to indicate that no other appellate route remains to a defendant within the state court system once the high court rules on a case.

An **appeal** by a convicted defendant asks that a higher court review the actions of a lower one. Courts within the appellate division, once they accept an appeal, do not conduct a new trial. Instead they provide a review of the case on the record. In other words, appellate courts examine the written transcript of lower-court hearings to ensure that those proceedings were carried out fairly and in accordance with proper procedure and state law.

State Court Administration

To function efficiently, courts require uninterrupted funding, adequate staffing, trained support personnel, a well-managed case flow, and coordination between levels and among jurisdictions. To oversee these and other aspects of judicial management, every state today has its own mechanism for court administration. Most make use of **state court administrators** who manage these operational functions. At the federal level, the federal court system is administered by the Administrative Office of the United State Courts (AO), located in Washington, D.C. Learn more about court administration and court administrators at *CJNow!* online.

Dispute Resolution Centers

Some communities have begun to recognize that it is possible to resolve at least minor disputes without the need for formal court hearings. **Dispute resolution centers**, which function to hear victim's claims of minor wrongs, such as passing bad checks, trespassing, shoplifting, and petty theft, function today in over 200 locations throughout the country.[1] Frequently staffed by volunteer mediators, such programs work to resolve disagreements (in which minor criminal offenses might otherwise be charged) without the need to assign blame. Mediation centers are often closely integrated with the formal criminal justice process and may substantially reduce the caseload of lower-level courts.

The Rise of the Federal Courts

Federal courts were created by the U.S. Constitution. As a result of constitutional mandates, congressional action, and other historical developments, today's federal judiciary consists of three levels: 1) U.S. district courts, 2) U.S. courts of appeals, and 3) the U.S. Supreme Court.

The lowest level of the federal court system consists of 94 district courts located in the 50 states (except for the District of Wyoming, which includes the Montana and Idaho portions of

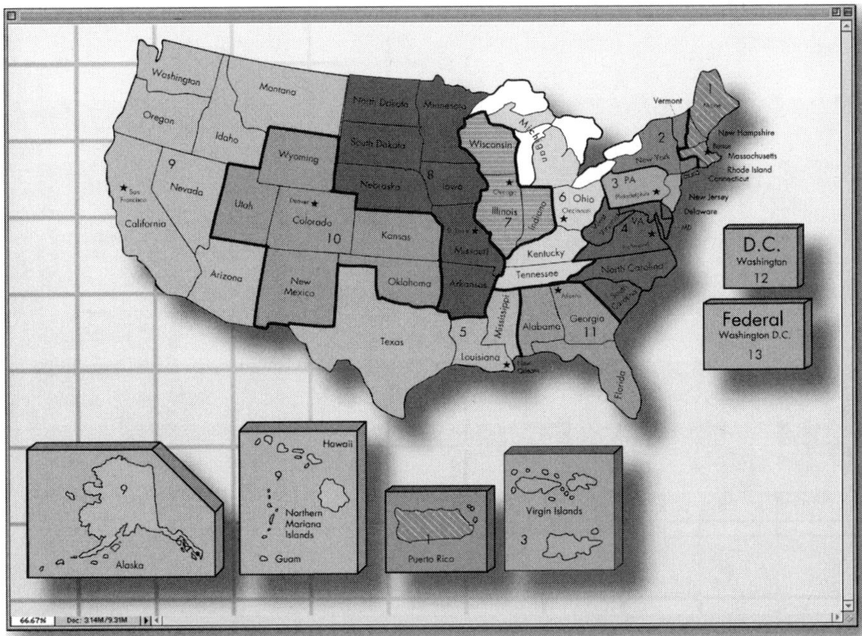

Figure 8-4 The 13 federal judicial circuits.

Yellowstone National Park); Puerto Rico; the District of Columbia; and the U.S. territories of Guam, the Virgin Islands, and the Northern Mariana Islands. District courts are the trial courts of the federal judicial system. They have original jurisdiction over all cases involving alleged violations of federal statutes.

The intermediate appellate courts in the federal judicial system are the courts of appeals.[2] Twelve of these courts have jurisdiction over cases from certain geographic areas. The Court of Appeals for the Federal Circuit has national jurisdiction over specific types of cases. The First through Eleventh Circuits each include three or more states, as illustrated by Figure 8-4.

At the apex of the federal court system stands the U.S. Supreme Court. The Court, which is located in Washington, D.C., consists of nine justices, eight of whom are referred to as associate justices. The ninth presides over the Court as the chief justice of the United States. (See Table 8-1 online.) The Supreme Court wields immense power. The Court's greatest authority lies in its capacity for **judicial review** of lower court decisions and state and federal statute. Learn more about the U.S. Supreme Court at *CJNow!* online.

Pretrial Activities

A number of court-related pretrial activities routinely take place before trial can begin. Although such activities (as well as the names given to them) vary between jurisdictions, they can be generally described as follows:

First Appearance

A first appearance, sometimes called an initial appearance or magistrate's review, occurs when defendants are brought before a judge to be: 1) given formal notice of the charges against them, 2) advised of their rights, 3) given the opportunity to retain a lawyer or to have one appointed to represent them, and (possibly) 4) afforded the opportunity for bail. Pretrial release may take the form of a cash bond, release on recognizance, a property bond, deposit bail, conditional release, third-party custody, unsecured or signature bond, or attorney affidavit. Although pretrial release is common practice (see Figure 8-5), some states have

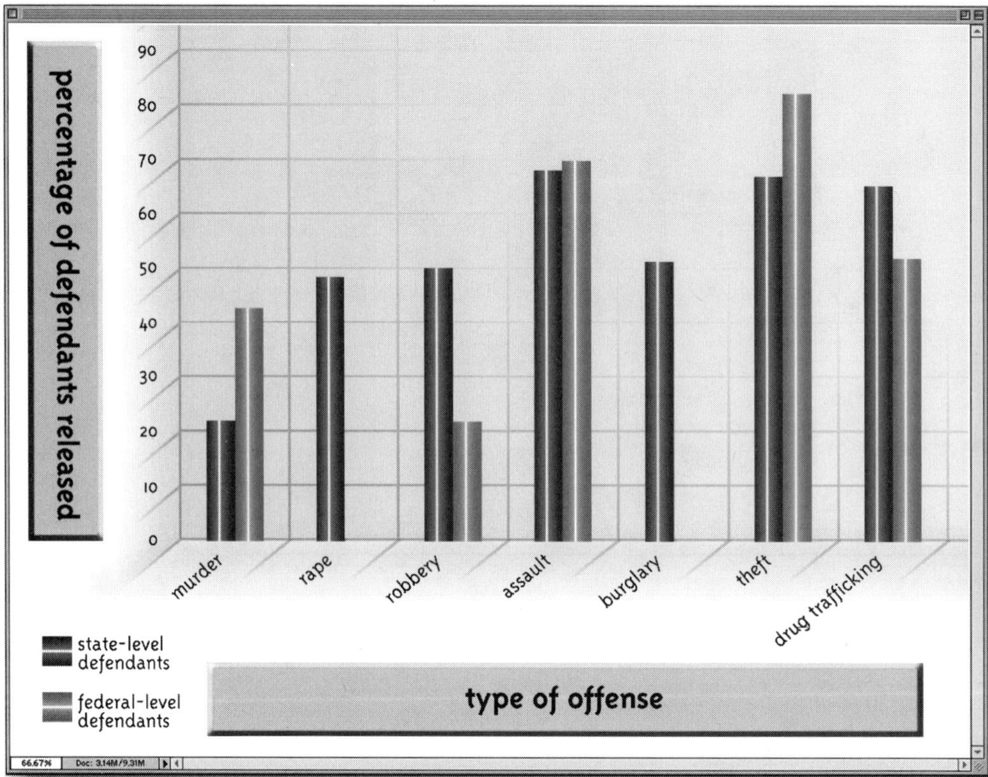

Figure 8-5 Proportion of state and federal felony defendants released prior to trial. *Sources:* Brian A. Reaves, *Felony Defendants in Large Urban Counties, 1994: State Court Processing Statistics* (Washington, D.C.,: Bureau of Justice Statistics, 1998); Brian A. Reaves and Jacob Perez, *Pretrial Release of Felony Defendants, 1992* (Washinton, D.C.: Bureau of Justice Statistics, November 1994); and Brian A. Reaves, *Pretrial Release of Felony Defendants* (Washington, D.C.: Bureau of Justice Statistics, February 1994). Note: Federal pretrial release statistics are not available for the crimes of rape and burglary.

enacted **danger laws**, which limit the right to bail for certain kinds of offenders.[3]

The Grand Jury

The federal government and about half of the states use grand juries as part of the pretrial process. Grand juries are composed of private citizens (often 23 in number) who hear evidence presented by the prosecution. Grand juries serve primarily as filters to eliminate from further processing cases for which there is not sufficient evidence. Grand jury hearings are held in secret, and the defendant is not afforded the opportunity to appear before the grand jury.[4] Grand juries have the power to subpoena witnesses and to mandate a review of books, records, and other documents crucial to their investigations.

After hearing the evidence, the grand jury votes on the indictment presented to it by the prosecution. The indictment is a formal listing of proposed charges. If the majority of grand jury members agree to forward the indictment to the trial court, it becomes a "true bill" upon which further prosecution will turn.

The Preliminary Hearing

States that do not use grand juries rely instead upon a preliminary hearing for charging defendants. In these jurisdictions, the prosecutor files an accusatorial document called an "information," or complaint, against the accused. A preliminary hearing is then held in order to determine whether there is probable cause to hold the defendant for trial. At this point, defendants who appear or claim to be mentally incompetent may be ordered to undergo further evaluation to determine their competency to stand trial. **Competency to stand trial** may become an issue when a defendant appears to be incapable of understanding the proceedings against him or is unable to assist in his own defense due to mental disease or defect.

Arraignment and the Plea

Once an indictment has been returned, or an information filed, the accused will be formally arraigned. Arraignment is generally a brief process with two purposes: 1) to once again inform the defendant of the specific charges against him or her, and 2) to allow the defendant to enter a **plea**. Generaly, three types of pleas to be entered: guilty, not guilty, and *nolo contendere* (no contest). A **no contest (*nolo contendere*)** plea is much the same as a plea of guilty. A defendant who pleads no contest is immediately convicted and may be sentenced just as though he or she had entered a plea of guilty. A no contest plea, however, is no admission of guilt and provides one major advantage to defendants: It may not be used as a later basis for civil proceedings which seek monetary or other damages against the defendant. Learn more about pretrial activities at *CJNow!* online.

What You Should Remember

- Throughout the United States there are two judicial systems. One consists of state and local courts established under the authority of state governments. The other is the federal court system, created by Congress under the authority of the Constitution of the United States. State courts have virtually unlimited power to decide nearly every type of case, subject only to the limitations of the U.S. Constitution, their own state constitutions, and state law. Federal courts have power to decide only those cases over which the Constitution gives them authority. The highest federal court, the U.S. Supreme Court, is located in Washington, D.C., and hears cases only on appeal from lower courts.
- The dual court system in America is the result of general agreement among the nation's founders about the need for individual states to retain significant legislative authority and judicial autonomy separate from federal control. Under this concept, the United States developed as a relatively loose federation of semi-independent provinces. New states joining the union were assured of limited federal intervention into local affairs. State legislatures were free to create laws, and state court systems were needed to hear cases in which violations of those laws occurred.
- The online version of this chapter also describes pretrial practices, including the first appearance (also called the initial appearance or magistrate's review), grand jury review or preliminary hearing (as the process by which an indictment may be returned is called in state's which do not use grand juries), and arraignment (during which the defendant is asked to enter a plea).

LIBRARY EXTRAS!

Library Extras! are suggested readings that are available digitally to readers of this guide. They may be accessed at the *CJNow!* Web site.

Library Extra! 8-1. *Federal Habeas Corpus Review: Challenging State Court Criminal Convictions* (USDOJ, 1995).

Library Extra! 8-2. *Prisoner Petitions in the Federal Courts*, 1980-96 (BJS, October 1997).

Library Extra! 8-3. *Survey of Judicial Salaries* (NCSC).

Library Extra! 8-4. "Therapeutic Jurisprudence and the Emergence of Problem-Solving Courts," *The National Institute of Justice Journal* (NIJ, July 1999).

ENDNOTES

[1] Martin Wright, *Justice for Victims and Offenders* (Bristol, PA: Open University Press, 1991), p. 56.

[2] Some of the materials in this section are adapted from the Administrative Office of the United States Courts, "Courts of Appeals," and "U.S. Court of Appeals for the Federal Circuit," Administrative Office of the United States Courts, World Wide Web site, July 27, 1995.

[3] According to Joseph B. Vaughn and Victor E. Kappeler, the first such legislation was the 1970 District of Columbia Court Reform and Criminal Procedure Act. See Vaughn and Kappeler, "The Denial of Bail: Pre-Trial Preventive Dention," *Criminal Justice Research Bulletin*, Vol. 3, no. 6 (Huntsville, TX: Sam Houston State University, 1987), p. 1.

[4] A few states now have laws that permit the defendant to appear before the grand jury.

Chapter 9

quick view

<< the courtroom work group and the criminal trial >>

Outline

- Introduction
- The Courtroom Work Group: Professional Courtroom Actors
- Outsiders: Nonprofessional Courtroom Participants
- The Criminal Trial

What You Should Learn

- The identities of the various types of professional courtroom actors in the courtroom work group and their roles.
- The identities of the various types of nonprofessional courtroom participants and their roles.
- The stages in a criminal trial.

- Methods that have been suggested for improving the adjudication process.
- The definitions of key terms that appear in boldface throughout this *Quick View* chapter. Definitions can be found online at http://www.cjnowonline.com.

Introduction

Hear the author introduce this chapter at *CJNow!* online.

To the public eye, criminal trials generally appear to be well managed and even dramatic events. Like plays on a stage, they involve many participants playing many different roles. Parties to the event can be divided into two categories: "professionals" and "outsiders." The "professional" category includes official courtroom actors, well versed in criminal trial practice, who set the stage for and conduct the business of the court. Judges, prosecuting attorneys, defense attorneys, public defenders, and others who earn a living serving the court fall into this category. Professional courtroom actors are also called the **courtroom work group**. Even within the adversarial framework of a criminal trial, the courtroom work group is dedicated to bringing the procedure to a successful close.

In contrast, "outsiders" are generally unfamiliar with courtroom organization and trial procedure. Most outsiders visit the court temporarily to provide information or to serve as members of the jury. Similarly, because of their temporary involvement with the court, defendant and victim are also outsiders, even though they may have more of a personal investment in the outcome of the trial than anyone else. Chapter 9 online examines the various roles of the many participants in a criminal trial, some which are summarized here.

The Courtroom Work Group: Professional Courtroom Actors

The Judge

The trial judge is probably the figure most closely associated with a criminal trial. The judge has the primary duty of ensuring justice. In the courtroom, the judge holds ultimate authority, ruling on matters of law, weighing objections from either side, deciding on the admissibility of evidence, and disciplining anyone who challenges the order of the court. In most jurisdictions, judges also sentence offenders after a verdict has been returned, and in some states judges serve to decide guilt or innocence for defendants who waive a jury trial.

Each state jurisdiction normally has a chief judge who, besides serving on the bench as a trial judge, must also manage the court system. Management includes hiring staff, scheduling sessions of court, ensuring the adequate training of subordinate judges, and coordinating activities with other courtroom actors. Chief judges usually assume their positions by virtue of seniority and rarely have any formal training in management. Hence, the managerial effectiveness of a chief judge is often a matter of personality and dedication more than anything else. Lean more about the duties of judges, their selection, and the problems associated with judicial misconduct in the online version of this chapter.

The Prosecuting Attorney

The prosecuting attorney—called variously the "solicitor," "district attorney," "state's attorney," "county attorney," "commonwealth attorney," and so on—is responsible for presenting the state's case against the defendant. Technically speaking, the prosecuting attorney is the primary representative of the people by virtue of the belief that violations of the criminal law are an affront to the public.

Another prosecutorial role has traditionally been that of quasi-legal advisor to local police departments. Because prosecutors are sensitive to the kinds of information needed for conviction, they may help guide police investigations and will exhort detectives to identify usable witnesses, uncover additional evidence, and the like. This role is limited, however, because police departments are independent of the administrative authority of the prosecutor and cooperation between them, although based on the common goal of conviction, is purely voluntary.

Once trial begins, the job of the prosecutor is to vigorously present the state's case against the defendant. Prosecutors introduce evidence against the accused, steer the testimony of witnesses "for the people," and argue in favor of conviction. Since defendants are presumed innocent until proven guilty, the burden of demonstrating guilt beyond a reasonable doubt rests with the prosecutor. Learn more about prosecutors and the wide discretion available to them in the online version of this chapter.

Defense Counsel

The defense counsel is a trained lawyer who may specialize in the practice of criminal law. The task of the defense attorney is to represent the accused as soon as possible after arrest and to ensure that the civil rights of the defendant are not violated through processing by the criminal justice system. Other duties of the defense counsel include testing the strength of the prosecution's case, being involved in plea negotiations, and preparing an adequate defense to be used at trial. In the preparation of a defense, criminal lawyers may enlist private detectives, experts, witnesses to the crime, and character witnesses. Some will perform aspects of the role of private detective or of investigator themselves. They will also review relevant court precedents in order to determine what the best defense strategy might be. To help attorneys know what is expected of them, ethical standards have been developed by various groups, most notably the American Bar Association.

A series of U.S. Supreme Court decisions have guaranteed that defendants unable to pay for private criminal defense attorneys will receive adequate representation at all stages of criminal justice processing. As a consequence, over 80% of all defendants in today's felony cases depend upon court-appointed attorneys, or **public defenders,** to represent them.[1] Most states now use one of three systems to deliver legal services to criminal defendants who are unable to afford their own: 1) court-assigned counsel, 2) public defenders, and 3) contractual arrangements. Learn more about the activities of criminal defense attorneys, including their professional ethics, and about indigent defense, at *CJNow!* online.

The Bailiff

Also called a court officer, **the bailiff**, another member of the professional courtroom work group, is usually an armed law enforcement officer. The job of the bailiff is to ensure order in the courtroom, announce the judge's entry into the courtroom, call witnesses, and prevent the escape of the accused (if the accused has not been released on bond). The bailiff also supervises the jury when it is sequestered and controls public and media access to the jury. Bailiffs in federal courtrooms are deputy U.S. marshals.

Local Court Administrators

Many states now employ trial court administrators whose job it is to facilitate the smooth functioning of courts in particular judicial districts or areas. Court administrators provide uniform court management, assuming many of the duties previously performed by chief judges, prosecutors, and court clerks. Where court administrators operate, the ultimate authority for running the court still rests with the chief judge. Administrators, however, are able to relieve the judge of many routine and repetitive tasks, such as record keeping, scheduling, case flow analysis, personnel administration, space utilization, facilities planning, and budget management. They may also serve to take minutes at meetings of judges and their committees. Juror management is another area in which trial court administrators are becoming increasingly involved. Effective court administrators are able to track lengthy cases and identify bottlenecks in court processing. They then suggest strategies to make the administration of justice increasingly efficient for courtroom professionals and more humane for lay participants. Learn more about court administrators and their activities at *CJNow!* online.

The Court Recorder

Also called the court stenographer or court reporter, the role of the court recorder is to create a record of all that occurs during trial. Accurate records are very important in criminal trial courts because appeals may be based entirely upon what went on in the courtroom. Especially significant are all verbal comments made in the courtroom, including testimony, objections, the rulings of the judge, the judge's instructions to the jury, arguments made by attorneys, and the results of conferences between the attorneys and the judge. Occasionally, the judge will rule that a statement should be "stricken from the record" because it is inappropriate or unfounded. The official trial record, often taken on a stenotype machine or audio recorder, may later be transcribed in manuscript form and will become the basis for any appellate review of the trial. Learn more about the role of the court recorder in the online version of this chapter.

Clerk of Court

The duties of the clerk of court (also known as the county clerk) extend beyond the courtroom. The clerk maintains all records of criminal cases, including all pleas and motions made both before and after the actual trial. The clerk also prepares a jury pool and issues jury summonses and subpoenas witnesses for both the prosecution and defense. During the trial, the clerk (or an assistant) marks physical evidence for identification as instructed by the judge and maintains custody of such evidence. The clerk also swears in witnesses and performs other functions as the judge directs. Some states allow the clerk limited judicial duties such as the power to issue warrants and to serve as judge of probate—overseeing wills and the administration of estates and handling certain matters relating to persons declared mentally incompetent.[2]

The Expert Witness

Most of the "insiders" we've discussed so far are either employees of the state or have ongoing professional relationships with the court (as in the case of defense counsel). Expert witnesses, however, may or may not have that kind of status, although some do. Expert witnesses are recognized for specialized skills and knowledge in an established profession or technical area. They must demonstrate their expertise through education, work experience, publications, and awards. By testifying at a trial they provide an effective way of introducing scientific evidence in such areas as medicine, psychology, ballistics, crime scene analysis, photography, and many other disciplines. An expert witness, like the other courtroom "actors" described in the online chapter, is generally a paid professional. And, like all other witnesses, they are subject to cross-examination. Unlike other ("lay") witnesses, they are allowed to express opinions and draw conclusions, but only within their particular area of expertise. Some well-known expert witnesses traverse the country and earn very high fees by testifying at one trial after another.

Outsiders: Nonprofessional Courtroom Participants

A number of people find themselves either unwilling or unwitting participants in criminal trials. Into this category fall defendants, victims, and most witnesses. Although they are "outsiders" who lack the status of paid professional participants, these are precisely the people who provide the "grist" for the judicial mill. Without them, trials could not occur, and the professional roles described earlier would be rendered meaningless.

Lay Witnesses

Nonexpert witnesses, otherwise known as lay witnesses, may be called by either the prosecution or defense. Lay witnesses may be eyewitnesses, who saw the crime being committed or who came upon the crime scene shortly after the crime had occurred. Another type of lay witness is the character witness, who provides information about the personality, family life, business acumen, and so on of the defendant in an effort to show that this is not the kind of person who would commit the crime he or she is charged with. Of course, the victim may also be a witness, providing detailed and sometimes lengthy testimony about the defendant and the event in question. The job of a witness is to provide accurate testimony concerning only those things of which he or she has direct knowledge.

Witnesses are officially notified that they are to appear in court to testify by a written document called a **subpoena**. Anyone who testifies in a criminal trial must do so under oath, in which some reference to God is made, or after affirmation,[3] where a pledge to tell the truth is used by those who find either "swearing" or a reference to God objectionable. All witnesses are subject to cross-examination, a process that is discussed in considerable detail in the online version of this chapter. A number of **victim assistance programs** (also called victim/witness assistance programs) have taken up a call for the rights of witnesses and are working to make the courtroom experience a more pleasant one for those who are called to testify.

Jurors

The U.S. Constitution requires jury trials in criminal cases, except where the right to trial is waived by the defendant. States have the authority to determine the size of criminal trial juries. Most states use juries composed of 12 persons and one or two alternates designated to fill in for jurors who are unable to continue due to accident, illness, or personal emergency. Some states allow for juries smaller than 12, and juries with as few as six members have survived Supreme Court scrutiny.[4] Ideally, the jury is to be a microcosm of society, reflecting the values, rationality, and common sense of the average person.

Jury duty is regarded as a responsibility of citizenship. Other than juveniles and certain job occupants such as police personnel, physicians, members of the armed services on active duty, and emergency services workers, persons called for jury duty must serve unless they can convince a judge that they should be excused for overriding reasons. Aliens, those convicted of a felony, and citizens who have served on a jury within the past two years are excluded from jury service in most jurisdictions.

The Role of the Victim in a Criminal Trial

Not all crimes have clearly identifiable victims. Some, like murder, do not have victims who survive. Where there is an identifiable surviving victim, however, he or she is often one of the most forgotten people in the courtroom. Although the victim may have been profoundly affected by the crime itself, and is often emotionally committed to the proceedings and trial outcome, he or she may not even be permitted to participate directly in the trial process. Although a powerful movement to recognize the interests of victims is in full swing in this country, it is still not unusual for crime victims to be totally unaware of the final outcome of a case which intimately concerns them. Victims, like witnesses, experience many hardships as they participate in the criminal court process. The trial process itself can make for a bitter experience. If victims take the stand, defense attorneys may test their memory, challenge their veracity, or even suggest that they were somehow responsible for their own victimization. Additional information on victims and victim's issues, including victim's assistance programs, is available at *CJNow!* online.

The Role of the Defendant in a Criminal Trial

The majority of criminal defendants are poor, uneducated, and often alienated from the philosophy which undergirds the American justice system. A common view of the defendant in a criminal trial is that of a relatively powerless person at the mercy of judicial mechanisms. Many defendants are just that. However, such an image is often far from the truth.

Defendants, especially those who seek an active role in their own defense, choreograph many courtroom activities. Experienced defendants, notably those who are career offenders, may be well versed in courtroom demeanor.

Every defendant who chooses to do so can substantially influence events in the courtroom. Defendants exercise choice in: 1) deciding whether or not to testify personally, 2) selecting and retaining counsel, 3) planning a defense strategy in coordination with their attorney, 4) deciding what information to provide to (or withhold from) the defense team, 5) deciding what plea to enter, and 6) determining whether or not to file an appeal, if convicted.

The Criminal Trial

Procedures in a modern courtroom are highly formalized. **Rules of evidence**, which govern the admissibility of evidence, and other procedural guidelines determine the course of a criminal hearing and trial. Significantly, criminal trials under our system of justice are built around an adversarial system and central to such a system is the advocacy model. Participating in the adversarial system are advocates for the state (the prosecution or district attorney) and for the defendant (defense counsel, public defender, etc.). The philosophy behind the **adversarial system** holds that the greatest number of just resolutions in all foreseeable criminal trials will occur when both sides are allowed to argue their cases effectively and vociferously before a fair and impartial jury. The system requires that advocates for both sides do their utmost, within the boundaries set by law and professional ethics, to protect and advance the interests of their clients (that is, the defendant and the state). The advocacy model makes clear that it is not the job of the defense attorney or the prosecution to judge the guilt of any defendant. Hence, even defense attorneys who are convinced that their client is guilty are still exhorted to offer the best possible defense and to counsel their client as effectively as possible.

As Figure 9-1 shows, trial chronology consists of eight stages: 1) trial initiation; 2) jury selection; 3) opening statements; 4) the presentation of evidence; 5) closing arguments; 6) the judge's charge to the jury; 7) jury deliberations; and 8) the verdict. Learn more about criminal trials, including types of evidence, and the advocacy model, at *CJNow!* online.

Figure 9-1 Stages in a criminal trial.

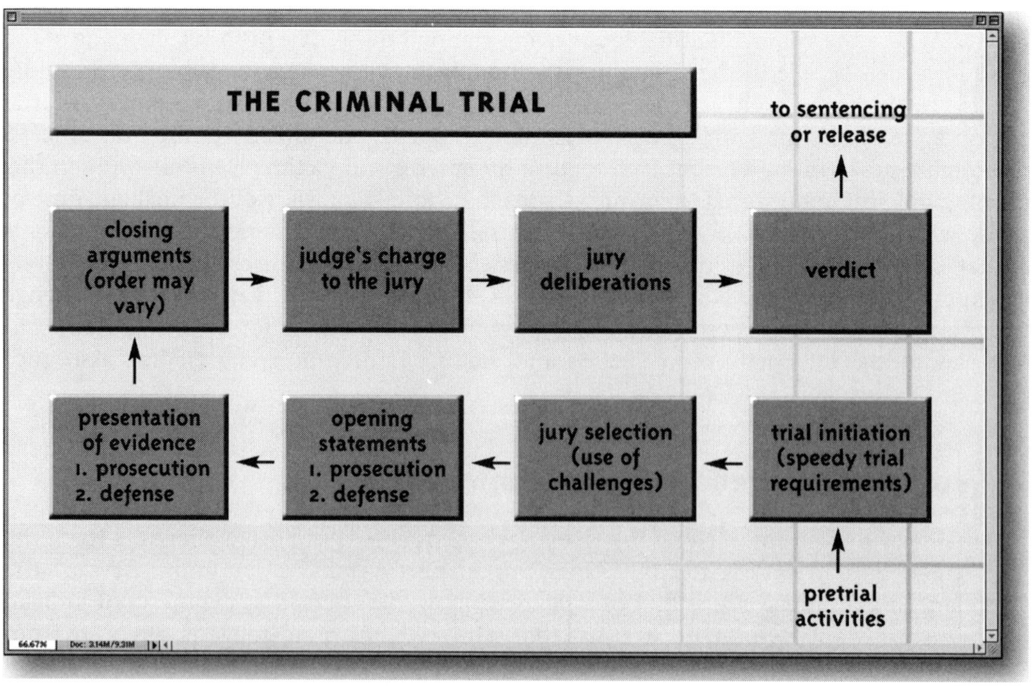

What You Should Remember

- The various types of professional actors in the courtroom work group are the judge (whose primary responsibility it is to ensure that justice prevails), the prosecuting attorney (who presents the state's case against the defendant), the defense attorney (who represents the defendant), the bailiff (who keeps order in the courtroom), the court recorder (who creates a record of the proceedings), the local court administrator (who schedules and manages the activities of the court), the clerk of courts (who maintains court records), and expert witnesses (who testify during trial).
- The various types of nonprofessional courtroom participants are lay witnesses (who provide testimony relevant to a case), jurors (who hear the evidence presented and make determinations of guilt or innocence), the victim, the defendant, and members of the press (who report on the proceedings).
- Trial chronology consists of eight stages: 1) trial initiation, 2) jury selection, 3) opening statements, 4) the presentation of evidence, 5) closing arguments, 6) the judge's charge to the jury, 7) jury deliberations, and 8) the verdict.
- Methods that have been suggested for improving the adjudication process include the use of professional jurors or judicial panels (in place of public juries); jurisdictional unification to avoid overlapping jurisdiction between courts; improved case processing, to include lessened personal costs for witnesses and jurors; and fairness in plea bargaining.

LIBRARY EXTRAS!

Library Extras! are suggested readings that are available digitally to readers of this guide. They may be accessed at the *CJNow!* Web site.

Library Extra! 9-1. *Felony Defendants in Large Urban Counties* (BJS, current volume).

Library Extra! 9-2. *Federal Pretrial Release and Detention* (BJS, current volume).

Library Extra! 9-3. *Indigent Defense* (BJS, 1996).

Library Extra! 9-4. *NIJ Survey of Prosecutors* (NIJ, 1995).

Library Extra! 9-5. *Trial Court Performance Standards* (BJA, 1997).

ENDNOTES

[1] "Pay the Costs of Justice," *USA Today*, March 30, 1993, p. 8A.

[2] See, for example, Joan G. Brannon, *The Judicial System in North Carolina* (Raleigh, NC: The Administrative Office of the Court, 1984), p. 14.

[3] *California* v. *Green*, 399 U.S. 149 (1970).

[4] *Williams* v. *Florida*, 399 U.S. 78, 90 S.Ct. 1893, 26 L.Ed. 2d 446 (1970).

Chapter 10

quick view

<< sentencing >>

Outline

- Crime and Punishment: Introduction
- The Philosophy of Criminal Sentencing
- Indeterminate Sentencing
- The Rise of Structured Sentencing
- Mandatory Sentencing
- Truth in Sentencing
- The Victim—Forgotten No Longer
- Traditional Sentencing Options

What You Should Learn

- The definition and nature of criminal sentencing.
- The five goals of contemporary criminal sentencing.

- The difference between indeterminate and structured sentencing, and the different types of structured sentencing models in use today.
- The nature of mandatory sentencing, and how it came about.
- The nature of truth in sentencing.
- The importance of federal sentencing guidelines.
- The nature and importance of the presentence investigation report.
- The history of victim's rights and services and the growing role of the victim in criminal justice proceedings.
- The four traditional sentencing options.
- The nature of arguments for and against the death penalty.
- The definitions of key terms that appear in boldface throughout this *Quick View* chapter. Definitions can be found online at http://www.cjnowonline.com.

Hear the author introduce this chapter at *CJNow!* online.

Crime and Punishment: Introduction

Sentencing is the imposition of a penalty upon a person convicted of a crime. Most sentencing decisions are made by judges, although in some cases, especially where a death sentence is possible, juries may be involved in a special sentencing phase of courtroom proceedings. The sentencing decision is one of the most difficult made by any judge or jury. Not only does it involve the future, and perhaps the very life, of the defendant, but society looks to sentencing to achieve a diversity of goals—some of which may not be fully compatible.

The online version of this chapter examines sentencing in terms of both philosophy and practice. It describes the goals of sentencing as well as the historical development of various sentencing models in the United States. The role of victims in contemporary sentencing practices is also discussed, and a detailed overview of victimization and victims' rights is provided.

The Philosophy of Criminal Sentencing

Modern sentencing practices are influenced by five goals, which weave their way through everyday sentencing practice. Each goal represents a quasi-independent sentencing philosophy, since each makes distinctive assumptions about human nature and holds implications for sentencing practice. The five goals of contemporary sentencing are:

1. Retribution
2. Incapacitation
3. Deterrence
4. Rehabilitation
5. Restoration

Retribution

Retribution is a call for punishment predicated upon a felt need for vengeance. It is the earliest known rationale for punishment. In its modern guise, retribution corresponds to the **just deserts** model of sentencing. The just deserts philosophy holds that offenders are responsible for their crimes. When they are convicted and punished, they are said to have gotten their "just deserts." Retribution sees punishment as deserved, justified, and even required, by the offender's behavior. The primary sentencing tool of today's just deserts model is imprisonment, but in extreme cases capital punishment (that is, death) may become the ultimate retribution. The goal of retribution is not deterrence, but satisfaction.

Incapacitation

Incapacitation, the second goal of criminal sentencing, seeks to protect innocent members of society from offenders who might do them harm if they were not prevented in some way. In ancient times mutilation and amputation of the extremities were sometimes used to prevent offenders from repeating their crimes. Modern incapacitation strategies separate offenders from the community in order to reduce opportunities for further criminality. Incapacitation is sometimes called the "lock 'em up approach" and forms the basis for the movement toward prison "warehousing," discussed in Chapter 12 online.

Both incapacitation and retribution are used as justifications for imprisonment. A significant difference between the two perspectives, however, lies in the fact that incapacitation requires only restraint—and not punishment.

Deterrence

Deterrence uses punishment as an example to convince people that criminal activity is not worthwhile. Its overall goal is crime prevention. **Specific deterrence** seeks to reduce the likelihood of recidivism (repeat offenses) by convicted offenders, whereas **general deterrence** strives to influence the future behavior of people who have not yet been arrested and who may be tempted to turn to crime.

Deterrence is one of the more "rational" goals of sentencing. It is rational because it is an easily articulated goal and also because it may be possible to objectively investigate the amount of punishment required to deter. Deterrence is compatible with the goal of incapacitation, since at least specific deterrence can be achieved through incapacitating offenders. However, although retribution is oriented toward the past and seeks to redress wrongs already committed, deterrence is a strategy for the future because it aims to prevent new crimes.

Rehabilitation

Rehabilitation seeks to bring about fundamental changes in offenders and their behavior. As in the case of deterrence, the ultimate goal of rehabilitation is a reduction in the number of criminal offenses. Whereas deterrence depends upon a "fear of the law" and the consequences of violating it, rehabilitation generally works through education and psychological treatment to reduce the likelihood of future criminality.

The term *rehabilitation*, however, may actually be a misnomer for the kinds of changes that its supporters seek. Rehabilitation literally means to return a person (or thing) to his or her previous condition. In the case of criminal offenders, however, it is unlikely that restoring many to their previous state will result in anything other than a more youthful type of criminality.

Restoration

Restoration is a sentencing goal that seeks to address this damage by making the victim and the community "whole again." Underlying the goal of restoration is the idea of **restorative justice**, which seeks to attain balance between the legitimate needs of the community, the offender, and the victim.

The "healing" of victims involves many aspects, ranging from victim assistance initiatives to legislation supporting victim compensation. Sentencing options which seek to restore the victim have focused primarily on restitution payments which offenders are ordered to make, either to their victims or to a general fund, which may then go to reimburse victims for suffering, lost wages, and medical expenses.

Some advocates of the restoration philosophy of sentencing point out that restitution payments and work programs which benefit the victim can also have the added benefit of rehabilitating the offender. The hope is that such sentences may teach offenders personal responsibility through structured financial obligations, job requirements, and regularly scheduled payments.

Indeterminate Sentencing

Whereas the *philosophy* of criminal sentencing is reflected in the goals of sentencing we have just discussed, different sentencing *practices* have been linked to each goal. During most of the twentieth century, for example, the rehabilitative goal has been influential. Since rehabilitation required that individual offenders' personal characteristics be closely considered in defining effective treatment strategies, judges were generally permitted wide discretion in choosing from among sentencing options. Although incapacitation is increasingly becoming the sentencing strategy of choice, many state criminal codes still allow judges to impose fines, probation, or widely varying prison terms, all for the same offense. These sentencing practices, characterized primarily by vast judicial choice, constitute an **indeterminate sentencing model**.

Indeterminate sentencing has both an historical and a philosophical basis in the belief that convicted offenders are more likely to participate in their own rehabilitation if they can reduce the amount of time they have to spend in prison. Inmates on good behavior will be released early, while recalcitrant inmates will remain in prison until the end of their terms. For that reason, parole generally plays a significant role in states which employ the indeterminate sentencing model. Indeterminate sentencing still plays a role in American criminal justice. Table 10-1 online shows the percent of imposed sentences that can be expected to be served in prison by offenders sentenced to prison by type of offense. Learn more about indeterminate sentencing at *CJNow!* online.

The Rise of Structured Sentencing

Beginning in the 1970s, a number of states moved to address concerns over **equity**, **proportionality**, and **social debt** in sentencing (see the online chapter for an explanation of these concepts) by developing a different model of sentencing known as **structured sentencing**. One form of structured sentencing, called **determinate sentencing**, requires that a convicted offender be sentenced to a fixed term that may be reduced by good time or earned time. Determinate sentencing states eliminated the use of parole and created explicit standards to specify the amount of punishment appropriate for a given offense. Determinate sentencing practices also specify an anticipated release date for each sentenced offender.

In response to the then-growing determinate sentencing movement, a few states developed **voluntary/advisory sentencing** guidelines. Such guidelines consist of recommended sentencing policies that are not required by law. They are usually based upon past sentencing practices and serve as guides to judges.

A third model of structured sentencing employs commission-based **presumptive sentencing** guidelines, which are usually developed by sentencing commissions rather than by legislatures and which give judges more leeway in deciding sentences than does determinate sentencing. Learn more about each type of sentencing, including critiques of each one at *CJNow!* online.

Mandatory Sentencing

Mandatory sentencing, which is actually another form of structured sentencing,[1] deserves special mention. **Mandatory sentencing** is just what its name implies—a structured sentencing scheme that allows no leeway in the nature of the sentence required and under which clearly enumerated punishments are mandated for specific offenses or for habitual offenders convicted of a series of crimes. Mandatory sentencing, because it is truly *mandatory*, differs from presumptive sentencing (discussed online) which allows for at least a limited amount of judicial discretion within ranges established by published guidelines. Some mandatory sentencing laws require only modest mandatory prison terms (for example, 3 years for armed robbery), while others are much more far-reaching

Typical of far-reaching mandatory sentencing schemes are three-strikes laws, (discussed in detail in the online chapter). Three-strikes laws (and, in some jurisdictions, two-strikes laws) require mandatory sentences (sometimes life in prison without the possibility of parole) for offenders convicted of a third serious felony. Such mandatory sentencing enhancements are aimed at deterring known and potentially violent offenders and are intended to incapacitate convicted criminals through long-term incarceration.

Mandatory sentencing has had significant consequences that deserve close attention. Among them are its impact on crime and the operation of the criminal justice system. The possible differential consequences for certain groups of people also bears examination. Some researchers[2] have found that under mandatory sentencing, officials tend to make earlier and more selective arrest, charging, and diversion decisions. They also tend to bargain less and to bring more cases to trial.

Truth in Sentencing

Truth in sentencing, which has been described as "a close correspondence between the sentence imposed upon those sent to prison and the time actually served prior to prison release,"[3] has become an important policy focus of many state legislatures and the federal congress. The Violent Crime Control and Law Enforcement Act of 1994 set aside $4 billion in federal prison construction funds (called "Truth in Sentencing Incentive Funds") for states which adopt truth in sentencing laws and are able to guarantee that certain violent offenders will serve 85% of their sentences. By 1999 twenty-seven states and the District of Columbia had met the 85% requirement.[4] Although most other states are moving toward practices which support truth in sentencing, there are some notable exceptions. Learn more about truth in sentencing, as well as the sentencing environment, presentence investigation reports, and federal sentencing guidelines at *CJNow!* online.

The Victim—Forgotten No Longer

In times past the concerns of victims were often forgotten. Thanks to a grass-roots resurgence of concern for the plight of victims, which began in this country in the early 1970s, the sentencing environment now frequently includes consideration of the needs of victims and their survivors. Changes began in 1982 when the President's Task Force on Victims of Crime[5] gave focus to the burgeoning victims' rights movement and urged the widespread expansion of victim assistance programs during what was then their formative period. The Task Force also recommended 68 specific programmatic and legislative initiatives for states and concerned citizens to pursue on behalf of crime victims. Recently, a victims' rights constitutional amendment was proposed by a bipartisan committee in the U.S. Congress. The text of the proposed amendment is reproduced in the online version of this chapter. Although a victims' rights amendment to the federal Constitution may not yet be reality, 32 states had passed their own victims' rights amendments as of January 1, 2000,[6] and significant federal legislation has already been adopted.

Much of the philosophical basis of today's victims' movement can be found in the restorative justice model, which was discussed briefly earlier in this chapter. **Restorative justice** emphasizes offender accountability and victim reparation. Restorative justice also provides the basis for victim compensation programs—which are another means of recognizing the needs of crime victims. See Table 10-2 online for a comparison of restorative justice with retributive justice.

An important consequence of the national victim-witness rights movement has been a call for the use of victim impact statements prior to sentencing. A victim impact statement generally takes the form of a written document which describes the losses, suffering, and trauma experienced by the crime victim or the victim's survivors. Judges are expected to consider such statements in arriving at an appropriate sanction for the offender. Learn more about victims, victims' rights, and victims' organizations at *CJNow!* online.

Traditional Sentencing Options

Assorted sentencing philosophies continue to permeate state-level judicial systems. Each state has its own sentencing laws, and frequent revisions of those statutes are not uncommon. Because of huge variations from one state to another in the laws and procedures which control the imposition of criminal sanctions, sentencing has been called "the most diversified part of the Nation's criminal justice process."[7] There is at least one common ground, however, that can be found in the four traditional sanctions which continue to dominate the thinking of most legislators and judges. The four traditional sanctions are: 1) imprisonment, 2) probation, 3) fines, and 4) death. Figure 10-1 shows the sentencing outcomes of persons convicted of felonies, while Figure 10-2 shows the increase in court-

Figure 10-1 The sentencing of convicted felons in state and federal courts by type of sentence. *Source:* Jodi M. Brown and Patrick A. Langan, *Felony Sentences in the United States, 1996* (Washington, D.C.: Bureau of Justice Statistics, 1999).

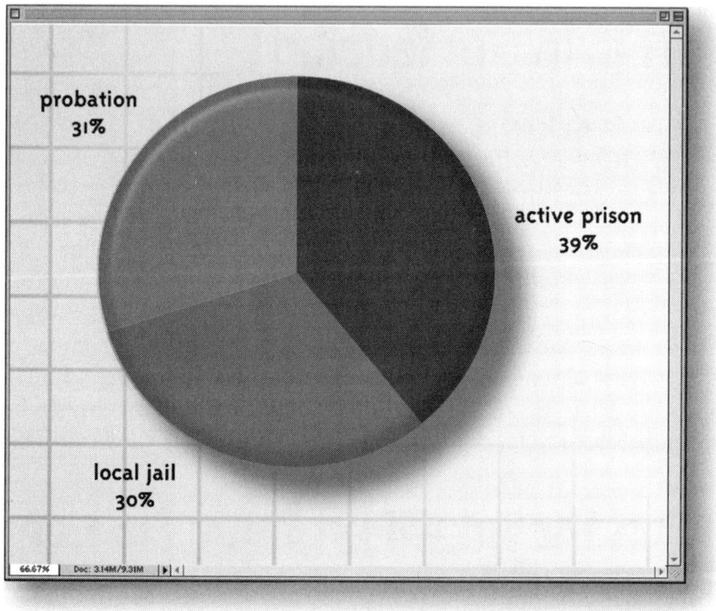

Figure 10-2 Court-ordered prison commitments, 1960–1996. *Source:* Jodi M. Brown and Patrick A. Langan, *Felony Sentences in the United States* (Washington, D.C.: Bureau of Justice Statistics, 1999 and other years).

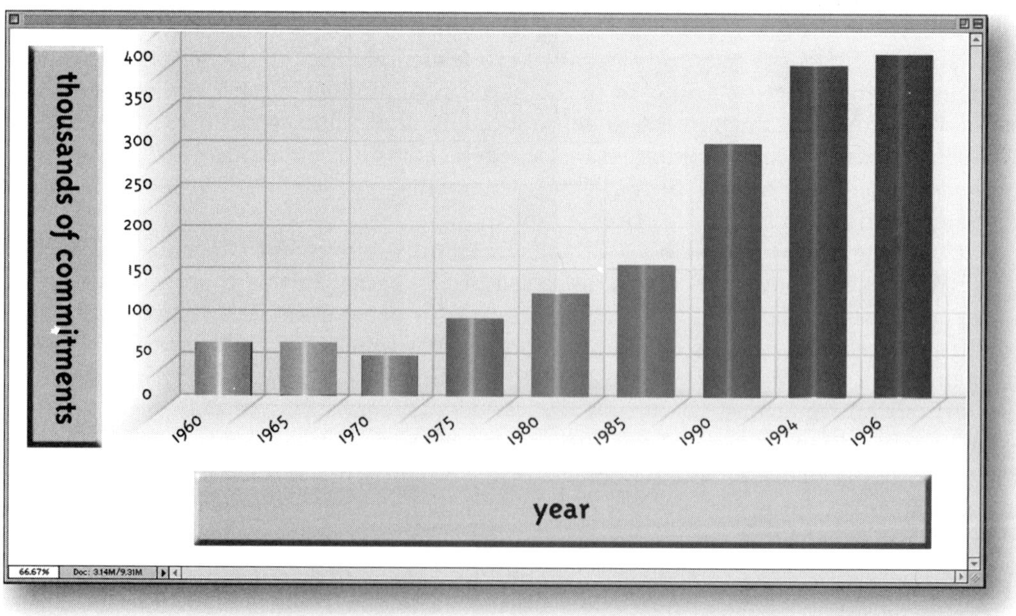

ordered prison commitments over time. You can learn more about traditional sanctions at *CJNow!* online; the paragraphs that follow contain additional information on capital punishment.

Death: The Ultimate Sanction

Some crimes are especially heinous and seem to cry out for extreme punishment. Consequently, many states today have statutory provisions that provide for a sentence of **capital punishment**. Since 1608, when records on capital punishment first became available, estimates are that more than 18,800 legal executions have been carried out in America.[8] Although capital punishment was widely used throughout the eighteenth and nineteenth centuries, the twentieth century has seen a constant decline in the number of persons legally executed in the United States. Between 1930 and 1967, when the U.S. Supreme Court ordered a nationwide stay of pending executions, nearly 3,800 persons were put to death. The years 1935 and 1936 were peak years, with nearly 200 legal killings each year. Executions declined substantially every year thereafter. Between 1967 and 1977 a *de facto* moratorium existed, with no executions carried out in any U.S. jurisdiction. Following the lifting of the moratorium, executions increased (see Figure 10-3). In 1993, 38 offenders were put to death, and 56 were executed nationwide in 1995. 1999 set a modern record for executions, with 98 executions—35 in Texas alone.

Today, 38 of the 50 states and the federal government have capital punishment laws. The number of crimes punishable by death under federal jurisdiction increased dramatically with passage of the Violent Crime Control and Law Enforcement Act of 1994—and now includes a total of about 60 offenses. Methods of imposing death vary by state. The majority of death penalty states authorize execution through lethal injection. Electrocution is the second most common means of dispatch, while hanging, the gas chamber, and firing squads have survived, at least as options available to the condemned, in a few states. For more information on capital punishment, including coverage of arguments for and against the death penalty, visit *CJNow!* online.

Figure 10-3 U.S. executions, 1976—2000, by state. *Source:* Death Penalty Information Center, data as of January 2, 1999.

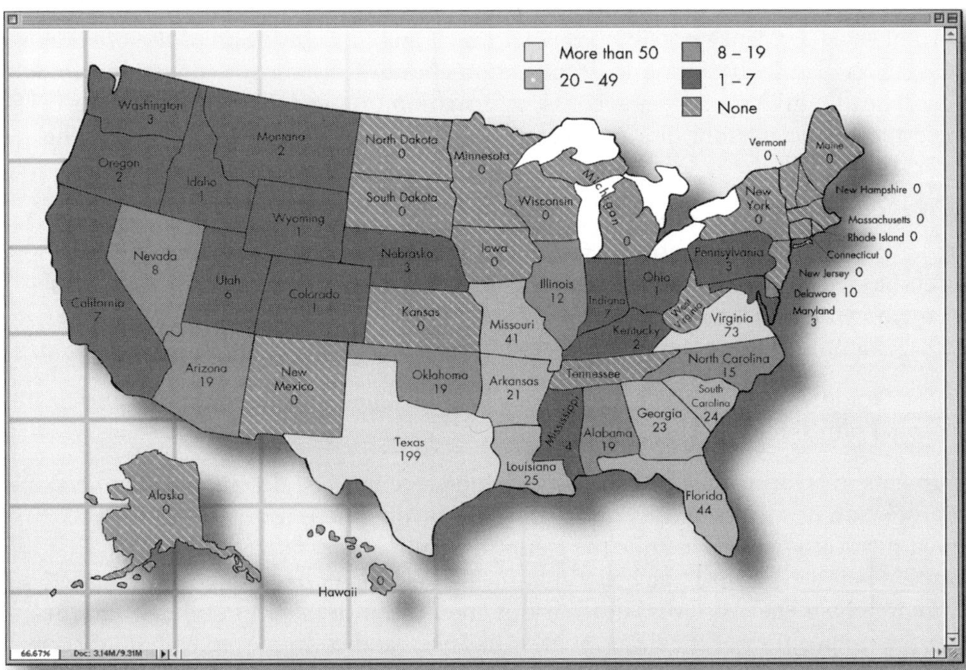

What You Should Remember

- Sentencing is the imposition of a penalty upon a person convicted of a crime.
- The five goals of contemporary criminal sentencing are retribution, incapacitation, deterrence, rehabilitation, and restoration.
- Indeterminate sentencing gives judges wide discretion in the imposition of criminal sentences, while structured sentencing limits judicial discretion and often requires sentences that are specified by law, or a specific range of sentencing options for given types of offenses. The different types of structured sentencing models in use today include determinate sentencing, voluntary/advisory sentencing, and presumptive sentencing.
- Mandatory sentencing is a structured sentencing scheme that allows no leeway in the nature of the sentence required and under which clearly enumerated punishments are mandated for specific offenses or for habitual offenders convicted of a series of crimes. Mandatory sentencing is the result of get-tough on crime attitudes that have been popular in American society over the last few decades.
- Truth in sentencing can be defined as a close correspondence between the sentence imposed upon those sent to prison and the time actually served in prison prior to release. Truth in sentencing requirements are now mandated by the federal government for states seeking certain types of federal funding and have influenced important policy decisions made by state legislatures and the federal Congress.
- Federal sentencing guidelines were mandated under Title II of the Comprehensive Crime Control Act, also known as the Sentencing Reform Act of 1984, which established the nine-member U.S. Sentencing Commission. Federal sentencing guidelines are important both because they guide federal judges in imposing sentences, and because they have become a model for many states that have embraced a structured sentencing model.
- Presentence reports are documents prepared by probation or parole officers for use by judges in determining appropriate sentences for convicted offenders. Presentence reports generally include personal information and identifying data describing the defendant, a chronology of the current offense and circumstances surrounding it, a record of the defendant's previous convictions (if any), a description of the offender's home life and family background, information about the offender's educational and physical health, military service records, information on the defendant's religious preference and financial condition, and (often) the sentencing recommendations of the officers submitting the report.
- Not long ago, crime was seen as an affront to the state, and the interests of victims were largely forgotten or ignored. Today, however, a growing interest in the rights of victims has led all states to pass some form of victims-rights legislation. Such legislation often includes the rights of crime victims to provide impact statements to the court. A victims' rights amendment to the U.S. Constitution is under consideration.
- The four traditional sentencing options are imprisonment, probation, fines, and death (or capital punishment).
- Arguments in favor of the death penalty include revenge, just deserts, and the need for the protection of society and its members from further victimization. Arguments against the death penalty include the claim that human life is sacred, the claim that execution is too expensive, the belief that the death penalty has often been imposed on innocent people, the claim that death is not an effective deterrent to others, and the belief that imposition of the death penalty has been and continues to be both discriminatory and arbitrary.

LIBRARY EXTRAS!

Library Extras! are suggested readings that are available digitally to readers of this guide. They may be accessed at the *CJNow!* Web site.

Library Extra! 10-1. *1996 National Survey of State Sentencing Structures* (NIJ, September 1998).

Library Extra! 10-2. *Balanced and Restorative Justice Philosophy* (OJJDP, not dated).

Library Extra! 10-3. *Capital Punishment*, (BJS, current volume).

Library Extra! 10-4. *Felony Sentences in the United States* (BJS, current volume).

Library Extra! 10-5. *National Assessment of Structured Sentencing* (BJA, 1996).

Library Extra! 10-6. *New Directions from the Field: Victim's Rights and Services in the 21st Century* (OVC, 1998).

Library Extra! 10-7. "Restorative Justice: Key Questions and Answers," *The National Institute of Justice Journal* (March 1998).

Library Extra! 10-8. *Three Strikes and You're Out: A Review of State Legislation* (NIJ, September 1997).

ENDNOTES

[1] Much of the material in this section is derived from Dale Parent, Terence Dunworth, Douglas McDonald, and William Rhodes, "Mandatory Sentencing," *NIJ Research in Action Series* (Washington, D.C.: NIJ, January 1997).

[2] Michael Tonry, *Sentencing Reform Impacts* (Washington, D.C.: National Institute of Justice, 1987).

[3] Lawrence A. Greenfeld, *Prison Sentences and Time Served for Violence* (Washington, D.C.: Bureau of Justice Statistics, April 1995).

[4] Paula M. Ditton and Doris James Wilson, "Truth in Sentencing in State Prisons," *BJS Special Report* (January 1999).

[5] President's Task Force on Victims of Crime, *Final Report* (Washington, D.C.: U.S. Government Printing Office, 1982).

[6] The last three states to adopt victim's rights constitutional amendments were Mississippi, Montana, and Tennessee. See the National Victim's Constitutional Amendment Network news page at http://www.nvcan.org/news.htm. Accessed January 10, 2000.

[7] *Report to the Nation on Crime and Justice*, 2nd ed. (Washington, D.C.: U.S. Department of Justice, 1988), p. 90.

[8] Capital Punishment Research Project, University of Alabama Law School.

Part 4

<< corrections >>

Chapter 11

PROBATION, PAROLE, AND COMMUNITY CORRECTIONS

Chapter 12

PRISONS AND JAILS

Chapter 13

PRISON LIFE

Chapter 11

quick view

<< probation, parole, and community corrections >>

Outline

- Introduction to Community Corrections
- What Is Probation?
- What Is Parole?
- Probation and Parole: The Pluses and Minuses
- The Legal Environment
- The Job of a Probation/Parole Officer
- Intermediate Sanctions
- The Future of Probation and Parole

What You Should Learn

- The difference between probation and parole and the history of both.
- Details of the legal environment surrounding the use of probation and parole, including the names of significant court cases in the area.

- A description of the federal probation system.
- The nature of the job of a probation/parole officer.
- The advantages of intermediate sanctions over more traditional forms of sentencing.
- The likely future of probation and parole.
- The definitions of key terms that appear in boldface throughout this *Quick View* chapter. Definitions can be found online at http://www.cjnowonline.com.

Hear the author introduce this chapter at *CJNow!* online.

Introduction to Community Corrections

Chapter 11 online takes a close look at the realities behind the practice of what we call "community corrections." **Community corrections**, also called **community-based corrections**, is a sentencing style that represents a movement away from traditional confinement options and an increased dependence upon correctional resources that are available in the community. Community corrections can best be defined as the use of a variety of court-ordered programmatic sanctions permitting convicted offenders to remain in the community under conditional supervision as an alternative to active prison sentences. Community corrections includes a wide variety of sentencing options such as probation, parole, home confinement, the electronic monitoring of offenders, and other new and developing programs—all of which are discussed in the online chapter.

What Is Probation?

Probation, which is one aspect of community corrections, is a sentence served while under supervision in the community.[1] Like other sentencing options, probation is a court-ordered sanction. Its goal is to allow for some degree of control over criminal offenders while using community programs to help rehabilitate them. Most of the alternative sanctions discussed in the online chapter are, in fact, predicated upon probationary sentences in which the offender is first placed on probation and then ordered to abide by certain conditions while remaining free in the community—such as participation in a specified program. Although probation can be directly imposed by the court in many jurisdictions, most probationers are technically sentenced first to confinement, but then immediately have their sentences suspended and are remanded into the custody of an officer of the court—the probation officer. Today, probation is the most commonly used form of criminal sentencing in the United States. Figure 11-1 shows that 58% of all persons under correctional supervision in the United States as of January 1, 1999, were on probation. Even violent offenders stand about a 1-in-5 chance of receiving a probationary term, as Figure 11-2 shows.

Figure 11-1 Persons under correctional supervision in the United States, by type of supervision. *Source: Probation and Parole in the United States* (Washington, D.C.: Bureau of Justice Statistics, August 1999). Note: Numbers do not total 100% due to rounding.

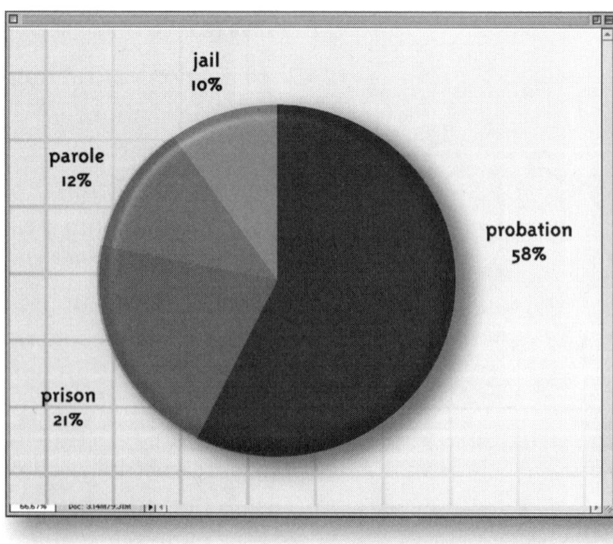

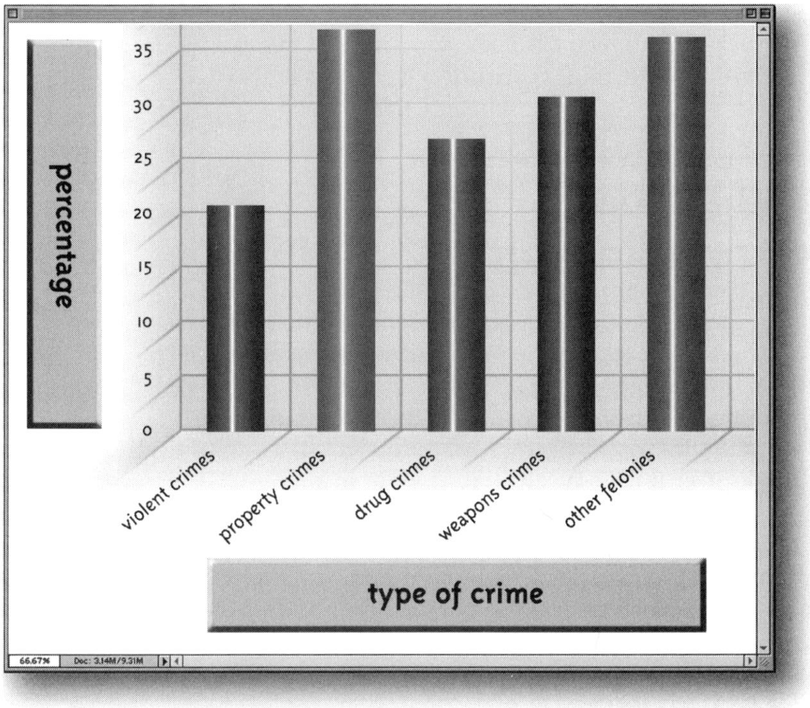

Figure 11-2 Percentage of convicted felony offenders receiving probation, by type of crime. *Source:* Jodi M. Brown and Patrick A. Langan, *Felony Sentences in the United States* (Washington, D.C.: Bureau of Justice Statistics, 1999).

Probation Conditions

Those sentenced to probation must agree to abide by court-mandated conditions of probation. Such conditions are of two types: general and specific. General conditions apply to all probationers in a given jurisdiction and usually include requirements that the probationer "obey all laws," "maintain employment," "remain within the jurisdiction of the court," "possess no firearm," "allow the probation officer to visit at home or at work," and so forth. As a general condition of probation, many probationers are also required to pay a fine to the court, usually in a series of installments. The fine is intended to reimburse victims for damages and to pay lawyers' fees and other costs of court. Special conditions may be mandated by a judge who feels that the probationary client is in need of particular guidance or control. Learn more about the conditions of probation, including the kinds of special conditions that might be imposed, at *CJNow!* online.

What Is Parole?

Parole is the supervised early release of inmates from correctional confinement. It differs from probation in both purpose and implementation. Whereas probationers generally avoid serving time in prison, offenders who are paroled have already been incarcerated. While probation is a sentencing option available to a judge, parole, in contrast, results from an administrative decision made by a legally designated paroling authority. Parolees comprise the smallest of the correctional categories shown in Figure 11-1 (other than "jail").

Parole Conditions

In those jurisdictions that retain discretionary parole, the conditions of parole remain very similar to the conditions agreed to by probationers. General conditions of parole usually include agreements not to willfully leave the state, as well as a blanket agreement to extradition requests from other jurisdictions. Parolees must also periodically report to parole officers, and parole officers may visit parolees at their homes and places of business—often arriving unannounced.

Failure to abide by the conditions of probation or parole may result in probation or parole **revocation**. As with probationers, parolees who are working can be ordered to pay fines and penalties. A provision for making **restitution** payments is also frequently included as a condition of probation or parole. Learn more at *CJNow!* online.

Probation and Parole: The Pluses and Minuses

Probation is used to meet the needs of offenders who require some correctional supervision short of imprisonment, while at the same time providing a reasonable degree of community protection. Parole fulfills a similar purpose for offenders released from prison. Both probation and parole provide a number of advantages over imprisonment, including: 1) lower costs, 2) increased employment, 3) the opportunity for restitution. 4) community support for offenders, 5) reduced risk of criminal socialization (while in prison), 6) increased use of community services, and 7) increased opportunity for rehabilitation. Any honest appraisal of probation and parole must recognize that they share a number of strategic drawbacks, such as 1) relative lack of punishment, 2) increased risk to the community, and 3) increased social costs. Learn more about the advantages and disadvantages of probation and parole at *CJNow!* online.

The Legal Environment

Ten especially significant U.S. Supreme Court decisions provide a legal framework for probation and parole supervision. Each is discussed in detail at *CJNow!* online. Among those that are discussed, the case of *Griffin* v. *Wisconsin* (1987)[2] may be the most significant. In *Griffin*, the U.S. Supreme Court ruled that probation officers may conduct searches of a probationer's residence without the need for either a search warrant or probable cause. According to the Court, "[a] probationer's home, like anyone else's, is protected by the Fourth Amendment's requirement that searches be 'reasonable.'" However, "[a] State's operation of a probation system . . . presents 'special needs' beyond normal law enforcement that may justify departures from the usual warrant and probable cause requirements." Probation, the Court concluded, is similar to imprisonment because it is a "form of criminal sanction imposed upon an offender after a determination of guilt." Similarly, in the 1998 case of *Pennsylvania Board of Probation and Parole* v. *Scott*,[3] the Court declined to extend the exclusionary rule to apply to searches by parole officers, even where such searches yield evidence of parole violations. Other court cases focus on the conduct of parole or probation **revocation hearings**, a topic that is covered in detail at *CJNow!* online.

The Job of a Probation/Parole Officer

The tasks performed by probation and parole officers are often quite similar. Some jurisdictions combine the roles of both into one job. The online chapter describes the duties of probation and parole officers, whether separate or performed by the same individuals. Probation/parole work consists primarily of four functions: 1) presentence investigations, 2) intake procedures, 3) needs assessment and diagnosis, and 4) the supervision of clients. Each function, along with the difficulties associated with the job of a probation/parole officer (including high **caseloads**) is discussed in detail in the online chapter.

Intermediate Sanctions

Significant new sentencing options have become available to judges in innovative jurisdictions over the past few decades. Many such options are called **intermediate sanctions** because they employ sentencing alternatives that fall somewhere between outright imprisonment and simple probationary release back into the community. They are also termed *alternative sentencing strategies*. The basic philosophy behind intermediate sanctions is this: When judges can find well-planned alternatives to imprisonment, the likelihood of a prison sentence is reduced. An analysis of alternative sentencing plans shows that they are accepted by judges in up to 80% of the cases in which they are recommended, and that as many as two-thirds of offenders who receive alternative sentences successfully complete them.[4]

Read more about intermediate, or alternative sanctions such as **shock probation**, **split sentencing**, boot camps, **mixed sentencing**, **community service**, intensive supervision, and home confinement and electronic monitoring—along with a description of the advantages and disadvantages of each—at *CJNow!* online.

The Future of Probation and Parole

Parole has been widely criticized in recent years. Citizen groups claim that it unfairly reduces prison sentences imposed on serious offenders. Academicians allege that parole programs can provide no assurances that criminals will not commit further crimes. Media attacks upon parole have centered on recidivism and have highlighted the so-called "revolving prison door" as representative of the failure of parole.

Official attacks upon parole have come from some powerful corners. Senator Edward Kennedy, for example, has called for the abolition of parole, as did former Attorney General Griffin Bell and former U.S. Bureau of Prisons Director Norman Carlson.[5] Prisoners have also challenged the fairness of parole, saying it is sometimes arbitrarily granted and creates an undue amount of uncertainty and frustration in the lives of inmates. Parolees have similarly complained about the unpredictable nature of the parole experience, citing their powerlessness in the parole contract.

Probation, although it has generally fared better than parole, is not without its critics. The primary purpose of probation has always been rehabilitation. Unfortunately for advocates of probation, however, the rehabilitative ideal holds far less significance today than it has in the past. The contemporary demand for "just deserts" appears to have reduced the tolerance society as a whole feels for even relatively minor offenders. Learn more about the possible future of probation and parole at *CJNow!* online.

What You Should Remember

- Probation is a court-ordered sentence of imprisonment that is suspended. Probation has a long and diverse history, but John Augustus (1784-1859), a Boston shoemaker, is generally recognized as the world's first probation officer.
- Parole is the conditional and (generally) supervised early release of a convicted offender from prison. Parole decisions are often made by parole boards or by parole commissions.
- The use of parole in this country began with the Elmira Reformatory in 1876 as part of a sentencing philosophy that stressed rehabilitation.
- Both probation and parole impose "conditions" upon defendants, requiring them to obey the law, meet with probation/parole officers, hold a job, and the like. Failure to abide by the conditions of probation or parole can result in rearrest and imprisonment.
- The online book discusses ten especially significant U.S. Supreme Court decisions that provide a legal framework for probation and parole supervision. The 1987 case of *Griffin* v. *Wisconsin* held that probation officers may conduct searches of a probationer's residence without the need for either a search warrant or probable cause. In the 1998 case of *Pennsylvania Board of Probation and Parole* v. *Scott*,[6] the Court declined to apply the exclusionary rule to searches by parole officers, even where such searches yield evidence of parole violations.

- The federal probation system, which is described in the online chapter, was created by Congress in 1925.
- The tasks performed by probation and parole officers are often quite similar. Probation/parole work consists primarily of four functions: 1) presentence investigations, 2) intake procedures, 3) needs assessment and diagnosis, and 4) the supervision of clients.
- Intermediate, or alternative, sanctions have three distinct advantages over more traditional forms of sentencing. Such sanctions are: 1) less expensive to operate on a per offender basis than imprisonment; 2) socially cost effective; and 3) flexibile in terms of resources, time of involvement, and place of service.
- While the future of probation looks bright, calls for the elimination of parole are widespread. Most such calls are based on claims that far too many parolees commit new crimes upon release.

LIBRARY EXTRAS!

Library Extras! are suggested readings that are available digitally to readers of this guide. They may be accessed at the *CJNow!* Web site.

Library Extra! 11-1. *Characteristics of Adults on Probation* (BJS, current volume).

Library Extra! 11-2. *Correctional Populations in the United States* (BJS, current volume).

Library Extra! 11-3. "Job Placement for Offenders: A Promising Approach to Reducing Recidivism and Correctional Costs," *The National Institute of Justice Journal* (NIJ, July 1999).

Library Extra! 11-4. "Probation in the United States: Practices and Challenges," *The National Institute of Justice Journal* (NIJ, September 1997).

Library Extra! 11-5. *State Court Sentencing of Convicted Felons* (NIJ, March 1998).

ENDNOTES

[1] President's Commission on Law Enforcement and Administration of Justice, *The Challenge of Crime in a Free Society* (Washington, D.C.: U.S. Government Printing Office, 1967).

[2] *Griffin* v. *Wisconsin*, 483 U.S. 868, 107 S.Ct. 3164 (1987).

[3] *Pennsylvania Board of Probation and Parole* v. *Scott*, No. 97-581 (1998).

[4] The Sentencing Project, *Changing the Terms of Sentencing: Defense Counsel and Alternative Sentencing Services* (Washington, D.C.: The Project, no date).

[5] James A. Inciardi, *Criminal Justice*, 2nd ed. (New York: Harcourt Brace Jovanovich, 1987), p. 664.

[6] *Pennsylvania Board of Probation and Parole* v. *Scott*, No. 97-581 (1998).

Chapter 12
quick view
<< prisons and jails >>

Outline

- Early Punishments
- The Emergence of Prisons
- Overcrowding
- Prisons Today
- Jails
- Private Prisons

What You Should Learn

- The nature and history of early punishments and their impact on modern correctional programs.
- The major characteristics of today's prisons.

- How jails fit into the correctional framework and what issues currently face jail administrators.
- The nature of the trend toward privatization in the corrections field.
- The definitions of key terms that appear in boldface throughout this *Quick View* chapter. Definitions can be found online at http://www.cjnowonline.com.

Early Punishments

Hear the author introduce this chapter at *CJNow!* online.

Prisons, as places where convicted offenders serve time as punishment for breaking the law, are a relatively new development in the handling of offenders. In fact, the emphasis upon *time served* as the essence of criminal punishment is scarcely 200 years old.

Prior to the emergence of imprisonment, convicted offenders were routinely subjected to fines, physical punishment, and often death. Corporal punishments were the most common form of criminal punishment used, and generally fit the doctrine of ***lex talionis*** (the law of retaliation). Also called "an eye for an eye, and a tooth for a tooth," this early rule of retaliation generally duplicated the offense, with the offender as the substitute victim. Hence, if a person blinded another, they were blinded in return. Murderers were themselves killed, with the form of execution sometimes being tailored to approximate the method they had used in committing the crime. Learn more about the corporeal punishments that preceded imprisonment, including flogging, mutilation, and branding, along with exile or banishment, and the diverse forms of public humiliation that were employed as criminal sanctions at *CJNow!* online.

Workhouses

A significant precursor of modern prisons was the sixteenth century workhouse. The 1500s were a time of economic upheaval in Europe, caused partly by wars and partly by the growing roots of the industrial revolution. By midcentury thousands of unemployed and vagrant people were scouring towns and villages seeking food and shelter. It was not long before they depleted the economic reserves of churches, which were the primary social relief agencies of the time.

In the belief that poverty was caused by laziness, governments were quick to create workhouses designed to instill "habits of industry" in the unemployed. The first workhouse in Europe opened in 1557, and by 1576 Parliament decreed that every county in England should build a workhouse. Although workhouses were forerunners of our modern prisons, they did not incarcerate criminal offenders—only vagrants and the economically disadvantaged. Nor were they designed to punish convicts, but served instead to reinforce the value of hard work.

The Emergence of Prisons

While the identity of the world's first true prison may never be known, we do know that at some point penalties for crime came to include incarceration. John Howard, an early prison reformer, mentions prisons housing criminal offenders in Hamburg, Germany; Berne, Switzerland; and Florence, Italy, in his 1777 book, *State of Prisons*.[1]

Near the end of the eighteenth century the concept of imprisonment as punishment for crime reached its fullest expression in the United States. Soon after they opened, U.S. prisons came to serve as models for European reformers searching for ways to humanize criminal punishment. For that reason, and in order to better appreciate how today's prisons operate, it is important to understand the historical development of the prison movement in the United States. Figure 12-1 portrays the stages through which American prisons progressed following introduction of the concept of incarceration as a punishment for crime around 1790. Stages shown in the figure are: 1) the Penitentiary Era (1790-1825), represented by the

prison era

	THE PENITENTIARY ERA	THE MASS (CONGREGATE) PRISON ERA	THE REFORMATORY ERA	THE INDUSTRIAL ERA	THE PUNITIVE ERA	THE TREATMENT ERA	THE COMMUNITY BASED (DECARCERATION) ERA	THE WAREHOUSING ERA	THE JUST DESERTS ERA
YEAR	1790	1825	1876	1890	1935	1945	1967	1980	1995
PHILOSOPHY	rehabilitation, deterrence	incapacitation, deterrence	rehabilitation	incapacitation, social restoration	retribution	rehabilitation	restoration, rehabilitation	incapacitation	retribution, incapacitation, deterrence
REPRESENTATIVE INSTITUTIONS	Philadelphia penitentiary eastern penitentiary (Cherry Hill, PA) western penitentiary (Pittsburgh)	New York state prison (Auburn, NY)	Elmira reformatory (Elmira, NY)	Auburn (NY) Sing Sing (NY) Statesville (IL) San Quentin (CA) Attica (NY)	Alcatraz (CA)	Marion (IL)	Massachusetts youth services halfway houses	most major prisons	emerging in Alabama, Mississippi, Virginia, Georgia, and rapidly spreading throughout the nation

Figure 12-1 Stages of prison development in the United States.

Pennsylvania system of imprisonment; 2) the Mass Prison Era (1825-1876), based upon the **Auburn system** of confinement; 3) the Reformatory Era (1876-1890), for which the Elmira Reformatory in New York stood as an example; 4) the Industrial Prison Era (1890-1935), characterized by various forms of inmate labor; 5) the Punitive Era (1935-1945), brought about by passage of the federal **Ashurst-Sumners Act** and other legislation designed to curtail prison labor; 6) the idealistic Era of Treatment (1945-1967), built upon a **medical model**; 7) the Community-Based Format (1967-1980), which made use of halfway houses and **work release** programs; 8) the era of Warehousing and Overcrowding (1980-1995), bred of high **recidivism** and founded upon the **nothing works doctrine**; and 9) the Just Deserts Era (1995-present), built upon a **justice model** with its emphasis on individual responsibility and accountability. Each historical era and the personalities who influenced it are discussed in detail in the online Chapter.

Overcrowding

As a consequence of the warehousing and just deserts eras, the American prison population grew dramatically (see Figure 12-2), and prisons everywhere became notoriously overcrowded (see Figure 12-3). Today, prison overcrowding remains a harsh reality in many jurisdictions, and prison officials have developed three definitions of prison capacity. **Rated capacity** refers to the size of the inmate population that a facility can handle according to the judgment of experts. **Operational capacity** is the number of inmates that a facility can effectively accommodate based on an appraisal of the institution's staff, programs, and services. **Design capacity** refers to the inmate population the institution was originally built to handle. Rated capacity estimates usually yield the largest inmate capacities, whereas design capacity (upon which many observations in the online chapter are based) typically shows the highest amount of overcrowding.

Some authors have identified the central problem of the present era as one of selective versus collective incapacitation.[2] Collective incapacitation is a strategy which would

Figure 12-2 U.S. prison population, historical and projected growth, 1960–2002. *Sources:* Greg Wees, "Inmate Population Expected to Increase 43% by 2002," *Corrections Compendium*, April 1996; and A. Beck and C.J. Mumola, *Prisoners in 1998* (Washington, D.C.: Bureau of Justice Statistics, 1999).

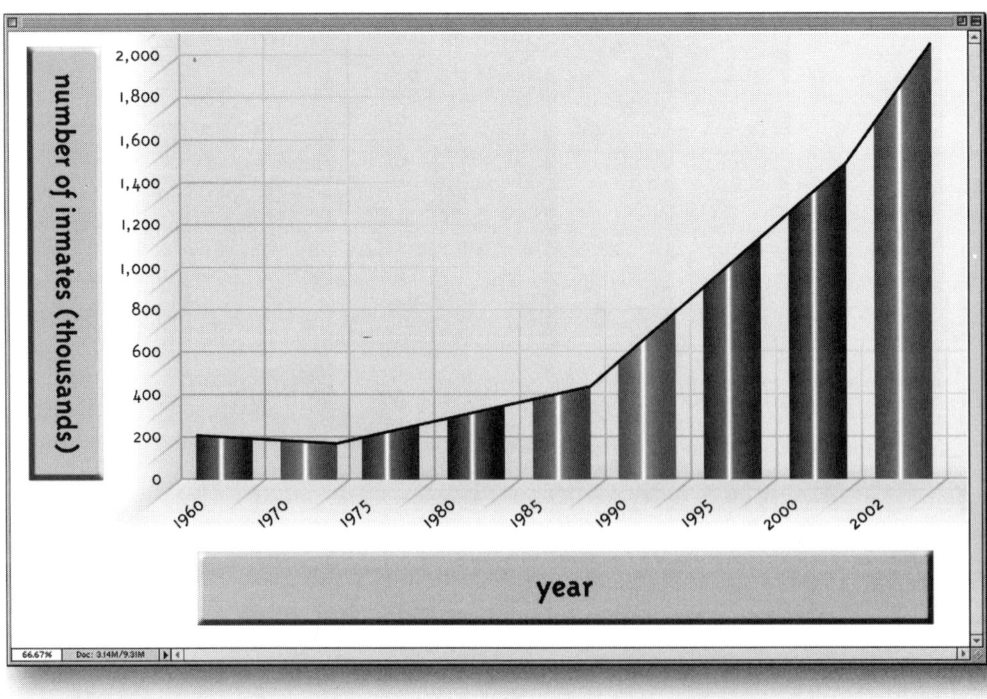

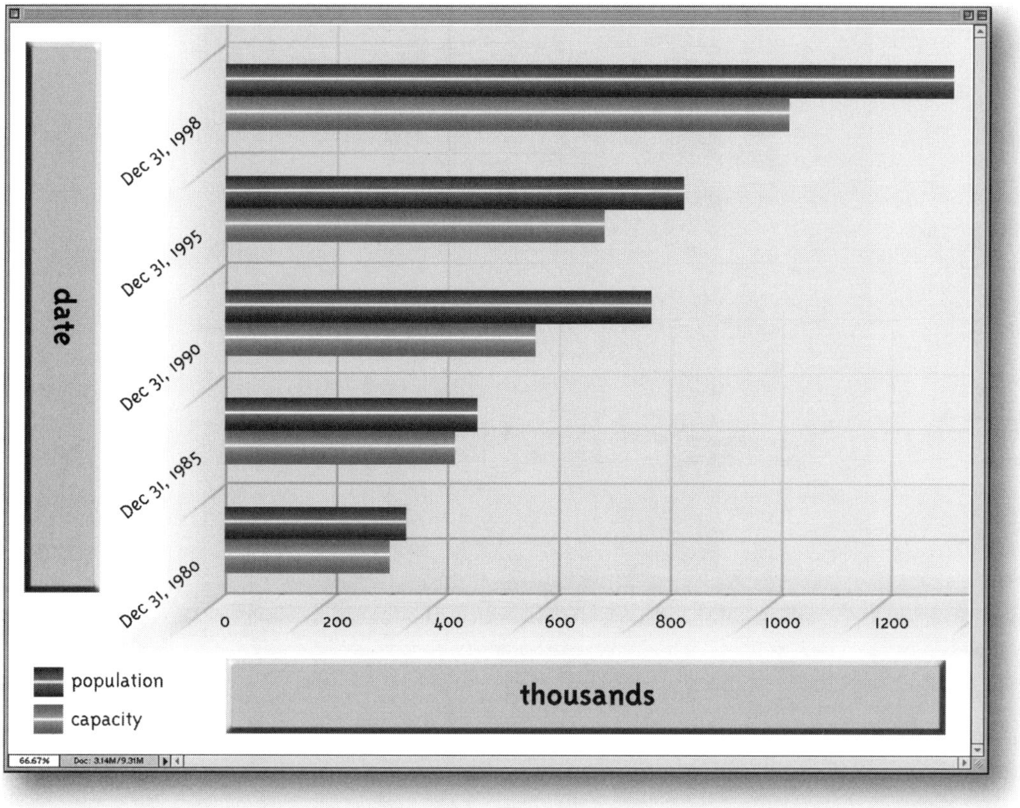

Figure 12-3 State and federal prison populations, inmates versus capacity, 1980–1998. *Source:* Bureau of Justice Statistics, *Correctional Populations in the United States* (Washington, D.C.: Bureau of Justice Statistics, various years).

imprison almost all serious offenders and is still found today in states which rely upon predetermined, or fixed, sentences for given offenses or for a series of specified kinds of offenses (as in the case of three-strikes legislation, which is discussed in the online chapter). Collective incapacitation is, however, prohibitively expensive as well as unnecessary in the opinion of many experts. Not all offenders need to be imprisoned because not all represent a continuing threat to society. But those who do are difficult to identify.[3]

In most jurisdictions where the just deserts initiative holds sway, selective incapacitation is rapidly becoming the rule. **Selective incapacitation** seeks to identify the potentially most dangerous criminals with the goal of selectively removing them from society.

Prisons Today

There are approximately 1,000 state and 80 federal prisons in operation across the country today. More are quickly being built as both the states and the federal government scramble to fund and construct new facilities. America's prison population has tripled since 1980, and its growth shows no signs of slowing. Slightly over 6.5% of those imprisoned are women.[4]

An examination of imprisonment statistics by race highlights the huge disparity between blacks and whites in prison. While only an estimated 868 white males are imprisoned in the United States for every 100,000 white males in their late 20s, latest figures show an incarceration rate of 8,630 black men for every 100,000 black males of the same age—*ten times* greater than the figure for whites![5] Worse yet, the rate of growth in such figures shows that the imprisonment rate of blacks increased dramatically over the past ten years, while the rate of white imprisonment has grown far less. Many of these statistics are displayed graphically in Figures 12-4 and 12-5. See *CJNow!* online for the latest numbers.

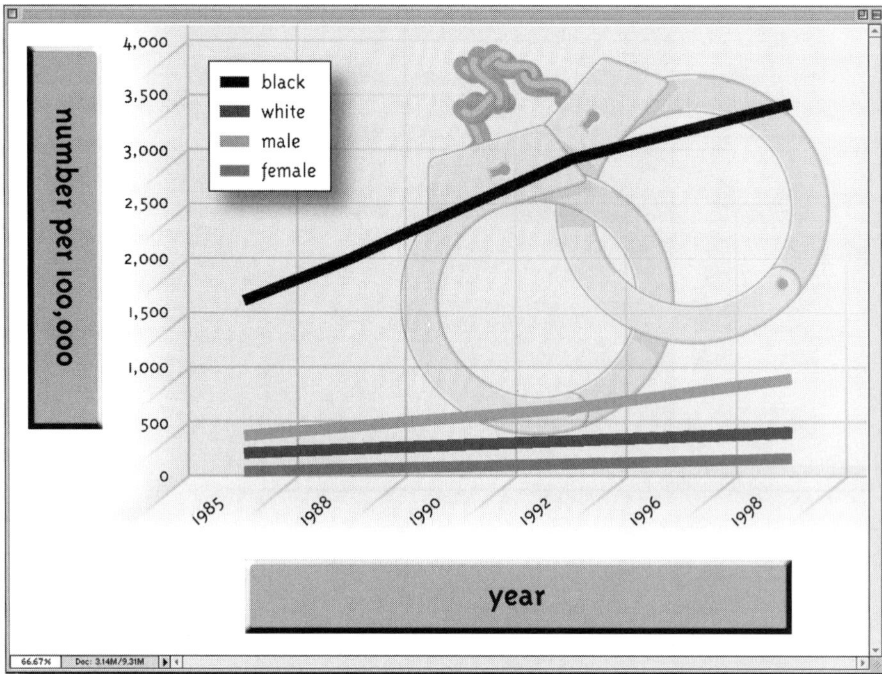

Figure 12-4 U.S. incarceration rates by race and sex. *Source:* Bureau of Justice Statistics.

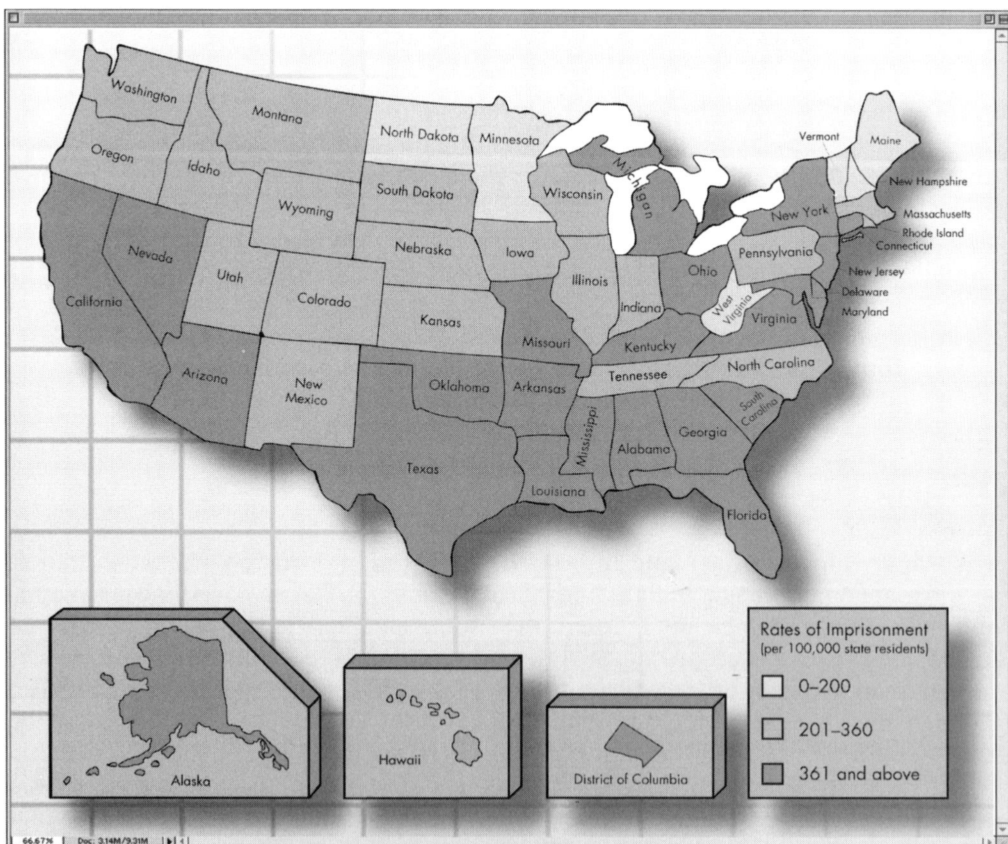

Figure 12-5 Rates of imprisonment in the United States.

The Federal Prison System

On May 14, 1930, the Federal Bureau of Prisons (BOP) was created under the direction of Sanford Bates. The Bureau inherited a preexisting federal system that was dramatically over-crowded. Many federal prisoners were among the most notorious criminals in the nation, and ideals of humane treatment and rehabilitation were all but lacking in the facilities of the 1930s. Director Bates began a program of improvements to relieve overcrowding and to increase the treatment capacity of the system. In 1933 the Medical Center for Federal Prisoners opened in Springfield, Missouri, with a capacity of around 1,000 inmates. Alcatraz Island began operations in 1934.

Today, the federal prison system classifies its institutions according to five security levels: 1) administrative maximum (ADMAX), 2) high security, 3) medium security, 4) low security, and 5) minimum security. High-security facilities are called United States Penitentiaries (USPs), medium- and low-security institutions are both called Federal Correctional Institutions (FCIs); and minimum-security prisons are termed Federal Prison Camps (FPCs). Minimum-security facilities (like Eglin Air Force Base, Florida; and Maxwell Air Force Base, Alabama) are essentially honor-type camps with barracks-like housing and no fencing. Low-security facilities in the federal prison system are surrounded by double chain-link fencing and employ vehicle patrols around their perimeters to enhance security. Medium-security facilities (like those in Terminal Island, California; Lompoc, California; and Seagoville, Texas) make use of similar fencing and patrols, but supplement it with electronic monitoring of the grounds and perimeter areas. High-security facilities (USPs such as those in Atlanta, Georgia; Lewisburg, Pennsylvania; Terre Haute, Indiana; and Leavenworth, Kansas) are architecturally designed to prevent escapes and to contain disturbances. They also make use of armed patrols and intense electronic surveillance. A separate federal prison category is that of Administrative Facility, consisting of institutions with special missions, which are designed to house all types of inmates. Most administrative facilities are Metropolitan Detention Centers (MDCs). MDCs, which are generally located in large cities close to federal courthouses, are the jails of the federal correctional system and hold inmates awaiting trial in federal court. Another five administrative facilities are termed Medical Centers for Federal Prisoners (MCFPs) and function as hospitals. The federal correctional system consists of 94 facilities existing either as single institutions or as Federal Correctional Complexes—that is, sites consisting of more than one type of correctional institution (see Figure 12-6). Learn more about the federal prison system at *CJNow!* online.

Figure 12-6 Long-term confinement facility locations in the federal correctional system, 1999. *Source:* Federal Bureau of Prisons. Note: Does not include Bureau of Prisons offices or Community Corrections Management (CCM) offices.

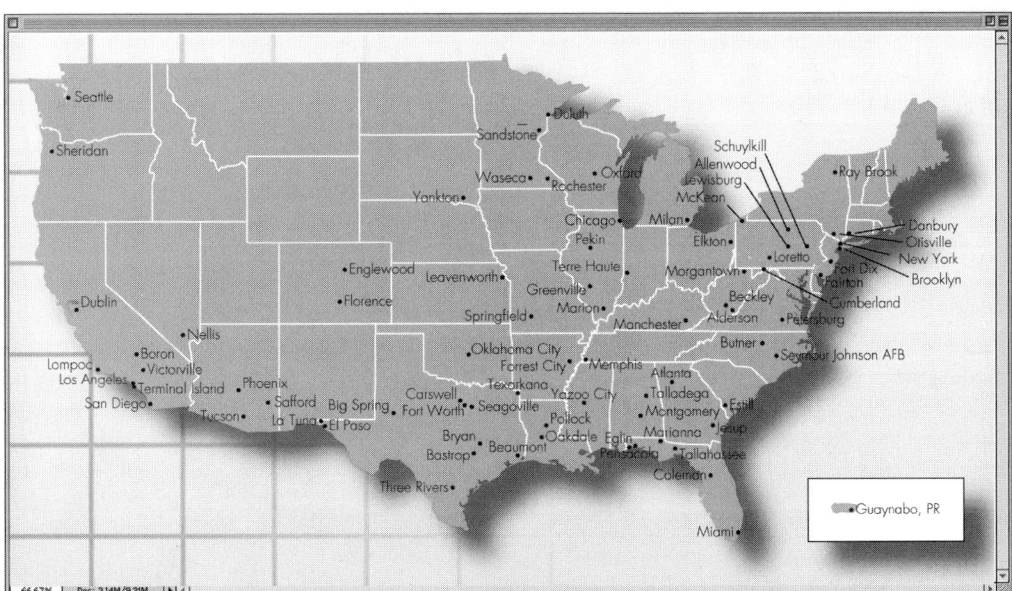

Recent Improvements

In the midst of frequent lawsuits, court-ordered changes in prison administration, and overcrowded conditions, outstanding prison facilities are being recognized through the American Correctional Association's program of accreditation. The ACA Commission on Accreditation has developed a set of standards which correctional institutions can use in self-evaluation. Those which meet the standards can apply for accreditation under the program. Another avenue toward improvement of the nation's prisons can be found in the National Academy of Corrections, the training arm of the National Institute of Corrections. Learn more about the ACA's accreditation pogram and the National Institute of Corrections at *CJNow!* online.

Jails

Jails are short-term confinement facilities which were originally intended to hold suspects following arrest and pending trial. Today, jails also house those convicted of misdemeanors who are serving relatively short sentences and felony offenders awaiting transportation to long-term confinement facilities. Jail authorities also supervise additional men and women in the community under the following programs: electronic monitoring; home detention without electronic monitoring; day reporting; community service; and weekender programs. See *CJNow!* for the latest statistics on these programs and on jail populations.

Not surprisingly, the nation's most populous states tend to have the most inmates. Almost half of the nation's jail population are housed in the jails of five states:[6] California, Texas, Florida, New York, and Georgia.

Jails have been called the "shame of the criminal justice system." Many are old, overcrowded, poorly funded, scantily staffed by underpaid and poorly trained employees, and given low priority in local budgets. The root cause of jail crowding can be found in a growing crime rate coupled with a punitive public attitude, which has heavily influenced correctional practice. Overcrowded prisons have also spilled over into jails. During the last few years, many states have begun using jails instead of prisons for the confinement of convicted felons, exacerbating the jail crowding problem still further. Symptomatic of problems brought on by overcrowding, the National Institute of Justice reported 234 suicides in jails across the nation during a recent year.[7] Jail deaths from all causes (which total about 650 annually) are shown in Figure 12-7. Learn more about jail crowding and jail conditions at *CJNow!* online.

Figure 12-7 Causes of jail deaths in the United States. *Source:* U.S. Department of Justice.

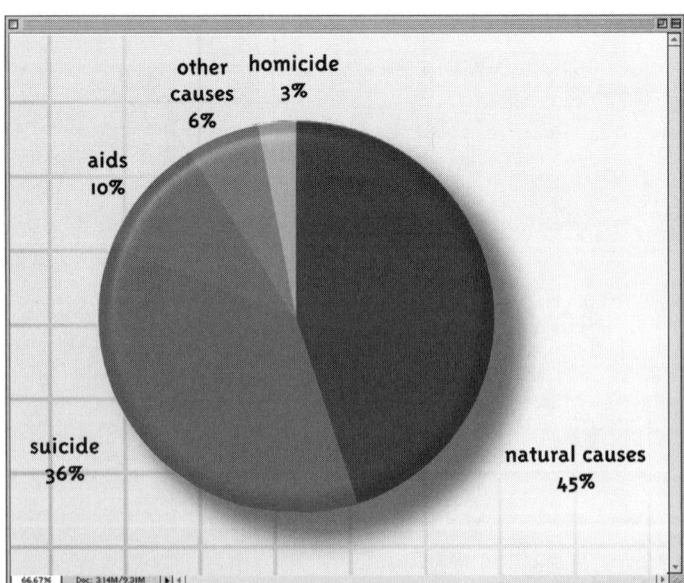

Direct Supervision Jails

In an effort to solve many of the problems which have dogged jails in the past, a new jail management strategy emerged during the 1980s. Called direct supervision (or podular/direct supervision, or PDS) this contemporary approach joins podular/unit architecture with a participative, proactive management philosophy. Often built in a system of "pods," or modular self-contained housing areas linked to one another, direct supervision jails eliminate the old physical barriers which separated staff and inmates. Gone are bars and isolated secure observation areas for officers. They are replaced by an open environment in which inmates and correctional personnel mingle with relative freedom. In a growing number of such "new-generation" jails, large reinforced Plexiglas® panels have supplanted walls and serve to separate activity areas, such as classrooms and dining halls, from one another. Soft furniture is often found throughout these institutions, and individual rooms take the place of cells, allowing inmates at least a modicum of personal privacy. In today's direct supervision jails, 16 to 46 inmates typically live in one pod, with correctional staffers present among the inmate population on an around-the-clock basis. While the number of direct supervision jails seems to be rapidly growing, such facilities are not without their problems. Learn more about direct supervision jails at *CJNow!* online.

Jails and the Future

In contrast to more visible issues confronting the justice system, such as the death penalty, gun control, the war on drugs, and big-city gangs, jails have received relatively little attention from the media and have generally escaped close public scrutiny. National efforts, however, to improve the quality of jail life are under way. Some changes involve adding crucial programs for inmates. Jail drug treatment programs, jail industries, jail volunteers, jail boot camps, jail standards, and **regional jails**—that is, jails that are built and run using the combined resources of a variety of local jurisdictions—are all discussed in detail in the online chapter.

Private Prisons

Although the prison **privatization** movement was slow to catch on at first, it has recently grown at a rapid pace—and the number of prisoners held in such institutions in expected to double over the next five years.[8] Today's privately-run prisons are operated by Corrections Corporation of America (CCA), U.S. Corrections Corporation, Wackenhut Corrections Corporation, and numerous other smaller companies. The growth rate of the private prison "industry" is over 35% annually[9]—comparable to the highest growth rates anywhere in the corporate sector.

Most states that use private firms to supplement their prison resources contract with such companies to provide a full range of custodial and other correctional services. States contract with private companies in order to reduce overcrowding, lower operating expenses, and avoid lawsuits targeted at state officials and employees. Many hurdles—both practical and legal—remain, however, before the privatization movement can effectively provide large-scale custodial supervision. Learn more about the privatization of both prisons and jails at *CJNow!* online.

What You Should Remember

- Today's overcrowded prisons are largely the result of historical efforts to humanize the treatment of offenders. Prior to the development of prisons, early punishments were often cruel and torturous. "Doing time for crime" is modern society's answer to the corporal punishments of centuries past.
- Prisons are long-term secure confinement facilities in which convicted offenders serve time as punishment for breaking the law.
- Prisons in the United States have evolved through nine stages: 1) the Penitentiary Era (1790-1825), 2) the Mass Prison Era (1825-1876), 3) the Reformatory Era (1876-1890),

4) the Industrial Prison Era (1890-1935), 5) the Punitive Era (1935-1945), 6) the Era of Treatment (1945-1967), 7) the Community-Based Format (1967-1980), 8) the era of Warehousing and Overcrowding (1980-1995), and 9) the Just Deserts Era (1995-present).

- Prisons today exist at both the state and federal level. Although most are overcrowded, prison populations continue to grow—fed in part by America's long-standing War on Drugs. Similarly, the just deserts philosophy, characterized by a "get-tough on crime" attitude, continues to swell prison populations.
- Jails are short-term confinement facilities which were originally intended to hold suspects following arrest and pending trial. They face many of the same problems as prisons, including overcrowding and burgeoning growth.
- The movement toward increased use of privately run correctional institutions, which began a few decades ago, has since expanded. Privatization continues to face many hurdles, however, not the least of which is the question of deciding who is ultimately responsible for the fate of inmates held in such facilities—the state or the corporations that run them.

LIBRARY EXTRAS!

Library Extras! are suggested readings that are available digitally to readers of this guide. They may be accessed at the *CJNow!* Web site.

Library Extra! 12-1. *Census of State and Federal Correctional Facilities* (BJS, current volume).

Library Extra! 12-2. *Prison and Jail Inmates* (BJS, current volume).

Library Extra! 12-3. *Two Views of Imprisonment Policies* (NIJ, July 1997).

ENDNOTES

[1] John Howard, *State of Prisons* (London, 1777), reprinted by E. P. Dutton, New York, 1929.

[2] D. Greenberg, "The Incapacitative Effect of Imprisonment, Some Estimates," *Law and Society Review*, Vol. 9 (1975), pp. 541-580. See also Jacqueline Cohen, "Incapacitating Criminals: Recent Research Findings," National Institute of Justice, *Research in Brief* (December 1983).

[3] For information on identifying dangerous repeat offenders, see M. Chaiken and J. Chaiken *Selecting Career Criminals for Priority Prosecution*, final report (Cambridge, MA: Abt Associates, 1987).

[4] Allen J. Beck and Christopher J. Mumola, *Prisoners in 1998* (Washington, D.C.: Bureau of Justice Statistics, 1999).

[5] Department of Justice press release, "The Nation's Prison Population Grew by 60,000 Inmates Last Year," August 15, 1999.

[6] U.S. Department of Justice press release, "The Nation's Jails Hold Record 490,442 Inmates," May 1, 1995.

[7] U.S. Department of Justice, "The Nation's Jails Hold Record 490,442 Inmates."

[8] Eric Bates, "Private Prisons: Over the Next 5 Years Analysts Expect the Private Share of the Prison 'Market' to More than Double," *The Nation*, Vol. 266, no. 1 (1998), pp. 11-18.

[9] Professor Charles Thomas, as cited in Joan Thompson, "Private Prisons," The Associated Press wire services, November 5, 1996.

Chapter 13

quick view

<< prison life >>

Outline

- Realities of Prison Life: The Male Inmate's World
- Realities of Prison Life: The Staff World
- Prison Riots
- Realities of Prison Life: Women in Prison
- Prisoner Rights
- Issues Facing Prisons Today

What You Should Learn

- The realities of prison life and prison subculture, as seen from the inmate's point of view.
- The realities of prison life from the staff's point of view, especially as seen by correctional officers.

- The stages in and causes of prison riots.
- The nature of the hands-off doctrine and the status of that doctrine today.
- The legal aspects of prisoners' rights and the names and consequences of precedent-setting U.S. Supreme Court cases in the area of prisoners' rights.
- The major problems and issues facing prisons today.
- The definitions of key terms that appear in boldface throughout this *Quick View* chapter. Definitions can be found online at http://www.cjnowonline.com.

Hear the author introduce this chapter at *CJNow!* online.

Realities of Prison Life: The Male Inmate's World

The online version of this chapter describes the realities of life in American prisons today, including prisoner lifestyles, prison subcultures, prison sexuality, prison violence, and inmate "rights" and grievance procedures. The online chapter also discusses both the world of the inmate and the staff world. A separate section on women in prison details the social structure of women's prisons, daily life in such facilities, and the various types of female inmates that have been identified in the academic literature.

Early studies of prison life focused primarily on maximum-security prisons for men. They treated correctional institutions as formal or complex organizations and employed the analytical techniques of organizational sociology, industrial psychology, and administrative science. By the 1960s, another approach to the study of prison life had been developed by Erving Goffman. Goffman coined the term **total institutions**, describing them as places where the same people work, play, eat, sleep, and recreate together on a daily basis. Such places include prisons, concentration camps, mental hospitals, seminaries, and other facilities in which residents are cut off from the larger society either forcibly or willingly. Total institutions are small societies. They evolve their own distinctive values and styles of life and place pressures on residents to fulfill rigidly proscribed behavioral roles.

Prison Subcultures

Generally speaking, the work of prison researchers built upon findings of other social scientists, who discovered that any group with similar characteristics, subject to confinement in the same place at the same time, develops its own subculture with specific components that govern hierarchy, behavioral patterns, values, and so on. **Prison subcultures**, also described in detail in the online chapter, provide the medium through which prison values are communicated and expectations made known. Prison subcultures develop independently of the plans of prison administrators, and inmates entering prison discover a social world not mentioned in the handbooks prepared by correctional staff. Inmate concerns, values, roles, and even language weave a web of social reality into which new inmates step and in which they must participate.

The socialization of new inmates into the prison subculture has been described as a process of **prisonization**. Different prisons share aspects of a common inmate culture,[1] so that prisonwise inmates who enter a new facility far from their home will already know the ropes. **Prison argot**, or language, provides one example of how widespread prison subculture can be. The terms used to describe inmate roles in one institution are generally understood in others. Lean more about prisonization, prison society, and prison subcultures at *CJNow!* online.

Prison Lifestyles and Inmate Types

Prison society is strict and often unforgiving. Even so, inmates are able to express some individuality through the choice of a prison lifestyle. John Irwin was the first well-known author to describe prison lifestyles, viewing them (like the subcultures of which they are a part) as adaptations to the prison environment.[2] Other writers have since elaborated on these coping mechanisms. The online chapter describes the following types of inmate lifestyles: 1) the mean dude (who adjusts to prison by bullying those around him), 2) the hedonist (whose life is built around the limited pleasures which can be had within the confines of prison), 3) the opportunist (who takes advantage of the positive experiences prison has to offer, such as schooling and trade training), 4) the retreatist (who attempts psychological escape from the realities of imprisonment), 5) the legalist (or jailhouse lawyer), 6) the radical (who portrays himself as a political prisoner), 7) the colonist (who thinks of prison as home), 8) the religious (who professes a strong spirituality), and 9) the realist (who sees confinement as a natural consequence of criminal activity). Learn more about each type of inmate at *CJNow!* online.

Realities of Prison Life: The Staff World

The flip side of inmate society can be found in the world of the prison staff. Staff roles encompass those of warden, psychologist, counselor, area supervisor, program director, instructor, and correctional officer—and in some large prisons, physician and therapist. Officers, generally considered the bottom of the staff hierarchy, may be divided into cellbock and tower guards, while some are regularly assigned to administrative offices where they perform clerical tasks.

Like prisoners, correctional officers undergo a socialization process that helps them to function according to the official and unofficial rules of staff society. As in years past, prison staffers are still most concerned with custody and control. Society expects correctional staff members to keep inmates in custody as the basic prerequisite of successful job performance. Of course, custody is necessary before any other correctional activities, such as instruction or counseling, can be undertaken. Control, the other major staff concern, ensures order, and an orderly prison is generally thought to be safe and secure. Learn more about custody and control, and the other concerns of correctional staffers at *CJNow!* online.

Types of Correctional Officers

Staff culture, in combination with pre-existing personalities, gives rise to a diversity of officer "types." Like the inmate typology we've already mentioned, correctional staff can be classified according to certain distinguishing characteristics. The online chapter discusses the following types of correctional officers: 1) the dictator (who uses prison rules to enforce his own personal brand of discipline), 2) the friend (who tries to fraternize with inmates, and approaches the issue of control by trying to be "one of the guys"), 3) the merchant (who participates in the inmate economy, supplying drugs, pornography, alcohol, and sometimes even weapons to inmates who can afford to pay for them), 4) the turnkey (who cares little for what goes on in the prison setting, and just gets by), 5) the climber (with an eye for promotion), and 6) the reformer (a "do-gooder" among officers, who believes that prison should offer positive opportunities for personal change). Learn more about each type of officer at *CJNow!* online.

The Professionalization of Correctional Officers

Correctional officers have generally been accorded low occupational status. Historically, the role of "prison guard" required minimal formal education and held few opportunities for professional growth and career advancement. Such jobs were typically low paying, frustrating, and often boring. Growing problems in our nation's prisons, including emerging issues of legal liability, however, increasingly require a well-trained and adequately equipped force of professionals. As correctional personnel have become better trained and more proficient, the old concept of "guard" has been supplanted by that of *corrections officer*. Learn more about the ongoing professionalization of corrections at *CJNow!* online.

Prison Riots

It is difficult to satisfactorily explain why prisoners riot, despite study groups which attempt to piece together the "facts" leading up to an incident. After the riot at Attica (described in the online chapter) the New York State Special Commission of Inquiry filed a report that recommended the creation of inmate advisory councils, changes in staff titles and uniforms, and other institutional improvements. The report emphasized "enhancing (the) dignity, worth, and self-confidence" of inmates. The New Mexico attorney general, in a final report on the violence at Santa Fe (see the online chapter for details), placed blame upon a breakdown in informal controls and the subsequent emergence of a new group of violent inmates among the general prison population.[3]

The "real" reasons for any particular prison riot are probably institution specific and may not allow for easy generalization. As a consequence, rioting in prison cannot be predicted.[4] Riots are generally unplanned and tend to occur spontaneously, the result of some relatively minor precipitating event.

Most modern facilities have incident management procedures and systems in place which are designed to be implemented in the event of disturbances. Such systems remove the burden of riot control from the individual officer, depending instead upon a systematic and deliberate approach developed to deal with a wide variety of correctional incidents. Learn more about prison riots and what can be done to help prevent them at *CJNow!* online.

Realities of Prison Life: Women in Prison

Figure 13-1 provides an overview of the total American prison population by gender and ethnicity. As it shows, women comprise only a minority of prisoners in this country. While there are still far more men imprisoned across the nation than women (approximately 16 men for every woman), the number of female inmates is rising quickly. Professionals working with imprisoned women attribute much of the rise in female prison populations to drugs. Figure 13-2 shows, in relative graphics, the proportion of men and women imprisoned for various kinds of offenses. The online chapter provides current statistics on the number of women in prison, and their relative proportion of the overall prison population.

Figure 13-1 Prison inmates by gender and ethnicity in state and federal prisons, 1998. *Source:* Allen J. Beck and Christopher J. Mumola, *Prisoners in 1998* (Washington, D.C.: Bureau of Justice Statistics, 1999).

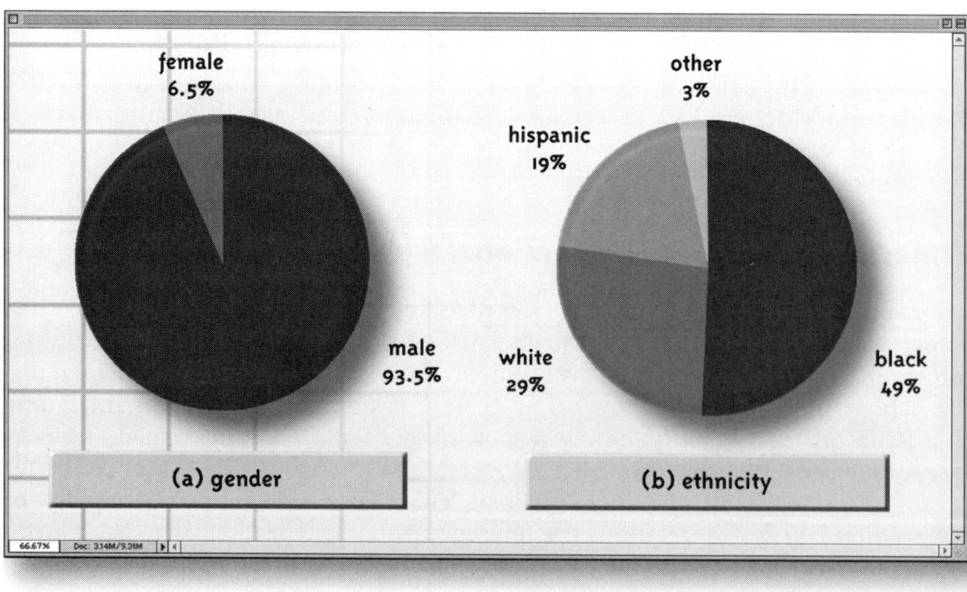

Most women inmates are housed in centralized state facilities known as "women's prisons," which are dedicated exclusively to the holding of female felons. Many states, however, particularly those with small populations, continue to keep women prisoners in special wings of what are otherwise institutions for men. Although there may be no "typical" prison for women and no perfectly "average" female inmate, the American Correctional Association's 1990 report by the Task Force on the Female Offender found that women's imprisonment could be generally described as follows:[5] 1) most prisons for women are located in towns with fewer than 25,000 inhabitants, 2) a significant number of facilities were not designed to house female inmates, 3) the number of female offenders being sent to prison is rising, 4) most facilities that house female inmates also house males, 5) not many facilities for women have programs especially designed for female offenders, 6) very few major disturbances or escapes are reported among female inmates, 7) substance abuse among female inmates is very high, 8) very few work assignments are available to female inmates, and 9) the number of female inmates without a high-school education is very high. Learn more about America's women inmates, the prisons that house them, and the programs that are available to them at *CJNow!* online.

Social Structure in Women's Prisons

Most studies of women's prisons have revealed a unique feature of such institutions, and that is the way that women inmates construct organized families from among the prison population. These artificially created quasi-kinship systems extend beyond simple "family" ties to the formation of huge, intricately related groups involving a large number of sexual as well as nonsexual relationships. In these groups the roles of "children," "in-laws," "grandparents," and so on are often explicitly recognized. Even "birth order" within a family can become an issue for these kinship groups. Such groups sometimes occupy a common household—usually a prison cottage or dormitory area—and the details of their existence is often well known to correctional staff. Learn more about families in women's prisons, the various types of female inmates that have been identified in the correctional literature, and violence in women's prisons at *CJNow!* online.

Figure 13-2 Prison inmates by gender and ethnicity in state and federal prisons, 1998. *Source:* Allen J. Beck and Christopher J. Mumola, *Prisoners in 1998* (Washington, D.C.: Bureau of Justice Statistics, 1999).

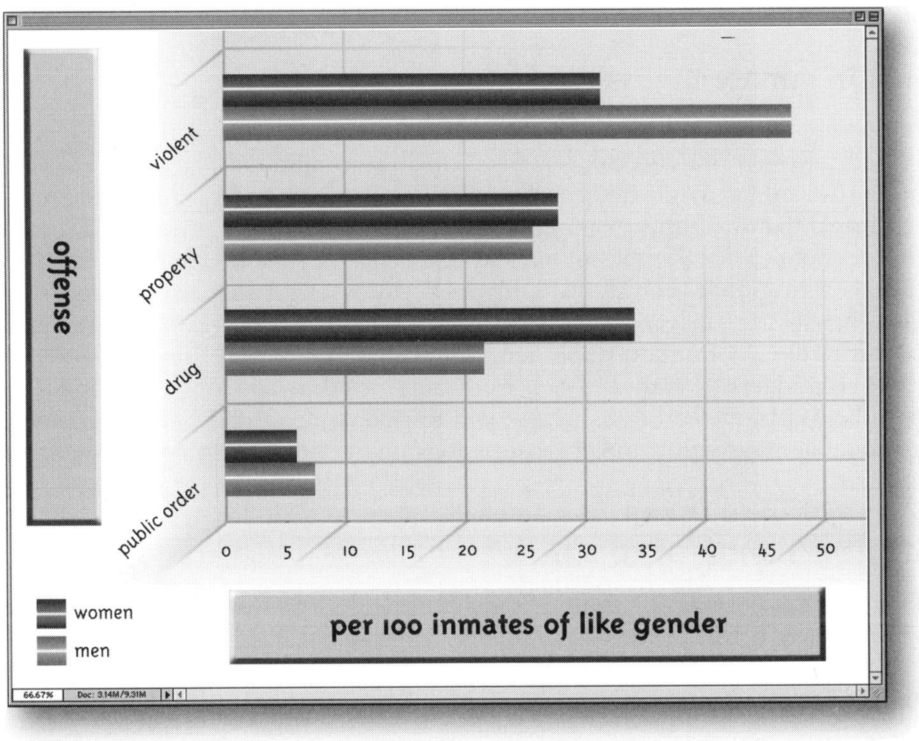

Prisoner Rights

Until the 1960s American courts took a neutral approach—commonly called the **hands-off doctrine**—toward the running of prisons. Judges assumed that prison administrators were sufficiently professional in the performance of their duties to balance institutional needs with humane considerations. The hands-off doctrine rested upon the belief that defendants lost most of their rights upon conviction, suffering a kind of **civil death.** Many states defined the concept of civil death through legislation which denied inmates the right to vote, hold public office, or even marry. Some states made incarceration for a felony a basis for uncontested divorce at the request of the noncriminal spouse.

The hands-off doctrine ended in 1969 when a federal court declared the entire Arkansas prison system unconstitutional after hearing arguments that conditions there constituted a form of cruel and unusual punishment.[6] The court's decision resulted from what it judged to be pervasive overcrowding and primitive living conditions. Stories about the system by longtime inmates claimed that a number of their fellow inmates had been beaten or shot to death by guards and buried over the years in unmarked graves on prison property.

The Legal Basis of Prisoners' Rights

Courts today are actively involved in the hearing of cases involving inmates' claims of rights violations. Most such claims, when they are made, are based upon constitutional guarantees found in the Bill of Rights. As a result of court decisions over the past few decades, it is today generally accepted that a prison inmate retains those rights that he or she would have in free society which are not inconsistent with his or her status as a prisoner or with the legitimate penological objectives of the corrections system. In other words, inmates have rights much the same as people who are not incarcerated, provided that the legitimate needs of the prison for security, custody, and safety are not compromised. Court decisions have declared that order maintenance, security, and rehabilitation are all legitimate concerns of prison administration, but that financial exigency and convenience are not.

Prisoner rights, because they are constrained by the legitimate needs of imprisonment, are actually more conditional rights than they are absolute rights. The Second Amendment to the U.S. Constitution, for example, grants citizens the right to bear arms. The right to arms is, however, necessarily compromised by the need for order and security in prison, and we would not expect a court to rule that inmates have a right to weapons.

Precedents in Inmate Rights

U.S. Supreme Court decisions of the last few decades can be interpreted along with a number of lower federal court findings to have established the conditional rights of prisoners shown in Table 13-1 online. While it is important to keep in mind the fact that the Supreme Court has indicated that institutional exigency can abbreviate any right, mere institutional convenience does not provide a sufficient basis for the denial of rights. Hence, inmate mail enjoys certain constitutional protections, and publications originating from outside of prison, such as newspapers, magazines, and special interest tracts, have generally been protected when mailed directly from the publisher. Other areas in which the conditional rights of inmates have been addressed by the U.S. Supreme Court include religious practice, visitation, legal access to the courts, medical care, privacy, and disciplinary and **grievance procedures.** Learn more about inmate rights and the court decisions upon which they are based at *CJNow!* online.

A Return to the Hands-Off Doctrine?

Some prisoner rights may soon be a thing of the past. In June 1991, in the case of *Wilson* v. *Seiter*,[7] an increasingly conservative U.S. Supreme Court signaled the beginning of what appears to be at least a partial return to the "hands-off" doctrine of earlier times. That case turned upon the "deliberate indifference" standard and, in effect, required that all future

Eighth Amendment challenges to prison conditions brought by inmates must show deliberate indifference by the officials responsible for the existence of those conditions before a court will hear the complaint.

The Prison Litigation Reform Act (PLRA),[8] passed by Congress in 1996, further limits the opportunity of inmates to raise constitutional claims about the conditions of their imprisonment. The PLRA: 1) requires inmates to pay a $120 federal-court filing fee, 2) limits the award of attorneys' fees in successful lawsuits brought by inmates, 3) requires judges to screen all inmate complaints against the federal government and to immediately dismiss those deemed frivolous or without merit, 4) revokes the good-time credits earned by federal prisoners toward early release if they file a malicious lawsuit, 5) bars prisoners from suing the federal government for mental or emotional injury unless there was also an associated physical injury, 6) mandates that court orders affecting prison administration cannot go any further than necessary to correct a violation of a particular inmate's civil rights, 7) makes it possible for state officials to have court orders lifted after two years unless there is a new finding of a continuing violation of federally guaranteed civil rights, and 8) mandates that any court order requiring the release of prisoners due to overcrowding be approved by a three-member court before it can become effective. Learn more about the PLRA and the growing conservativism of federal courts in the area of prisoners' rights at *CJNow!* online.

Issues Facing Prisons Today

Prisons are society's answer to a wide range of social problems. They house outcasts, misfits, and some highly dangerous people. While prisons provide a part of the answer to the question of crime control, they also face problems of their own. A number of those special issues facing prisons today are described in the online chapter; an overview of a few of those issues follows.

AIDS

Best estimates place the reported HIV-infection rate among U.S. prison inmates at 2,300 cases per 100,000[9]—many times that of the general population. In fact, AIDS has become the leading cause of death among prisoners.[10] While not all inmates are infected during confinement, authorities say that the virus is spread behind bars through homosexual activity (including rape), intravenous drug use, and the sharing of tainted tattoo and hypodermic needles. The fact that inmates tend to have histories of high-risk behavior before entering prison, especially intravenous drug use, however, probably means that many are infected before coming to prison and helps to explain much of the huge difference in infection rates. Learn more about AIDS in prison at *CJNow!* online.

Geriatric Offenders

Many persons already in prison, including those in their middle years, will be serving longer sentences because of the harsh sentencing laws that have been passed during the last decade. Longer sentences and mandatory life without parole laws are bringing about a relentless increase in the number of elderly prisoners being held at both the federal and state levels. Some experts predict an explosion in the number of elderly prisoners in coming decades.

The "graying" of America's prison population has a number of causes, including: 1) the general aging of the American population, which is reflected inside prisons; 2) new sentencing policies such as "three-strikes," "truth in sentencing," and mandatory minimum laws that send more criminals to prison for longer stretches; 3) a massive prison building boom that, since the 1980s, has provided space for more inmates, reducing the need to release prisoners to alleviate overcrowding; and 4) dramatic changes in parole philosophies and practices,[11] with state and federal authorities phasing out or canceling parole programs, thereby forcing institutions to hold inmates with life sentences until they die. Learn more about long-termers and geriatric inmates, including the problems they face and the programs that have been established to meet their needs at *CJNow!* online.

Mentally Ill Inmates

The mentally ill are another inmate category with special needs. Some mentally ill inmates are neurotic or have personality problems. Others have serious psychological disorders which may have escaped earlier diagnosis (at trial) or which did not provide a legal basis for the reduction of criminal responsibility. Unfortunately, few states have any substantial capacity for the psychiatric treatment of mentally disturbed inmates.

Mentally deficient inmates constitute still another inmate group with special needs. Some studies estimate the proportion of mentally deficient inmates at about 10%.[12] Such inmates are less likely to complete training and rehabilitative programs successfully than are other inmates. They also evidence difficulty in adjusting to the routines of prison life. Learn more about the issues associated with the handling and treatment of mentally and psychiatrically challenged individuals at *CJNow!* online.

What You Should Remember

- Studies of prison life have detailed the existence of prison subcultures, or inmate worlds, replete with inmate values, social roles, and lifestyles.
- New inmates who are socialized into prison subculture are said to undergo the process of "prisonization." Prisonization involves, among other things, learning the language of prison—commonly called prison argot.
- Prison society functions to fill the needs of inmates—many of which arise from the deprivations brought about by imprisonment.
- Correctional officers undergo a socialization process that helps them to function according to the official and unofficial rules of staff society. The primary focus of staff culture is on institutional security and the control of inmates.
- Prison riots have a variety of causes. They generally evolve through five stages: 1) explosion, 2) organization, 3) confrontation, 4) termination, and 5) reaction and explanation.
- For many years courts throughout the nation assumed a "hands-off" approach to prisons, rarely intervening in the day-to-day administration of prison facilities. That changed in the late 1960s when the hands-off era ended and the U.S. Supreme Court began to identify inmate rights mandated by the U.S. Constitution.
- The rights of prisoners that have been identified by U.S. courts include the right to physical integrity, an absolute right to be free from unwarranted corporeal punishments, certain religious rights, and limited procedural rights such as those involving access to attorneys and to the courts.
- Today's prisons reflect problems and challenges that exist in the larger society of which they are a part. HIV-infected inmates, geriatric offenders, homosexual inmates, and the mentally ill all constitute special groups within the inmate population that require additional attention.

LIBRARY EXTRAS!

Library Extras! are suggested readings that are available digitally to readers of this guide. They may be accessed at the *CJNow!* Web site.

Library Extra! 13-1. "Can Telemedicine Reduce Spending and Improve Prisoner Health Care?" *The National Institute of Justice Journal* (NIJ, April 1999).

Library Extra! 13-2. *HIV in Prisons and Jails* (BJS, current volume).

Library Extra! 13-3. *Resolution of Prison Riots* (NIJ, October 1995).

Library Extra! 13-4. *Women Offenders: Programming Needs and Promising Approaches* (NIJ, August 1998).

Library Extra! 13-5. *Work in American Prisons: Joint Ventures with the Private Sector* (NIJ, not dated).

Library Extra! 13-6. *Women in Prison* (BJS, current volume).

ENDNOTES

[1] Gresham M. Sykes, *The Society of Captives: A Study of a Maximum Security Prison* (Princeton, NJ: Princeton University Press, 1958), p. xiii.

[2] John Irwin, *The Felon* (Englewood Cliffs, NJ: Prentice Hall, 1970).

[3] *Report of the Attorney General on the February 2 and 3, 1980 Riot at the Penitentiary of New Mexico* (two parts), June and September 1980.

[4] Steve Dillingham and Reid Montgomery, "Prison Riots: A Corrections Nightmare Since 1774," in Michael Braswell, et al., *Prison Violence in America* (Cincinnati, OH: Anderson, 1985), pp. 19-36.

[5] American Correctional Association, Task Force on the Female Offender, *The Female Offender: What Does the Future Hold?* (Washington, D.C.: St. Mary's Press, 1990).

[6] *Holt* v. *Sarver*, 309 F.Supp. 362 (E.D. Ark 1970).

[7] *Wilson* v. *Seiter et al.*, 501 U.S. 294 (1991).

[8] Public Law 104-134.

[9] Laura Maruschak, *HIV in Prisons and Jails* (Washington, D.C.: Bureau of Justice Statistics, 1997).

[10] Dennis Cauchon, "AIDS in Prison: Locked Up and Locked Out," *USA Today*, March 31, 1995, p. 6A.

[11] See, Jim Krane, "Demographic Revolution Rocks U.S. Prisons," APB Online, April 12, 1999. Web posted at http://www.apbonline.com/safestreets/oldprisoners/mainpris0412.html. Accessed January 5, 2000.

[12] Robert O. Lampert, "The Mentally Retarded Offender in Prison," *The Justice Professional*, Vol. 2, no. 1 (Spring 1987), p. 61.

Part 5

<< special issues >>

Chapter 14

quick view

<< juvenile justice >>

Outline

- Introduction
- Juvenile Justice Throughout History
- The Problems of Children Today
- Significant Court Decisions Affecting Juveniles
- The Juvenile Justice Process Today

What You Should Learn

- The history and evolution of the juvenile justice system in the Western world.
- The reasons for studying juvenile justice and juvenile delinquency.
- The categories of children in today's juvenile justice system.

- The nature of the problems faced by juveniles in the United States today.
- The names of important U.S. Supreme Court decisions of relevance to juvenile justice, and their effects on the handling of juveniles by the system.
- The similarities and differences between the juvenile and adults systems of justice.
- The definitions of key terms that appear in boldface throughout this *Quick View* chapter. Definitions can be found online at http://www.cjnowonline.com.

Hear the author introduce this chapter at *CJNow!* online.

Introduction

On average, about 20% of all arrests in any year are of juveniles,[1] and juveniles under the age of 18 have a higher likelihood of being arrested for robbery and UCR index property crimes than any other age group. Figure 14-1 shows FBI statistics on juvenile arrests for selected offense categories. Similarly, Figure 14-2 forecasts the number of homicides that can be expected to be committed by offenders aged 14-17 through the year 2004 if recent trends in offending rates persist.

The fact that juveniles account for a relatively large percentage of all crimes committed in this country provides one important reason for studying juvenile justice. Of equal significance is the fact that reports indicate that many adult criminals began their illegal activities while young.

The online version of this chapter has four purposes. First, it describes the **juvenile justice system** from its historical beginnings to the present. Second, it compares the juvenile and adult systems as they currently operate. Third, it describes in detail the agencies, processes, and problems of the juvenile justice system itself. Fourth, the online chapter considers some of the issues raised by critics of the current system and describes many of the changes that are now afoot.

A major source of information on juvenile justice is the Office of Juvenile Justice and Delinquency Prevention (OJJDP). Learn more about the results of OJJDP research on juvenile crime and the juvenile justice system at *CJNow!* online.

Figure 14-1 Juvenile involvement in crime versus system totals, 1998.
Source: Federal Bureau of Investigation, *Crime in the United States, 1998* (Washington, D.C.: U.S. Governement Printing Office, 1999).

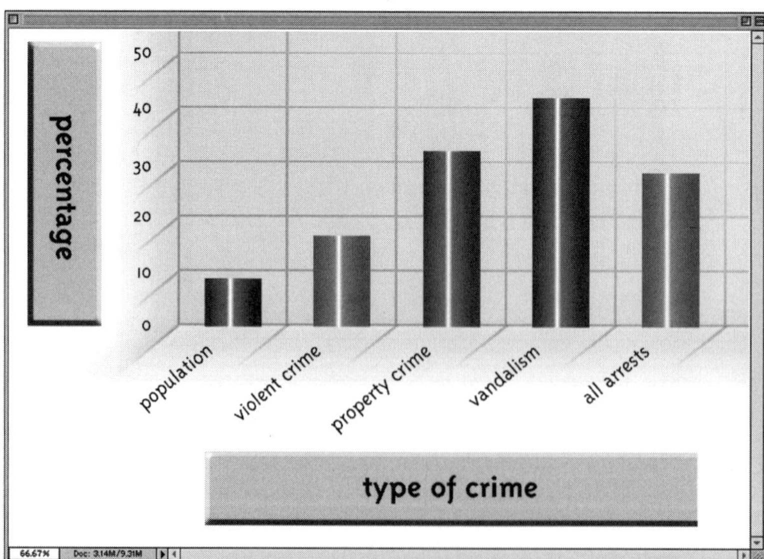

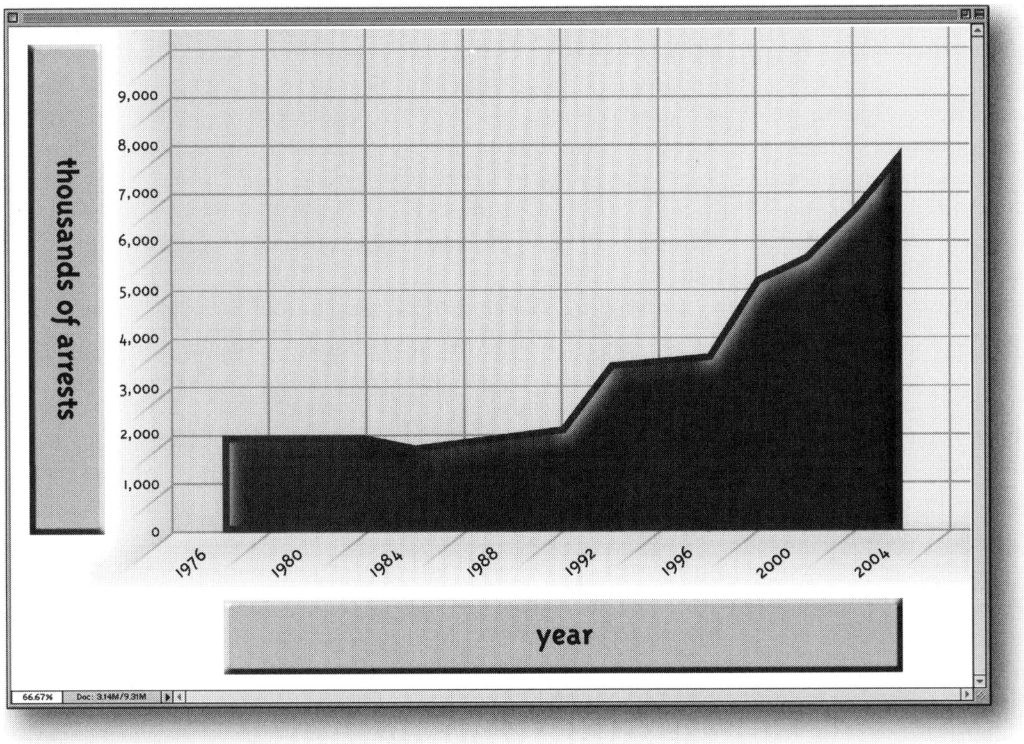

Figure 14-2 Number of homicides by offenders aged 14 to 17, projections through 2004. *Source:* James Alan Fox, *Trends in Juvenile Violence* (Washington, D.C.: Bureau of Justice Statistics, 1996), p. 15.

Juvenile Justice Throughout History

Earliest Times

A study of the history of the Western world shows that children who committed crimes in centuries past could expect no preferential treatment because of their youth. Youngsters were typically adjudicated and punished alongside adults. In like fashion, little distinction was made between criminality and **delinquency** or other kinds of undesirable behavior.

European court philosophy for dealing with juveniles derived from an early Roman principle called ***parens patriae***. *Parens patriae* allowed the king, or the state, to take the place of parents in dealing with children who broke the law.

Juveniles in Early America

Early American solutions to the problems of delinquency were much like those of the English. Puritan influence in the colonies, with its heavy emphasis upon obedience and discipline, led to a frequent use of jails and prisons for both juveniles and adults. Legislation reflected the biblical Ten Commandments and often provided harsh punishments for transgressors of almost any age.

Around the middle of the 1800s, a child savers movement began in America. The movement espoused a philosophy of productivity and eschewed idleness and unprincipled behavior. One product of the child savers movement was the reform school—a place for delinquent juveniles which embodied the atmosphere of a Christian home. Learn more about the child savers movement and the reform school concept at *CJNow!* online.

The Juvenile Court Era

In a major leap forward, the 1899 Illinois Juvenile Court Act created juvenile courts which were separate in form and function from adult criminal courts. In order to avoid the lasting stigma of criminality, the law applied the term *delinquent* rather than *criminal* to adjudicated youthful offenders. The act specified that *the best interests of the child* were to guide juvenile court judges in their deliberations. In effect, the judge was to serve as an advocate for the juvenile, seeking to guide the development of the child in socially desirable directions. Concerns with guilt or innocence took second place to the betterment of the child. The 1899 law also abandoned strict adherence to the due process requirements of adult prosecutions, allowing informal procedures designed to scrutinize the child's situation. By sheltering the juvenile from the punishment philosophy of the adult system, the Illinois act emphasized reformation in place of retribution.

A national juvenile court movement, modeled after the Illinois law, transformed the country beginning in the early 1900s. It was based upon five philosophical principles, or beliefs, that: 1) the state is the "higher or ultimate parent" of all children, 2) children are worth saving and nonpunitive procedures should be used to save them, 3) children should be nurtured and protected from the stigmatizing impact of formal adjudicatory procedures, 4) justice, to accomplish the goal of reformation, needs to be individualized for each child, and 5) the use of noncriminal procedures are necessary in order to give primary consideration to the needs of the child.

By the time of the Great Depression, most states had expanded juvenile statutes to include the following six categories of children that are still used today in most jurisdictions to describe the variety of children subject to juvenile court jurisdiction:

1. **Delinquent children** were those who violated the criminal law. If they were adults, the word "criminal" would have been applied to them.
2. **Undisciplined children** were said to be beyond parental control, as evidenced by their refusal to obey legitimate authorities, such as school officials and teachers. They needed state protection.
3. **Dependent children** typically had no parents or guardians to care for them, or had been abandoned or placed for adoption in violation of the law.
4. **Neglected children** were defined as those who did not receive proper care from their parents or guardians. They may have suffered from malnutrition, not been provided with adequate shelter, or not received a proper upbringing.
5. **Abused children** included those who suffered physical abuse at the hands of their custodians—a category which was later expanded to include emotional and sexual abuse, as well.
6. **Status offenders**, a special category which was to lead to many later disputes, embraced children who violated laws written only for children.

Explanations of Delinquency

As states implemented innovative efforts to handle problem children, researchers began to investigate the causes of juvenile misbehavior. One of the first comprehensive social scientific explanations for delinquency, advanced in the 1920s, was known as **social ecology**. The social ecology approach focused on the misbehavior of lower-class youth and saw delinquency primarily as the result of **social disorganization**. Another explanation for delinquency was offered by **opportunity theory**. Developed in the 1960s, opportunity theory saw delinquency as resulting from the lack of availability of legitimate opportunities for success. About the same time, **cohort** analysis came into use as a technique for identifying the determinants of delinquency. Cohort analysis usually begins at birth and traces the development of a population which shares common characteristics until they reach a certain age. Read more about systematic explorations of delinquency, including the results of the Program of Research on the Causes and Correlates of Juvenile Delinquency, sponsored by the U.S. Department of Justice's Office of Juvenile Justice and Delinquency Prevention (OJJDP), at *CJNow!* online.

The Post-Juvenile Court Era

Juvenile court era philosophy continues to support much of the contemporary system of American juvenile justice. The juvenile justice system in the United States today, however, is in the midst of transition. Extensive media coverage of violent crimes in predominantly urban neighborhoods has fueled perceptions that violence committed by juveniles has reached epidemic proportions and that no community is immune to random acts of violence committed by young people—especially those involving a weapon. Visit *CJNow!* online to learn more about the movement presently underway to change the workings of the American juvenile justice system.

The Problems of Children Today

Besides delinquency, but in some ways contributing to it, are a vast array of other problems facing children today. Many of these problems are quite different from those that existed when the juvenile court was formed. Problems with which today's children must deal include: 1) a lack of clear purpose, 2) drug and alcohol abuse (see Figure 14-3), 3) violence in the school, home, and media, 4) gangs and gang-related violence, 5) peer pressures, 6) neglect at the hands of would-be caregivers, and 7) sexual and physical abuse (see Figure 14-4). These and other problems facing children today are discussed in detail at *CJNow!* online.

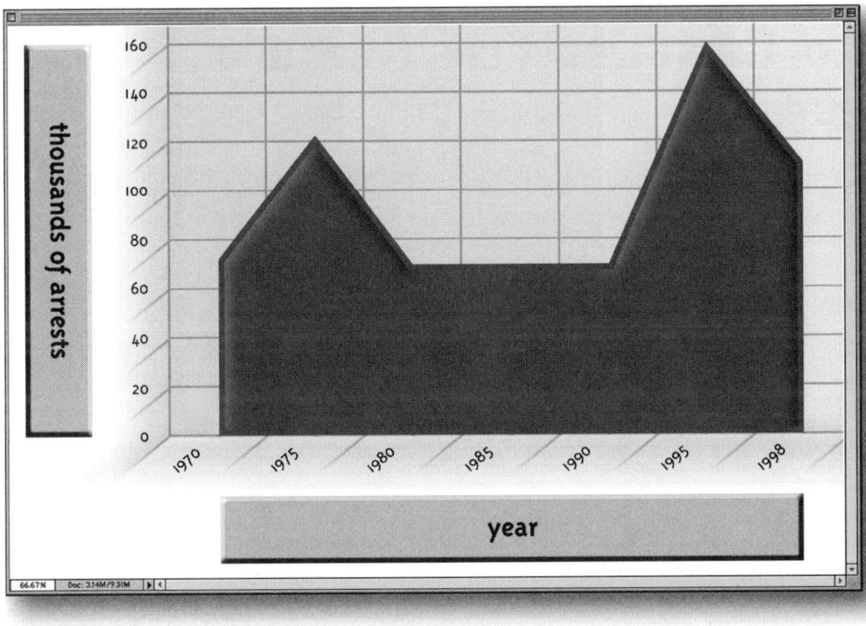

Figure 14-3 Drug-related arrests of juveniles, 1970–1998. *Source:* Federal Bureau of Investigation, *Crime in the United States* (Washington, D.C.: U.S. Governement Printing Office, various years).

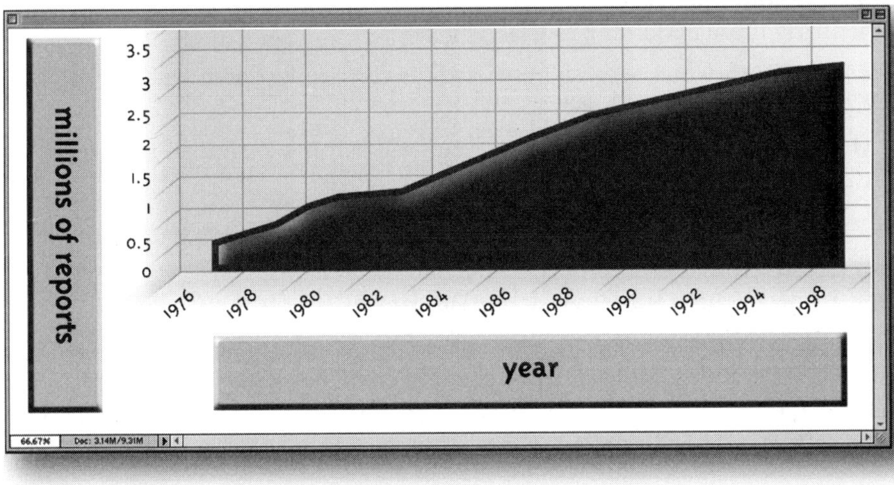

Figure 14-4 Reports of child abuse and neglect, 1976–1998. *Source:* National Committee to Prevent Child Abuse.

What Can Be Done?

Many who have studied the problems of juveniles return to basic solutions involving such things as the quality of family life, neighborhood economic conditions, proper socialization, and supportive social institutions. Recently, for example, the Office of Juvenile Justice and Delinquency Prevention (OJJDP) published a "Policymaker's Guide," based upon the findings of a metastudy,[2] which summarized many other studies that had been conducted over decades. The report concluded that 1) there is "a positive relationship between parental conflict and delinquency," 2) "the effect of broken homes on delinquency is real and consistent," 3) the tendency toward delinquency and other problems is enhanced for children living in low-income families, 4) "physical abuse of children leads them into violence later in life," and 5) "children who have criminal parents are at greater risk of becoming delinquent themselves." The study authors suggested that "a healthy home environment, one in which parents and children share affection, cohesion, and involvement, reduces the risk of delinquency," and of other childhood problems, within both one- or two-parent families, and "parental rejection appears to be one of the most significant predictors of delinquency." The report noted that "parents play a critical role in moral development," and that "the quality of [parental] supervision is consistently and strongly related to delinquency" and other childhood problems. Learn more about what is being done to address the problems of children today, including details from the Coordinating Council on Juvenile Justice and Delinquency Prevention's (CCJJDP) new *National Juvenile Justice Action Plan*,[3] at *CJNow!* online.

Significant Court Decisions Affecting Juveniles

Throughout the first half of the twentieth century, the U.S. Supreme Court followed a "hands-off" approach to juvenile justice, much like its early approach to prisons (which is described in Chapter 13 online). The adjudication and further processing of juveniles by the system was left mostly to specialized juvenile courts or local appeals courts. It was not until the 1960s that the Court began close legal scrutiny of the principles underlying the juvenile justice system itself. The online chapter provides a detailed discussion of some of the most important juvenile justice Supreme Court cases in recent years. Among them are:

- *Kent* v. *U.S.* (1966),[4] which ended the "hands-off" era in juvenile justice.
- *In re Gault* (1967),[5] which made available to juveniles many of the same due process rights that adults have when facing criminal prosecution.
- *In re Winship* (1970),[6] which required juvenile courts making determinations of delinquency to operate under the same evidentiary standards as adult courts.
- *McKeiver* v. *Pennsylvania* (1971),[7] which reinforced the long-accepted practice of conducting juvenile adjudicatory hearings in the absence of certain due process considerations, particularly those pertaining to trial by jury.
- *Breed* v. *Jones* (1975),[8] which severely restricted the conditions under which transfers from juvenile to adult courts may occur.
- *Schall* v. *Martin* (1984),[9] which held that preventive detention cannot be imposed upon a juvenile without 1) prior notice, 2) an equitable detention hearing, and 3) a statement by the judge setting forth the reason(s) for detention.

A Summary of Differences in Adult and Juvenile Justice

Juvenile court philosophy brings with it a number of significant differences from the adult system. Among them are 1) a reduced concern with legal issues of guilt or innocence and an emphasis on the child's best interests; 2) an emphasis on treatment rather than punishment; 3) privacy and protection from public scrutiny through the use of sealed records, laws

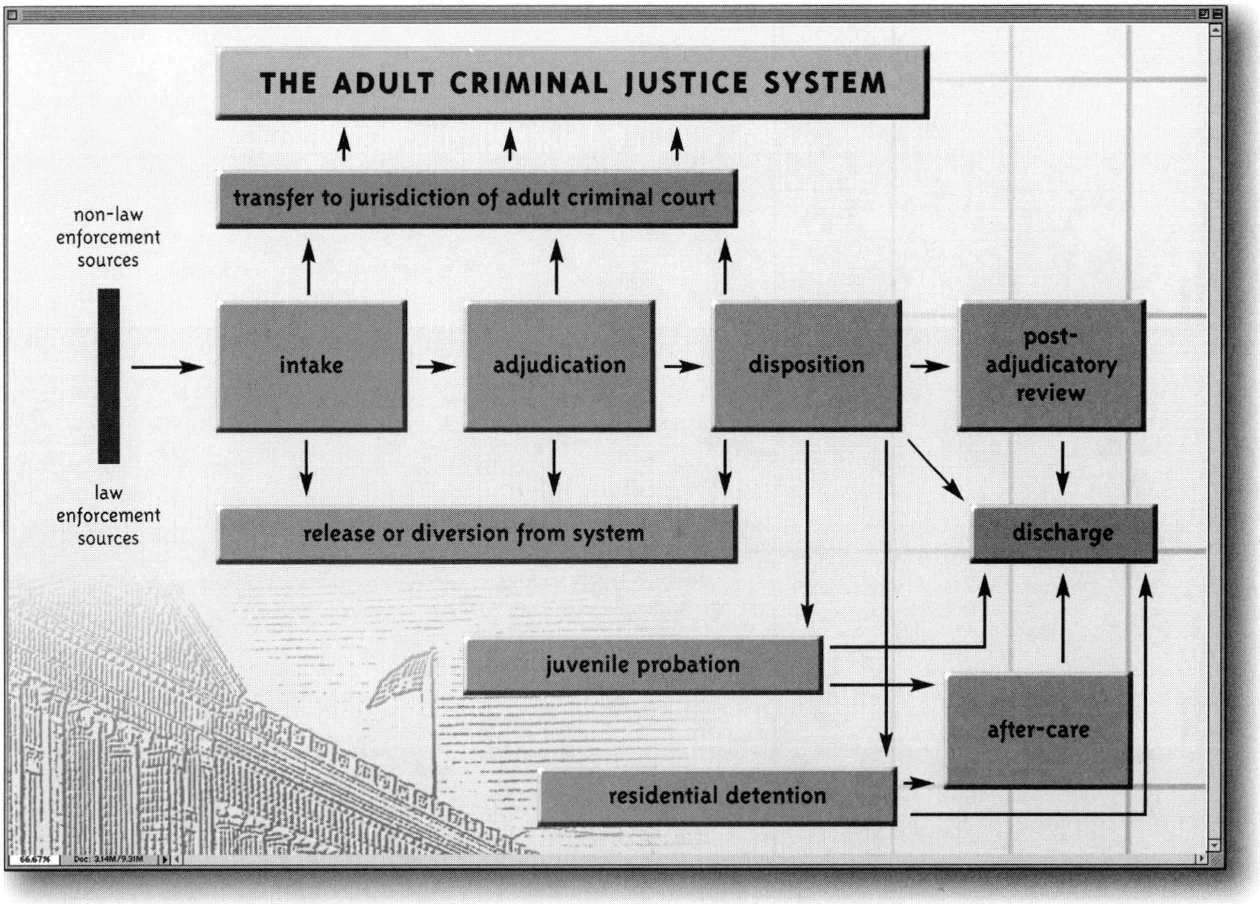

Figure 14-5 The juvenile justice process.

against publishing the names of juvenile offenders, and so forth; 4) use of the techniques of social science in dispositional decision making, rather than sentences determined by a felt need for punishment; 5) no long-term confinement, with most juveniles being released from institutions by their twenty-first birthday, regardless of offense; 6) separate facilities for juveniles; and 7) broad discretionary alternatives at all points in the process. This combination of court philosophy and due process requirements has created a unique justice system for juveniles, which takes into consideration the special needs of young people while attempting to offer reasonable protection to society. The juvenile justice process is diagrammed in Figure 14-5.

Because existing juvenile court philosophy has come under increasing fire in recent years by those who point to growing levels of violence among juvenile offenders, the juvenile justice system of the twenty-first century will likely be quite different from the one we know today. See the online chapter for details on various future possibilities.

The Juvenile Justice Process Today

Modern juvenile court jurisdiction rests upon the offender's age and conduct. The majority of states today define a child subject to juvenile court jurisdiction as a person who has not yet turned 18. A few states set the age at 16, and several use 17. Figure 14-6 shows the upper ages of children subject to juvenile court jurisdiction in delinquency matters, by state. When they reach their 18th birthday, children in most states leave the purview of juvenile court and become subject to the jurisdiction of adult criminal courts.

Depending upon the laws of the state and the behavior involved, the jurisdiction of the juvenile court may be exclusive. Exclusive jurisdiction applies when the juvenile court is the

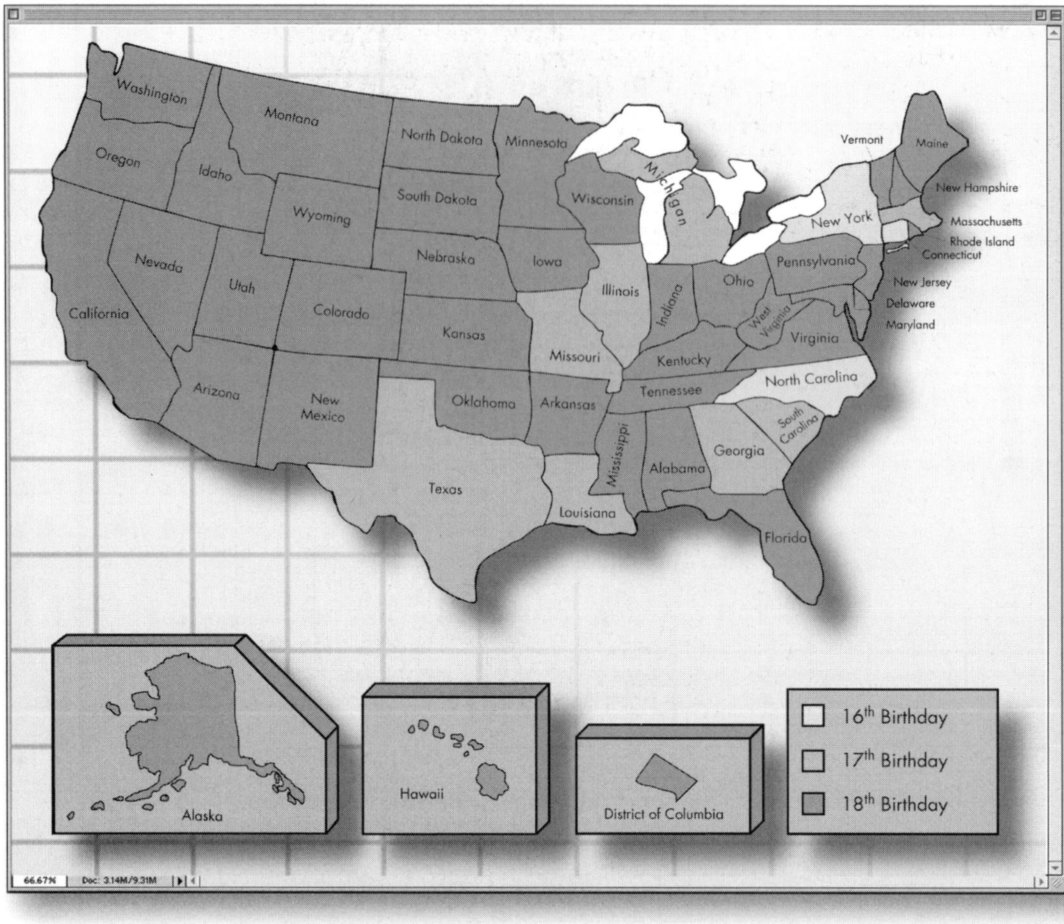

Figure 14-6 Limit of juvenile court jurisdiction over young offenders, by state.

only court that has statutory authority to deal with children for specified infractions. For example, status offenses such as truancy normally fall within the exclusive jurisdiction of juvenile courts. Delinquency, which involves violations of the criminal law, however, is often not within the juvenile court's exclusive jurisdiction. All 50 states, the District of Columbia, and the federal government have judicial waiver provisions which allow for juveniles who commit serious crimes to be bound over to criminal court. Some states specify that juvenile courts have no jurisdiction over certain excluded offenses. Delaware, Louisiana, and Nevada, for example, allow no juvenile court jurisdiction over children charged with first-degree murder.

How the System Works

The juvenile justice system can be viewed as a process which, when carried to completion, moves through four stages. Those stages are: 1) **intake**, 2) adjudication (involving **adjudicatory hearings**), 3) disposition (involving **dispositionary hearings**), and 4) postadjudication review. Though organizationally similar to the adult criminal justice process, the juvenile system is far more likely to maximize the use of discretion and to employ diversion from further formal processing at every point in the process. Each stage of juvenile justice system processing is described in detail at *CJNow!* online.

Secure Institutions for Juveniles

Juveniles who evidence the potential for serious new offenses may be ordered to participate in rehabilitative programs within a secure environment such as a youth center or training school. Most confined juveniles are held in semisecure facilities designed to look less like prisons and more like residential high school campuses. Most states, however, operate at

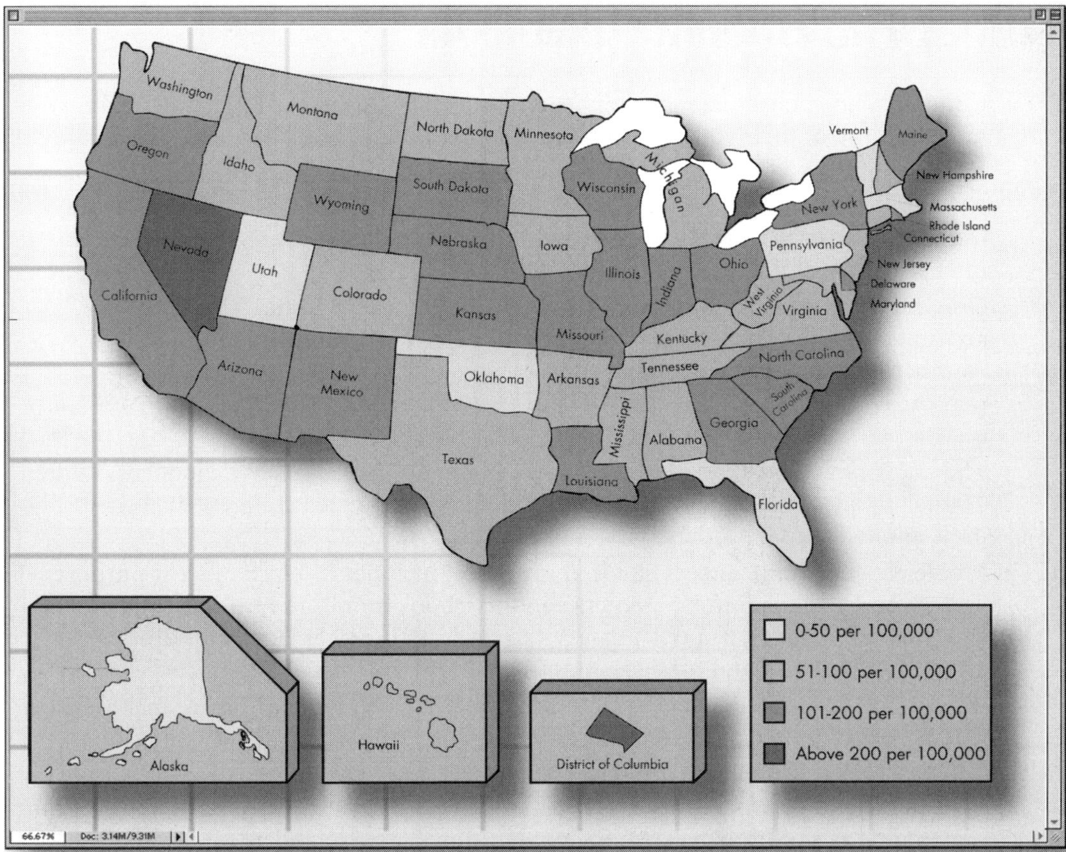

Figure 14-7 Juvenile custody rates, by state.

least one secure facility for juveniles, intended as a home for the most recalcitrant youthful offenders. Halfway houses, boot camps,[10] ranches, forestry camps, wilderness programs, group homes, and state-hired private facilities also hold a proportion of the total number of juveniles reported under confinement. Children placed in group homes continue to attend school and live in a familylike environment in the company of other adjudicated children, shepherded by "house parents." Figure 14-7 shows juvenile custody rates by state.

The operative philosophy of custodial programs for juveniles focuses squarely on the rehabilitative ideal. Juveniles are usually committed to secure facilities for indeterminate periods of time, with the typical stay being less than one year. Release is often timed to coincide with the beginning or end of the school year. Learn more about the confinement of juveniles, including the characteristics of juveniles in confinement, and the sad facts of overcrowding in juvenile facilities at *CJNow!* online.

Dissatisfaction with Today's System

The juvenile justice system is not without its critics, and a huge potential for reform of the system now looms on the horizon. An emerging recognition of the fact that a small number of "hard-core" delinquents are responsible for repeated serious criminal activity, combined with a concern for public safety, has laid the groundwork for a burgeoning reform movement which focuses on three areas: 1) lessening the degree of privacy which surrounds juvenile proceedings; 2) increasing penalties associated with certain kinds of delinquent acts; and 3) reducing diversionary opportunities for habitual, violent, and serious offenders. The overall thrust of the present-day juvenile justice reform movement is to bring about changes which would recognize the harm suffered by victims of delinquency, and which would result in juveniles being treated more like adults. Learn more about juvenile justice system reforms at *CJNow!* online.

What You Should Remember

- Children who committed crimes in past centuries could expect no preferential treatment because of their youth. They were adjudicated and punished alongside adults.
- Modern juvenile court philosophy derives from the early Roman principle of *parens patriae. Parens patriae* was adopted by the juvenile court movement in this country at the beginning of the twentieth century. It requires juvenile courts to act in the best interests of the child.
- One important reason for studying juvenile delinquency is that juvenile crime accounts for a relatively large percentage of all crimes committed in this country. Another is that such crime may be increasing, and a third has to do with the fact that calls for changes to the juvenile justice system are now being heard from many quarters.
- The categories of juveniles in the American system of justice are: 1) delinquent children, 2) undisciplined children, 3) dependent children, 4) neglected children, 5) abused children, and 6) status offenders.
- Problems with which today's children must deal include: 1) a lack of clear purpose, 2) drug and alcohol abuse, 3) violence in the school, home, and media, 4) gangs and gang-related violence, 5) peer pressures, 6) neglect at the hands of would-be caregivers, and 7) sexual and physical abuse.
- Important U.S. Supreme Court decisions of relevance to juvenile justice include: *Kent* v. *U.S.* (1966), *In re Gault* (1967), *In re Winship* (1970), *McKeiver* v. *Pennsylvania* (1971), *Breed* v. *Jones* (1975), and *Schall* v. *Martin* (1984).
- Juveniles who face processing by the justice system today are guaranteed many of the same rights as adults facing criminal prosecution. These include a right to notice of the charges against them, a right to counsel, a right to confront and cross-examine witnesses against them, and protection against self-incrimination.
- Juvenile court philosophy brings with it a number of differences from the adult system. Among them are: 1) a reduced concern with legal issues of guilt or innocence and an emphasis on the child's best interests, 2) an emphasis on treatment rather than punishment, 3) privacy and protection from public scrutiny through the use of sealed records and laws against publishing the names of juvenile offenders, 4) use of social science techniques in dispositional decision making, rather than sentences determined by a felt need for punishment, 5) no long-term confinement, with most juveniles being released from institutions by their twenty-first birthday, regardless of offense, 6) separate facilities for juveniles, and 7) broad discretionary alternatives at all stages in the process.

LIBRARY EXTRAS!

Library Extras! are suggested readings that are available digitally to readers of this guide. They may be accessed at the *CJNow!* Web site.

Library Extra! 14-1. *Causes and Correlates of Delinquency Program* (OJJDP, April 1999).

Library Extra! 14-2. *Developmental Pathways in Boys' Disruptive and Delinquent Behavior* (OJJDP, December 1997).

Library Extra! 14-3. *Indicators of School Crime and Safety, 1998* (BJS, October 1998).

Library Extra! 14-4. *National Youth Gang Survey* (OJJDP, current volume).

Library Extra! 14-5. *Offenders in Juvenile Court* (OJJDP, current volume).

Library Extra! 14-6. *Prosecuting Gangs: A National Assessment* (NIJ, 1995).

Library Extra! 14-7. *State Legislative Responses to Violent Juvenile Crime* (OJJDP, November 1998).

Library Extra! 14-8. *Youth Gangs: An Overview* (OJJDP, August 1998).

ENDNOTES

[1] Where "juvenile" refers to persons under 18 years of age.

[2] Kevin N. Wright and Karen E. Wright, *Family Life, Delinquency, and Crime: A Policymaker's Guide: Research Summary* (Washington, D.C.: Office of Juvenile Justice and Delinquency Prevention, 1994).

[3] Coordinating Council on Juvenile Justice and Delinquency Prevention, *Combating Violence and Delinquency—The National Juvenile Justice Action Plan* (Washington, D.C.: U.S. Government Printing Office, 1996).

[4] *Kent* v. *U.S.*, 383 U.S. 541 (1966).

[5] *In re Gault*, 387 U.S. 1 (1967).

[6] *In re Winship*, 397 U.S. 358 (1970).

[7] *McKeiver* v. *Pennsylvania*, 403 U.S. 528 (1971).

[8] *Breed* v. *Jones*, 421 U.S. 519 (1975).

[9] *Schall* v. *Martin*, 467 U.S. 253 (1984).

[10] See, for example, Blair B. Bourque, Robert C. Cronin, Daniel B. Felker, Frank R. Pearson, Mei Han, and Sarah M. Hill, "Boot Camps for Juvenile Offenders: An Implementation Evaluation of Three Demonstration Programs," *An NIJ Research in Brief* (Washington, D.C.: National Institute of Justice, 1996).

Chapter 15

quick view

<< drugs and crime >>

Outline

- The Drug Problem and the Criminal Justice System
- What Are Drugs—and Who Is Using Them?
- Drugs, Crime, and Social Problems
- Solving the Drug Abuse Problem

What You Should Learn

- The nature of the criminal justice system's response to the drug problem in America.
- The history of drug abuse and the history of anti-drug abuse legislation in America.
- The different types of drugs that are illegally used in this country, as well as the effects and legal classifications of each.
- The nature of the link between drugs and other social problems, including different forms of criminal activity.

- The nature of various efforts to respond to the drug problem and the assessed effectiveness of each.
- The definitions of key terms that appear in boldface throughout this *Quick View* chapter. Definitions can be found online at http://www.cjnowonline.com.

The Drug Problem and the Criminal Justice System

Hear the author introduce this chapter at *CJNow!* online.

Drug abuse is pervasive in American society, and the values that support it have become entrenched among large segments of the American population. Consequently, a dramatic increase in drug-related crime and the corresponding expansion of both drug laws and efforts at enforcement over the last few decades have had a significant impact on all aspects of our justice system. About 70% of all first offenders in federal prisons, for example, are serving drug sentences (see Figure 15-1). On both the state and federal levels, drug offenders account for a large portion of those processed by the criminal justice system today, and many of those arrested report having been under the influence of drugs at the time they committed their crimes (see Figure 15-2).

Drug Abuse: More than an Individual Choice

The online textbook devotes an entire chapter to drug-related crime because it has such a pervasive and far-reaching impact, not only on the criminal justice system but also on all of American society. The online chapter notes that 1) drug abuse accounts for a large proportion of present-day law violations; 2) drug abuse contributes to many other types of criminal activity, including smuggling, theft, robbery, and murder, 3) drug abuse has led to a huge number of arrests, clogged courtrooms, and overcrowded prisons, 4) as a consequence, drug abuse has placed tremendous strain on the criminal justice system, and 5) the fight against it has become one of the most expensive activities ever undertaken by federal, state, and local governments.

The online chapter says that drug crime may be the major challenge facing the nation's criminal justice system and state and federal criminal justice policy makers today. The chapter

Figure 15-1 Percentage of federal prisoners sentenced for drug offenses, 1970–1998. *Source: Sourcebook of Criminal Justice Statistics Online*, Table 6-52.

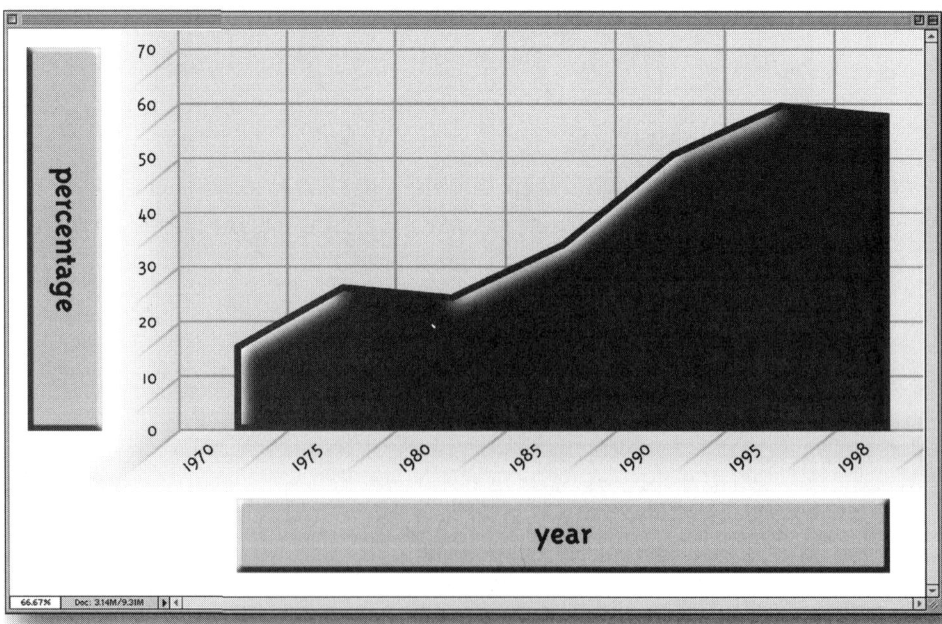

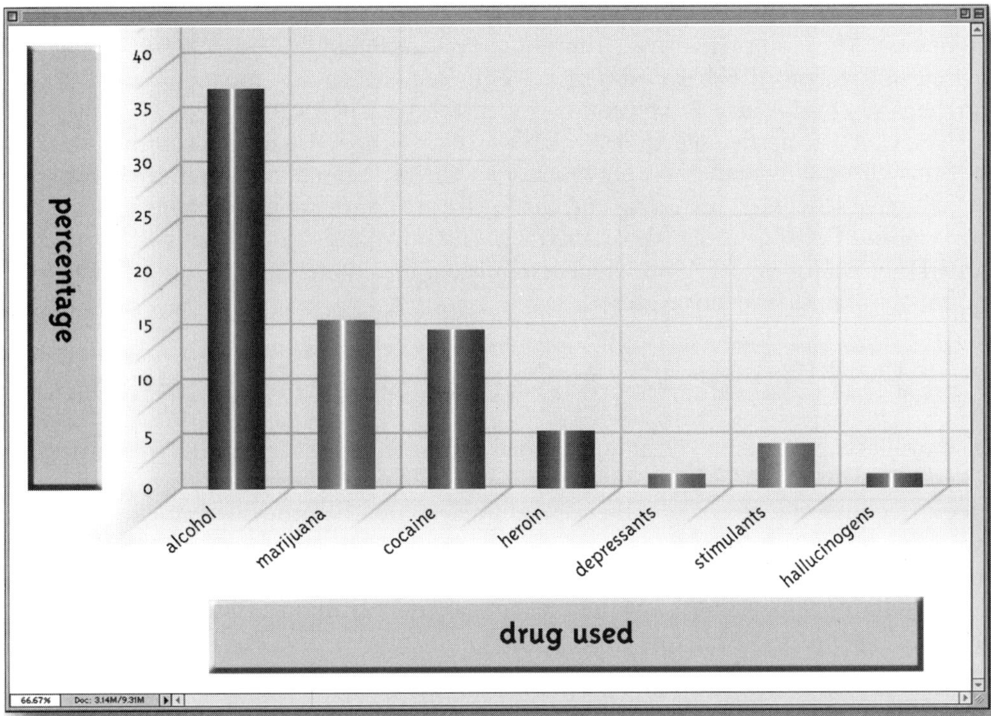

Figure 15-2 Percentage of state prisoners admitting drug use immediately prior to crime commission, by type of drug. *Source:* Bureau of Justice Statistics, *Substance Abuse and Treatment of State and Federal Prisoners, 1997* (Washington, D.C.: BJS, January 1999).

begins with an analysis of what constitutes a drug, moves through a history of drug abuse in America, and then describes the various categories of major **controlled substances**. The link between drugs and other forms of crime is also explained, and solutions to solving the problem of drug abuse are described.

What Is a Drug?

Common usage holds that a **drug** may be any ingestible substance which has a noticeable effect upon the mind or body. Drugs may enter the body via injection, inhalation, swallowing, or even by direct absorption through the skin or mucous membranes. Some drugs, like penicillin and tranquilizers, are useful in medical treatment, whereas others, like heroin and cocaine, are attractive only to recreational users or to those who are addicted to them.

In determining what substances should be called "drugs," it is important to recognize the role that social definitions of any phenomenon play in our understanding of it. Hence, what Americans today consider to be drugs depends more upon social convention or agreed-upon definitions than it does upon any inherent property of the "drugs" themselves. The use of alcohol serves as an example in the online chapter, and the current extent of alcohol use in this country is explored. Powerful drugs, those with the ability to produce substantially altered states of consciousness and with a high potential for addiction, occupy the "high ground" in social and legal condemnation. Among them are **psychoactive substances**, such as heroin, peyote, mescaline, LSD, and cocaine. The online chapter traces the history of various drugs in the United States and describes historical legislation curtailing the use of those substances.

Significant legislative initiatives that are discussed online include the **Harrison Act**, which was passed in 1914. It required persons dealing in opium, morphine, heroin, cocaine, and specified derivatives of these drugs to register with the federal government and to pay a tax of $1.00 per year. The only people permitted to register were physicians, pharmacists, and members of the medical profession. Nonregistered drug traffickers faced a maximum fine of $2,000 and up to five years in prison. The Narcotic Control Act of 1956 increased penalties for drug trafficking and possession and made the sale of heroin to anyone under age 18 a capital offense. The Comprehensive Drug Abuse Prevention and Control Act was passed in 1970, and still forms the basis of federal enforcement efforts today. Title II of the Comprehensive Drug Abuse Prevention and Control Act is the Controlled Substances Act (CSA). The CSA sets up five schedules which classify psychoactive drugs according to their degree of psychoactivity and abuse potential. Visit *CJNow!* online to learn more about each of the CSA's five schedules, including current legislation concerning "date rape drugs" such as Rohypnol and GHB (gammahydroxybutyrate), and other anti-drug abuse laws—including the Anti-Drug Abuse Act of 1988 which established a national **Drug Czar** cabinet-level position within the federal government.

What Are Drugs—and Who Is Using Them?

The sale of illegal drugs is a $57 billion annual industry in the United States.[1] Some perspective can be gained on this figure by recognizing that Americans spend approximately $44 billion on alcohol products and another $37 billion on tobacco products annually.[2]

According to a federal study released recently,[3] 13 million Americans were "current" users of illegal drugs—defined as those "having used an illicit drug in the month before the survey." Ten million people reported using marijuana, and 6 million of those were found to be "frequent" marijuana users (defined as "use on at least 51 days during the past year"). Around 1.75 million used cocaine in various forms, and 608,000 were classified as "hard-core" cocaine addicts. Many users reported using more than one drug, either alone or in combination, while the illegal use of inhalants, hallucinogens, heroin, and the nonmedical use of psychotherapeutics accounted for the remainder of the total number of reported users. As the Office of National Drug Control Policy (ONDCP) points out, however, federal studies typically underestimate the number of hard-core drug abusers in the country because they fail to survey the homeless, prisoners, people living at colleges, active-duty military personnel, and those in mental and other institutions. ONDCP estimates that there are 2.1 million hard-core cocaine addicts and 600,000 heroin addicts in the country[4]—figures well above those provided by national surveys.

Another way to measure the size of the drug problem in America is to analyze the dollars spent to combat it. In 1981, for example, total federal spending for all drug control efforts, including enforcement activities, educational programs, and treatment, totaled $1.5 billion. By 1989 the figure had risen to $6.7 billion and reached $12.2 billion in 1993. Fiscal year 2000 federal expenditures on drug control activities stood at $16.7 billion and are planned to increase to $17.3 by 2003.[5] State budgetary allowances for drug control activities, which are considerable, are not included in these figures.

A number of agencies report on the amount of various types of drugs which enter the country or are produced here. One such group, the National Narcotics Intelligence Consumers Committee (NNICC), was established in 1978 to coordinate the collection and analysis of foreign and domestic strategic drug-related intelligence. Members of the NNICC include the DEA, FBI, CIA, IRS, INS, Coast Guard, and other federal agencies charged with drug law enforcement. NNICC data describe the availability and use of marijuana, cocaine, PCP, and heroin. Other dangerous drugs and the money laundering schemes of drug traffickers are also a focus of NNICC activity. NNICC and DEA data for each of the major drug categories, including marijuana, cocaine, heroin, and other psychoactive substances are described in the online chapter. See Table 15-1 at *CJNow!* online for an overview of these and other drugs and their effects.

Drugs, Crime, and Social Problems

The drug problem in the United States is not simply one of drug use. The manufacture, possession, sale, and use of controlled substances are related to a variety of criminal activities and produce other large-scale social problems. A number of these problems are examined briefly in this guide. Details are available at *CJNow!* online.

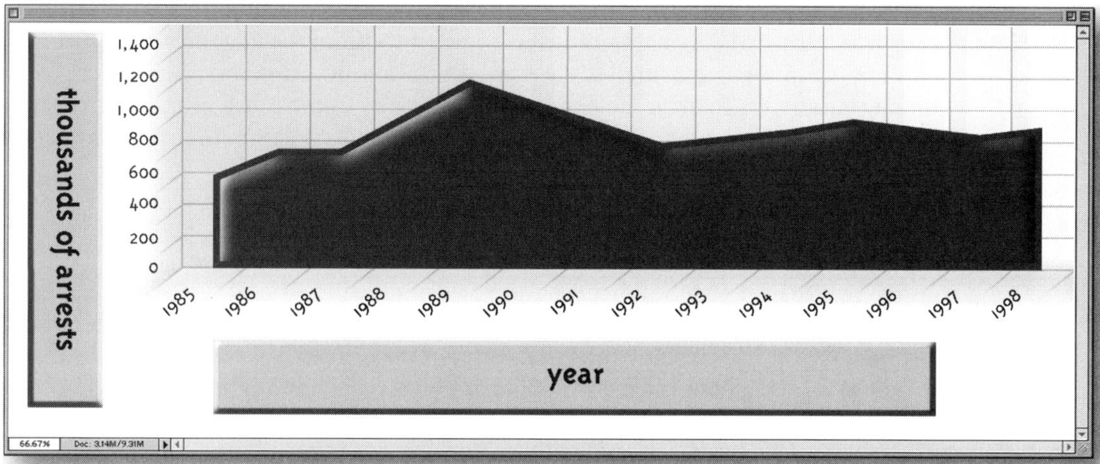

Figure 15-3 Adult arrests for drug-law violations, 1985–1998. *Source:* Federal Bureau of Investigation, *Crime in the United States* (Washington, D.C.: U.S. Government Printing Office, various years).

Drugs and Crime

The link between drugs and crime has at least three dimensions: 1) the possession, use, or sale of controlled substances which directly violates antidrug laws; 2) crimes committed by drug users in order to obtain more drugs, or crimes committed by persons whose judgment is altered by drugs; and 3) organized criminal activities in support of the drug trade and associated money laundering activities. Drugs and crimes are linked in other ways, as well. A recent report[6] by the Office for National Drug Control Policy (ONDCP), for example, claims that 5.2% of all homicides are "related to narcotic drug law" violations.

Figure 15-3 shows the number of persons over the age of 18 who were arrested in the United States in 1998 for drug law violations (excluding alcohol). Seventy-five percent of all arrests nationally were for possession of controlled substances; the remainder were for sale, possession, or manufacture. A close examination of official statistics reveals considerable regional variation. Overall, drug arrest rates are highest in the Western part of the country and lowest in the South.[7] A comprehensive effort designed to gauge the degree of drug use among criminal offenders is the NIJ's Arrestee Drug Abuse Monitoring program (ADAM). ADAM, formerly known as the Drug Use Forecasting (DUF) program, utilizes anonymous interviews and voluntary biological specimens from randomly selected male and female arrestees in 75 cities across the country. Learn more about the results of the ADAM program and other drug survey findings at *CJNow!* online.

Money Laundering

Because cash can flow into the hands of dealers in huge amounts, it can be difficult to spend. Few people buy houses, cars, and other "big-ticket" items with cash, and cash transactions arouse suspicion. **Money laundering** is the name given to the process used by drug dealers to hide the source of their revenues in order to avoid taxes and to disguise the financial evidence of drug dealing. Drug profits are laundered by converting them into other assets, such as real estate, stocks and bonds, racehorses, diamonds, gold, or other valuables. The NNICC says that millions of dollars in drug monies are laundered through commercial banks and other financial institutions each year, with major money laundering operations flourishing in South Florida and Los Angeles.[8] Other estimates put the laundered amount as high as $300 billion.[9] The Police Executive Research Forum (PERF) estimates that profits in excess of $100 billion a year are generated in the United States through narcotics trafficking and related underworld activities.[10] PERF also points out that successful money laundering can be accomplished only with the cooperation of lawyers, accountants, stockbrokers, realtors, and other investment advisers.

In an effort to catch money launderers, U.S. banking law requires financial institutions to report deposits in excess of $10,000. Traffickers attempt to avoid the law through techniques known as smurfing and structuring. Learn more about money laundering, the techniques used by money launderers to avoid detection, court cases of significance in the money laundering area, and efforts being made by the federal government to combat money laundering at *CJNow!* online.

Narcoterrorism

Some authors have identified a link between major drug traffickers and terrorist groups.[11] A number of South American traffickers appear especially willing to finance the activities of terrorist groups as a way of purchasing protection for themselves and their operations. The insurgents with whom they deal have their own political agendas, including the disruption of society, the overthrow of constitutional governments, and the spread of radical political ideas.

The link between drug traffickers and political insurgents has been termed **narcoterrorism**. Narcoterrorism, simply defined, is the involvement of terrorist organizations and insurgent groups in the trafficking of narcotics. The symbiotic relationship which exists between terrorist organizations and drug traffickers is mutually beneficial. Insurgents derive financial benefits from their support role in drug trafficking, while the traffickers themselves receive protection and benefit from the use of terrorist tactics against foes and competitors. Contemporary insurgent organizations with links to drug dealers probably include: 1) the 19th of April Movement (M-19) operating in Colombia, 2) Peru's *sendero luminoso* (shining path), 3) the Revolutionary Armed Forces of Colombia, and 4) the large Farabundo Marti National Liberation Front (FMLN), which has long sought to overthrow the elected government of El Salvador.[12] Learn more about narcoterrorism, including international efforts to combat it, at *CJNow!* online.

Lost Productivity and Police Corruption

Drug abuse has many personal and social costs that extend beyond its impact on the criminal justice system. Among them are lost productivity (estimated as high as $60 billion annually[13]), poor job performance, medical claims, the corruption of public officials, the loss of human life, and disease.

The potential for official corruption posed by widespread drug abuse is another area in which social costs may be substantial. In 1999, for example, former Justice Department attorney and Harvard Law School graduate Michael Abbell was sentenced in federal court in Miami to more than seven years in prison after being convicted of multiple counts of racketeering activity. The charges stemmed from his support of the cocaine-smuggling operations of the infamous "Cali cartel," the major source of cocaine in the United States.[14] Justice Department officials proved that Abbell knowingly served international drug traffickers at the highest level for years and that he distributed cartel monies to underlings to keep them from testifying against their bosses. Learn more about the corruption potential that illegal drugs hold at *CJNow!* online.

Solving the Drug Abuse Problem

The online chapter identifies six general strategies from among the many techniques for attacking the drug problem that have been proposed. They are 1) strict enforcement, 2) asset forfeiture, 3) interdiction, 4) crop control, 5) education and treatment, and 6) legalization or decriminalization.

Conservative politicians generally opt for a strict program of antidrug law enforcement and costly drug sentences, with the goal of removing dealers from the streets, disrupting supply lines, and eliminating sources of supply. Unfortunately, legal prohibitions appear to have done little to discourage widespread drug abuse. Those who look to strict law enforcement as a primary drug control strategy usually stress the need for secure borders, drug testing to identify users, and stiff penalties to discourage others from drug involvement.

Forfeiture, an enforcement strategy that federal statutes and some state laws support, is discussed in detail in the online chapter and bears special mention in this guide. Federal antidrug forfeiture statutes authorize judges to seize "all monies, negotiable instruments, securities, or other things of value furnished or intended to be furnished by any person in exchange for a controlled substance . . . (and) all proceeds traceable to such an exchange."[15] Forfeiture statutes find a legal basis in the "relation-back" doctrine. The relation-back doctrine assumes that because the government's right to illicit proceeds relates back to the time they are generated, anything acquired through the expenditure of those proceeds also belongs to the government.

The first federal laws to authorize forfeiture as a criminal sanction were both passed in 1970. They were the Continuing Criminal Enterprise statute, commonly called the CCE, and the Organized Crime Control Act. A section of the Organized Crime Control Act, known as the **RICO** statute (for Racketeer Influenced Corrupt Organizations), was designed to prevent criminal infiltration of legitimate businesses and has since been extensively applied in federal drug smuggling cases. In 1978, Congress authorized civil forfeiture of any assets acquired through narcotics trafficking in violation of federal law. Many states modeled their own legislation after federal law and now have similar statutes.

Interdiction involves efforts aimed at stopping drugs from entering the United States. The Coast Guard, Border Patrol, and Customs agents have played the most visible roles in interdiction efforts over the last few decades. Interdiction strategies in the fight against drugs, however, are almost doomed to failure by the sheer size of the task. Although most enforcement efforts are focused on international airports and major harbors, the international boundary of the United States extends for over 12,000 miles. Rough coastline, sparsely populated desert, and dense forests provide natural barriers to easy observation and make detection of controlled substances entering the country very difficult. Add to this the fact that over 420 billion tons of goods and more than 270 million people cross over the American border annually and the job of interdiction becomes more complicated still.[16] Because even minute quantities of most drugs can be highly potent, the interdiction strategy suffers from the proverbial "needle in the haystack" predicament.

Crop control strategies attempt to limit the amount of drugs available for the illicit market by targeting foreign producers. Crop control in source countries generally takes one of two forms. In the first, government subsidies (often with U.S. support) are made available to farmers to induce them to grow other kinds of crops. Sometimes illegal crops are bought and burned. The second form of control depends upon aerial spraying or ground-level crop destruction.

Although every proposed solution to the drug crisis has its difficulties, many people believe that education, aimed at preventing drug abuse, provides the best solution to the problem. Drug education programs can be found in schools, churches, and youth groups and may be provided by police departments, social service agencies, hospitals, and private citizens groups. Media advertisements against drugs also make use of educational principles. Project DARE (the Drug Abuse Resistance Education Program), is probably the nation's best-known school-based antidrug education program, although doubts have recently been raised about its effectiveness.

One of the most hopeful antidrug treatment programs is the **drug court**. Modern drug courts, or court-based drug abuse treatment programs, are often modeled after a Dade County (Florida) innovation begun in 1989 which has come to be known as the "Miami Drug Court model." Nonviolent first-time drug offenders are routinely diverted to mandatory treatment programs, with required periodic drug testing. A failure to comply with court-ordered treatment, or a return to drug use, results in harsher punishments, including imprisonment.

Often regarded as the most "radical" approach to solving the drug problem, **decriminalization** and legalization have been proposed repeatedly and in recent years seem to be gaining at least a modicum of respectability. Although the words decriminalization and legalization are often used interchangeably, there is a significant difference. Legalization refers to the removal of all legal strictures from the use or possession of the drug in question. Manufacture and distribution might still be regulated. Decriminalization, on the other hand, substantially reduces penalties associated with drug use, but may not eliminate drugs entirely.

Learn more about each drug control strategy, including arguments for and against both legalization and decriminalization, at *CJNow!* online.

What You Should Remember

- Drug crimes and drug-related crimes account for a large proportion of all crimes committed in this country.
- The history of drug abuse and anti-drug abuse legislation in America is replete with examples of the ongoing criminalization of substances that once were legal. Decisions about which drugs to outlaw have rested largely on popular opinion combined with political recognition of distinctively American viewpoints.
- The first major piece of federal anti-drug legislation was the Harrison Act of 1914, which required persons dealing in opium, morphine, heroin, cocaine, and specified derivatives of those drugs to register with the federal government and to pay a tax. Other early federal legislation included the Marijuana Tax Act of 1937, and the Narcotic Control Act of 1956.
- Recent anti-drug legislation includes the Comprehensive Drug Abuse Prevention and Control Act of 1970, the Anti-Drug Abuse Act of 1988, and the Drug-Free Communities Act of 1997.
- Whereas many substances can be classified as drugs, the online chapter and most state and federal laws concern themselves primarily with marijuana, cocaine, heroin (and their derivatives), and other psychoactive substances such as LSD. Each of these types of drugs has been classified under federal legislation into a series of "schedules" defined by law.
- While the manufacture, importation, sale, and use of illegal drugs account for a substantial number of law violations, many other offenses are also linked to drug use. Among them are thefts of all kinds, burglary, assault, and murder. Such crimes are often committed by people under the influence of drugs, and who may be committed to support continued drug use.
- Six strategies for attacking the drug problem are discussed in the online chapter. They are 1) strict enforcement, 2) asset forfeiture, 3) interdiction, 4) crop control, 5) education and treatment, and 6) legalization or decriminalization.

LIBRARY EXTRAS!

Library Extras! are suggested readings that are available digitally to readers of this guide. They may be accessed at the *CJNow!* Web site.

Library Extra! 15-1. *ADAM Annual Report on Drug Use Among Adult and Juvenile Arrestees* (ADAM, current volume).

Library Extra! 15-2. *The National Drug Control Strategy* (ONDCP, current volume).

Library Extra! 15- 3. *National Household Survey on Drug Abuse*, (SAMHSA, current volume).

Library Extra! 15-4. *National Narcotics Intelligence Consumers Committee* (NNICC) Report: The Supply of Illicit Drugs to the United States (DEA, current volume).

Library Extra! 15-5. *Pulse Check: National Trends in Drug Abuse*, (ONDCP, current volume).

Library Extra! 15-6. The U.S. Controlled Substances Act.

ENDNOTES

[1] Office of National Drug Control Policy, "ONDCP Finds Americans Spent $57 Billion in One Year on Illegal Drugs," ONDCP press release, 1997.

[2] Office of National Drug Control Policy, *What America's Users Spend on Illegal Drugs* (Washington, D.C.: ONDCP, 1991) p. 4.

[3] U.S. Department of Health and Human Services, *National Household Survey on Drug Abuse: Main Findings 1996* (Washington, D.C.: U.S. Government Printing Office, 1997).

[4] Carolyn Skorneck, "Drug Use," The Associated Press wire services, July 20, 1994.

[5] Office of National Drug Control Policy, *The National Drug Control Strategy 1999* (Washington, D.C.: ONDCP, 1999).

[6] ONDCP, *The National Drug Control Strategy: Executive Summary*, April 1995, p. 12.

[7] Federal Bureau of Investigation, *Crime in the United States 1998* (Washington, D.C.: U.S. Government Printing Office, 1999).

[8] National Narcotics Intelligence Consumers Committee, *The NNICC Report 1996* (Washington, D.C.: Drug Enforcement Administration 1997).

[9] Clifford L. Karchmer and Douglas Ruch, "State and Local Money Laundering Control Strategies," *NIJ Research in Brief* (Washington, D.C.: National Institute of Justice, 1992), p. 1.

[10] Clifford L. Karchmer, *Illegal Money Laundering: A Strategy and Resource Guide for Law Enforcement Agencies* (Washington, D.C.: Police Executive Research Forum, 1988), p. iv.

[11] Daniel Boyce, "Narco-Terrorism," *FBI Law Enforcement Bulletin* (October 1987), p. 24; and James A. Inciardi, "Narcoterrorism: A Perspective and Commentary," in Robert O. Slater and Grant Wardlaw, eds., *International Narcotics* (London: Macmillan/St. Martins, 1989).

[12] U.S. Department of State, *Terrorist Group Profiles* (Washington, D.C.: U.S. Government Printing Office, 1989).

[13] Jack Kelley, "Poll: On-Job Drug Use Is Significant," *USA Today*, December 13, 1989, p. 1A.

[14] See "Former DOJ Lawyer Jailed for Money Laundering," APB News. Web posted at http://www.apbonline.com/911/1999/06/19/abbell0619_01.html. Accessed January 10, 2000.

[15] 21 U.S.C. § 881(a)(6).

[16] Mark Moore, *Drug Trafficking*, a National Institute of Justice Crime File Study Guide (Washington, D.C.: U.S. Government Printing Office, 1988), p. 3.

Chapter 16

quick view

<< multinational criminal justice >>

Outline

- The Transnational Perspective
- The Chinese Justice System
- Islamic Criminal Justice
- Criminal Justice in England and Wales
- International Criminal Justice Organizations

What You Should Learn

- The nature of comparative criminology and the problems inherent in cross-cultural comparisons of crime.
- The main characteristics of the Chinese justice system.
- The central features of Islamic criminal justice.

- Important characteristics of the criminal justice system in England and Wales.
- The identity of different international criminal justice organizations and their roles in international crime fighting.
- The definitions of key terms that appear in boldface throughout this *Quick View* chapter. Definitions can be found online at http://www.cjnowonline.com.

Hear the author introduce this chapter at *CJNow!* online.

The Transnational Perspective

Criminologists who study crime and criminal justice on a cross-national level are referred to as **comparative criminologists**, and their field is called comparative criminology or **comparative criminal justice**. Comparative criminal justice is becoming increasingly valued for the insights it provides. By contrasting native institutions of justice with similar institutions in other countries, procedures and problems which have been taken for granted under one system can be reevaluated in the light of world experience. As communications, rapid travel, and other technological advances effectively "shrink" the world, we find ourselves in a nearly ideal situation of being able to learn firsthand about the criminal justice systems of other countries and to use that information to improve our own.

The online chapter explains the value of comparative criminology for students of criminal justice, points to the problems which arise in comparing data among and between nations, and explores criminal justice systems in three parts of the world: China, England, and the Middle East. International police agencies are also described, and the role of the United Nations in the worldwide fight against crime is discussed. Visit *CJNow!* online to learn more.

Ethnocentrism and the Study of Criminal Justice

The study of criminal justice in the United States has been largely **ethnocentric**. The word *ethnocentric* literally means centered on one's own culture. Because people are socialized from birth into a particular culture, they tend to prefer their own culture's way of doing things over that of any other. Native patterns of behavior are seen as somehow "natural" and therefore better than foreign ones. The same is true for values, beliefs, and customs. People tend to think that the religion they were born into holds a spiritual edge over other religions, that their values and ethical sense are superior to those of others, and that the fashions they wear, the language they speak, and the rituals of daily life in which they participate are somehow better than comparable practices elsewhere. Ethnocentric individuals rarely stop to think that people elsewhere in the world probably cling to their own values, beliefs, and standards of behavior with just as much fervor as they do. Hence, ethnocentrism is not a uniquely American phenomenon.

Problems with Data

The crime rates of different nations are difficult to compare because of 1) differences in the way specific crimes are defined, 2) diverse crime reporting practices, and 3) political and other influences on the reporting of statistics to international agencies.[1]

Definitional differences create what may be the biggest problem. For cross-national comparisons of crime data to be meaningful, it is essential that the reported data share conceptual similarities. Unfortunately, that is rarely the case. Nations report offenses according to the legal criteria by which arrests are made and under which prosecution can occur. Switzerland, for example, includes bicycle thefts in its reported data on what we call "auto theft" because Swiss data gathering focuses more on the concept of personal transportation than it does upon the type of vehicle stolen. Social, cultural, and economic differences between countries compound such difficulties.

Reporting practices also vary substantially between nations. INTERPOL (the International Criminal Police Organization) and the United Nations are the only international organizations which regularly collect crime statistics from a large number of countries. Both agencies can only request data and have no way of checking on the accuracy of the data reported to them. Learn more about the problems associated with international crime and justice data at *CJNow!* online.

The Chinese Justice System

The People's Republic of China (PRC), with a land area of 3,691,502 square miles and a population of more than 1.2 billion people, is the largest nation on earth. Some people predict that in the twenty-first century, as the Chinese economy awakens and its massive military might makes itself felt, it will become the world's most important nation. For that reason students of criminal justice should have some understanding of the Chinese justice system and of the cultural assumptions that underlie it.

The Chinese justice system is structured along jurisdictional lines similar to those in the United States. At the highest level, the Chinese justice system is built around four national offices: the Ministry of Public Security, the Supreme People's Court, the People's **Procuratorate**, and the Ministry of Justice. Article 5 of the Chinese constitution specifies that the procuratorate is directly responsible for supervising the administration of criminal justice throughout the country, including the investigation of crimes, the activities of the courts, the police and correctional institutions, and initiation of prosecution.

Chinese police agencies fall under the authority of the Ministry of Public Security, and Courts in China are hierarchically organized. The Supreme People's Court is the highest court in China. It deals with cases which may have an impact on the entire country. Most cases come before the Court on appeal. The Court is divided into three sections: criminal court, which deals with felony violations of the law, mostly on appeal, and death penalty reviews; civil affairs court; and economic court. At the opposite judicial extreme, the Basic People's Court operates at the county level as the court with original jurisdiction over most criminal cases.

Defendants may choose to be represented in Chinese courts by an attorney, a relative or a friend, or may choose to represent themselves. If they desire, a lawyer will be appointed for them. Attorneys in China, however, have a far different role from that of their American counterparts. While they work to protect the rights of the defendant, attorneys have a responsibility to the court which transcends their duties to the accused. Defense lawyers are charged with helping the court render a just verdict.[2] The Chinese believe that vigorous defense strategies such as those found in the adversarial framework of Western justice can lead to criminals escaping responsibility.

The Chinese justice system also depends greatly on People's Mediation Committees. By virtue of the large number of cases they resolve, **mediation committees** may be the most important component of justice in modern China. Mediation committees generally consist of from five to seven people, with judicial assistants assigned to them by the Bureau of Justice, the courts, and the procuratorates.[3] They are officially guided by law and government policy. Their power, however, comes from the force of public opinion. Education and persuasion are their primary tools. Learn more about the Chinese system of criminal justice, including Chinese corrections, the widespread use of capital punishment, and the impact of international law at *CJNow!* online.

Islamic Criminal Justice

Islamic law (or *Shari'ah* in Arabic, which means "path of God") forms the basis of theocratic judicial systems in Kuwait, Saudia Arabia, the Sudan, Iran, and Algeria. Other Arabic nations, such as Egypt, Jordan, and Iraq, recognize substantial elements of Islamic law in their criminal justice systems, but also make wide use of Western and nontheocratic legal principles. Islamic law is based upon four sources. In order of importance these sources are 1) the Koran (also spelled "Quran" and "Qur'an"), or Holy Book of Islam, which Muslims believe is the word of God, or "Allah;" 2) the teachings of the Prophet Mohammed; 3) a consensus of the clergy in cases where neither the Koran nor the prophet directly address an issue; and 4) reason or logic which should be used when no solution can be found in the other three sources.[4]

Islamic law recognizes seven *Hudud* (sometimes called *Hodood* or *Huddud*) crimes—or crimes based on religious strictures. *Hudud* crimes are essentially violations of "natural law" as interpreted by Arab culture. Divine displeasure is thought to be the basis of crimes defined as *Hudud*, and *Hudud* crimes are often said to be crimes against God (or, more specifically, "God's rights"). Four *Hudud* crimes for which punishments are specified in the Koran are 1) making war upon Allah and His messengers, 2) theft, 3) adultery, and 4) false accusation of fornication or adultery. Three other *Hudud* offenses are mentioned by the Koran, for which no punishment is specified—1) "corruption on the earth," 2) drinking of alcohol, and 3) highway robbery—and the punishments for these crimes are determined by tradition.[5] The seven *Hudud* offenses and associated typical punishments are shown in Table 16-1 online. "Corruption on Earth" is a general category of religious offense, not well understood in the West, which includes activities such as embezzlement, revolution against lawful authority, fraud, and "weakening the society of God."

The religious aspect of Islamic law makes for strict punishment of moral failure. Sexual offenders, even those who engage in what may be considered essentially victimless crimes in Western societies, are subject to especially harsh treatment. The Islamic penalty for fornication, for example, is 100 lashes. Men are stripped to the waist, women have their clothes bound tightly, and flogging is carried out with a leather whip. Adultery carries a much more severe penalty: flogging and stoning to death.

Under Islamic law even property crimes can be severely punished. Thieves who are undeterred by less serious punishments may eventually suffer amputation of the right hand.

All crimes other than *Hudud* fall into an offense category called ***tazirat***. *Tazir* crimes are regarded as any action not considered acceptable in a spiritual society. They include crimes against society and against individuals, but not against God. *Tazir* crimes may call for *Quesas* (retribution) or *Diya* (compensation or fines). Crimes requiring *Quesas* are based on the Arabic principle of "an eye for an eye, a nose for a nose, a tooth for a tooth," and generally require physical punishments up to and including death. *Quesas* offenses may include murder, manslaughter, assault, and maiming. Learn more about Islamic justice, including Islamic courts and punishments, at *CJNow!* online.

Criminal Justice in England and Wales

The country of England is quite small—only a little larger than the state of New Jersey, but with a population of around 40 million people. One of the original participants in the industrial revolution, it remains a highly industrialized nation. England is linked closely to its neighbors—Wales, Scotland, and Northern Ireland—an alliance which created the political entity of "Great Britain" and which today is officially known as the "United Kingdom of Great Britain." Because England is a much more open society than either China or Iran, a far greater amount of descriptive detail is available about the criminal justice system there.

British crime surveys mirror their American counterparts, and the Research and Statistics Department of the Home Office makes reports of crime freely available to researchers. Major crimes in England and Wales are termed "notifiable offenses," the counterpart of "Part I" or "Index Offenses" in the United States.

In recent years public opinion polls have identified crime as the number one concern of the British voting public. By any measure, crime would appear to be high in England. In 1997,[6] for example, the British Crime Survey (BCS) estimated that there were nearly 16,500,000 crimes committed against adults living in households in England and Wales in 1997. The Survey found 3.3 million violent crimes and 10.1 million property crimes. Given the size of the British population, these statistics mean that fully 34% of all people living in England and Wales were in some way victimized by criminal activity in 1997.

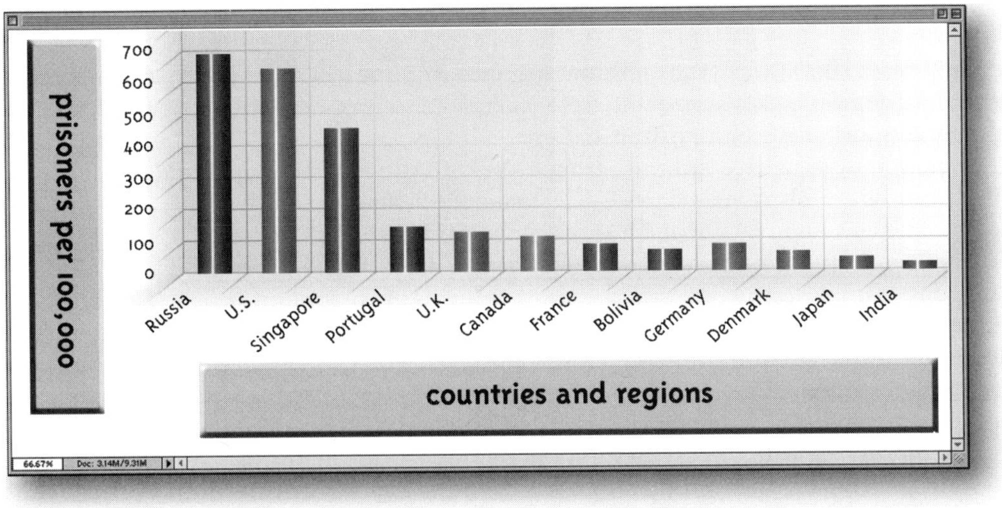

Figure 16-1 International incarceration rates of selected countries. *Source:* Roy Walmsley, *World Prison Population List* (London: Home Office, 1999).

Modern Criminal Law in England

In November 1994, a powerful nationwide conservative emphasis led to passage of the Criminal Justice and Public Order Act 1994 (CJA) in England. The CJA marked a return to a get-tough English anticrime policy. The CJA selectively criminalized what had previously been especially serious violations of the civil law, made it easier to catch and convict criminals, made it harder for repeat offenders to get bail, and restricted, at least to some degree, the rights of criminal defendants. The CJA also gave British courts wider powers to sentence persistent offenders between the ages of 12 and 14 and effectively doubled the maximum possible sentence youthful offenders could receive. As in the United States, which sports the second highest incarceration rate among democratic nations (see Figure 16-1), the call for longer sentences for English convicts has come up against the reality of prison crowding. Learn more about the British system of justice, including the police (and **New Scotland Yard**), courts, prisons, and recent legislation at *CJNow!* online.

International Criminal Justice Organizations

The United Nations (UN), composed of 185 member states and based in New York City, is the largest and most inclusive international body in the world. Through its Crime Prevention and Criminal Justice Program, the United Nations continues to advance the cause of crime prevention and to disseminate useful criminal justice information. The Program's 40-member State Commission on Crime Prevention and Criminal Justice, and its secretariat, the Crime Prevention and Criminal Justice Branch of the United Nations Offices at Vienna, provide forums for ongoing discussions of justice practices around the world. The Program has regional links throughout the world, sponsored by supportive national governments which have agreed to fund the Program's work. The European Institute for Crime Prevention and Control (HEUNI), for example, provides the Program's regional European link in a network of institutes operating throughout the world. Other network components include the United Nations Interregional Crime and Justice Research Institute (UNICRI) in Rome, Italy; an Asian regional institute (UNAFEI) in Tokyo, Japan; ILANUE, based in San Jose, Costa Rica, which focuses on crime problems in Latin America and the Caribbean; an African institute (UNAFRI) in Kampala, Uganda; Australia's AIC in Canberra; an Arabic institute (ASSTC) in Riyadh, Saudi Arabia; and other centers in Siracusa, Italy, and in Vancouver and Montreal, Canada. Learn more about the role of the United Nations in the fight against international crime at *CJNow!* online.

Transnational Organized Crime

Transnational crime (also, **transnational organized crime**), and the internationally organized criminal groups that support it, have emerged as one of the most pressing challenges of the early twenty-first century. Transnational crime refers to unlawful activity undertaken and supported by organized criminal groups operating across national boundaries.

In the words of Robert S. Gelbard, U.S. Assistant Secretary for International Narcotics and Law Enforcement Affairs: "The main threat now is transnational organized crime. It comes in many forms: drug trafficking, money laundering, terrorism, alien smuggling, trafficking in weapons of mass destruction, fraud and other forms of corruption." "These problems all have one critical element in common," says Gelbard, "they threaten the national security of all states and governments—from our closest allies to those that we find most repugnant. No country is safe. International criminal organizations all seek to establish pliant governments that can be manipulated through bribery and intimidation. They respect no national boundaries and already act with virtual impunity in many parts of the world."[7] Worse still, entire nations may become rogue countries, or quasi-criminal regimes where criminal activity runs rampant and wields considerable influence over the national government. As this guide goes to press, Russia, for example, appears to be fast approaching such status through an intertwining of the goals of organized criminal groups and official interests that run to the top levels of government. The number of organized criminal groups operating in Russia is estimated to be over 12,000.[8] Learn more about the globalization of crime and what the United States and other countries are doing to combat transnational crime at *CJNow!* online.

INTERPOL and Europol

The International Criminal Police Organization (INTERPOL), headquartered in Lyon, France, traces its origins back to the first International Criminal Police Congress of 1914, which met in Monaco. INTERPOL, however, did not officially begin operations until 1946, when the end of World War II brought about a new spirit of international harmony. Today, 176 nations belong to INTERPOL.[9] The U.S. INTERPOL unit is called the "U.S. National Central Bureau" (USNCB) and is a separate agency within the U.S. Department of Justice.

INTERPOL's primary purpose is to act as a clearinghouse for information on offenses and suspects who are believed to operate across national boundaries. INTERPOL does not have its own field investigators. The agency has no powers of arrest or of search and seizure in member countries. Instead, INTERPOL draws upon the willingness of local and national police forces to lend support to its activities. The headquarters staff of INTERPOL consists of around 250 individuals, many with prior police experience, who direct data gathering efforts around the world and who serve to alert law enforcement organizations to the movement of suspected offenders within their jurisdiction. Learn more about INTERPOL and other international criminal justice organizations, including Europol (the European Police Office), at *CJNow!* online.

What You Should Remember

- The international perspective helps U.S. law enforcement agencies, court personnel, correctional officials, and policymakers benefit from exposure to innovative crime prevention, investigative, and treatment strategies found throughout the world.
- A number of barriers continue to limit the applicability of cross-national studies on crime, including the unavailability of detailed, up-to-date, and reliable international information on crime rates, victimization, and adjudication.
- Ethnocentrism, a hesitancy on the part of some people to consider any personal or professional viewpoints other than that of their own culture, reduces the likelihood for serious analysis of even the limited international information that is available.
- The modern Chinese criminal justice system is somewhat similar in structure to that of the United States. Chinese police officers investigate crimes, make arrests, and present

suspected offenders to the court for trial. Differences exist, however, in the role of defense attorneys and in the widespread use of informal mediation committees at the local level.

- Islamic criminal justice is largely based upon religious tradition. It distinguishes between *Hudud* crimes (those against God), and *tazir* crimes (crimes against society and against individuals). Islamic courts sometimes impose physical punishments that may seem barbaric by Western standards.
- Unlike justice practices in many parts of the world, the criminal justice system of England and Wales is largely open to study. While the crime rate in England is high, so, too, are incarceration rates. Recent laws, however, have given British police officers greater authority than at any time in the recent past.
- The United Nations plays an important role in the fight against international and transnational crime through its Crime Prevention and Criminal Justice Program. Other international crime fighting organizations of note include the International Criminal Police Organization (INTERPOL) and the European Police Office (Europol).

LIBRARY EXTRAS!

Library Extras! are suggested readings that are available digitally to readers of this guide. They may be accessed at the *CJNow!* Web site.

Library Extra! 16-1. *The British Crime Survey* (London: Home Office, current volume).

Library Extra! 16-2. *Crime and Justice in the U.S. and England and Wales* (BJS, current volume).

Library Extra! 16-3. *Global Report on Crime and Justice* (United Nations, 1999).

Library Extra! 16-4. *The International Crime Victimization Survey* (London: Home Office, current volume).

Library Extra! 16-5. "Thinking Globally to Act Locally," *National Institute of Justice Journal* (NIJ, February 1996).

Library Extra! 16-6. *World Prison Populations List* (London: Home Office, 1999).

Library Extra! 16-7. *World Factbook of Criminal Justice Systems* (BJS, various years).

ENDNOTES

[1] Adapted from Carol B. Kalish, "International Crime Rates," a Bureau of Justice Statistics *Special Report* (Washington, D.C.: Bureau of Justice Statistics, 1988).

[2] Robert Lilly, "Forks and Chopsticks: Understanding Criminal Justice in the PRC," *Criminal Justice International* (March/April 1986), pp. 14-15.

[3] Zhenxiong (Joseph) Zhou, "An Introduction to the Present Legal System of the People's Republic of China," *North Carolina Criminal Justice Today*, Vol. IV, no. 6 (Salemburg: NC Justice Academy, 1987), p. 13.

[4] Parviz Saney, "Iran," in Elmer H. Johnson, ed., *International Handbook of Contemporary Developments in Criminology* (Westport, CT: Greenwood, 1983), p. 359.

[5] This section owes much to Matthew Lippman, "Iran: A Question of Justice?" *Criminal Justice International*, 1987, pp. 6-7.

[6] Catriona Mirrlees-Black, Tracey Budd, Sara Patridge and Pat Mayhew, *The 1998 British Crime Survey* (London, England: Home Office, 1998).

[7] Robert S. Gelbard, "Foreign Policy after the Cold War: The New Threat—Transnational Crime," address at St. Mary's University, San Antonio, Texas, April 2, 1996.

[8] Barbara Starr, "A Gangster's Paradise," ABCNEWS.com, September 14, 1998.

[9] See U.S. Department of Justice, "INTERPOL Member Countries," Web posted at http://www.usdoj.gov/usncb/countrytext.htm. Accessed January 19, 2000.

Chapter 17

quick view

<< the future of criminal justice >>

Outline

- Introduction
- Technology and Criminal Justice
- Terrorism
- Technology and Individual Rights

What You Should Learn

- An appreciation for the important role that technology has played and will continue to play in the fight against crime and the quest for criminal justice.
- Some details about the historical roots of terrorism, what motivates terrorists, and the government's attempts to prevent and control the spread of terrorism.
- The threats to individual rights inherent in the increased use of advanced technology.

- The definitions of key terms that appear in boldface throughout this *Quick View* chapter. Definitions can be found online at http://www.cjnowonline.com.

Introduction

Hear the author introduce this chapter at *CJNow!* online.

Rapidly expanding technologies, including computer networking, digital access to enormous amounts of information, and the use of innovative investigative tools such as DNA fingerprinting, are shaping many of the practical aspects of the twenty-first century criminal justice system—from new forms of crime to the way in which evidence is gathered. Even so, the criminal justice system of the near future will look much like the system we know today. It will rest upon constitutional mandates and will be responsive to court precedent. The system itself will remain recognizable through its backbone of subsystems: the police, courts, and corrections. Deterrence, apprehension, and reformation will continue to serve as the philosophical trilogy guiding the day-to-day operations of criminal justice agencies. New issues will arise, but most of them will be resolved within the context of the question which has guided American criminal justice since its inception: how to ensure public safety while guaranteeing justice in a free society.

Coming changes in the fabric of American society will necessitate some predictable, large-scale system responses. Many demographic, ideological, and behavioral transformations, such as widespread illegal drug use and a greater social acceptance of certain victimless crimes, have already occurred and are now firmly rooted in substantial segments of American society. In the area of drugs, much is already known. Drug culture has been studied, the impact of drug abuse on society is becoming clear, and the economic and human costs of drugs have been charted. Because the battle lines in the "war on drugs" are firmly drawn, a picture of drug abuse and the system's response to it can be provided, as we have done in an earlier chapter. Only the final outcome of the "war" is still unknown.

Less clear, however, are changes yet to come, changes we can only now begin to discern. The online version of this chapter attempts to identify some of these coming changes and to predict what impact they will have on American criminal justice. Perhaps the two most significant sources of change will be technology and the continuing evolution of society and social values.

Technology and Criminal Justice

We live in a world governed by rapid change. Technology and science are the modern-day engines of change, and they continue to run relentlessly forward. The impact of change on all areas of human life has been dramatic. The automobile and the airplane have made the world a smaller place, and journeys that would have required months a century ago can now be made in a day. Radio, television, and the Internet have transformed the planet into a "global village," in which every human being can be in touch with events of importance as they happen anywhere around the globe. Computers have dramatically altered the rate at which information is being produced, so much so that precedence is given today to storing information rather than using it. Coming software, it is hoped, will do a better job of sorting through accumulated information, distinguishing the significant from the mundane and permitting us to make use of that which is of interest.

Advancing technology, along with legislation designed to control it, will create crimes never before imagined. The future will see a race between technologically sophisticated offenders and law enforcement authorities as to who can wield the most advanced skills on either side of the age-old battle between crime and justice. Learn more about the future of American criminal justice at *CJNow!* online.

Criminalistics: Past, Present, and Future

The use of technology in the service of criminal *investigation* is a subfield of criminal justice referred to as **criminalistics**. Criminalistics applies scientific techniques to the detection and evaluation of criminal evidence. Police crime scene analysts and laboratory personnel versed in criminalistics are referred to as **criminalists**. Modern criminalistics had its beginnings with the need for the certain identification of individuals.

The first "modern" system of personal identification was created by Alphonse Bertillon. Bertillon was the director of the Bureau of Criminal Identification of the Paris Police Department during the late 1800s. The Bertillon system of identification made the assertion that certain bodily aspects, such as eye color, skeletal size and shape, and ear form, did not change substantially after physical maturity had been reached. It combined physical measurements with the emerging technology of photography.

Fingerprints, produced by contact with the ridge patterns in the skin on the fingertips, became the subject of intense scientific study in the mid-1840s. While their importance in criminal investigation today seems obvious, it was not until the 1880s that scientists began to realize that each person's fingerprints were unique and unchangeable over a lifetime. The use of fingerprints in identifying offenders was popularized by Sir Francis Galton and officially adopted by Scotland Yard in 1901. By the 1920s fingerprint identification was in use in police departments everywhere, having quickly replaced the anthropometric system of Bertillon.

Modern criminalistics also depends heavily upon **ballistics**, the analysis of weapons, ammunition, and projectiles; medical pathology, to determine the cause of injury or death; **forensic anthropology**, to reconstruct the likeness of a decomposed or dismembered body; **forensic entomology**, or the study of insect behavior to determine issues such as the time of death of a corpse; the photography of crime scenes (now often done with video or digital cameras); plaster and polymer casting of tire tracks, boot prints, and marks made by implements; polygraph (the "lie detector") and voice-print identification; as well as a plethora of other techniques. Learn more about the advancing science of criminalistics, including the use of artificial intelligence, **expert systems**, and computer-based training, at *CJNow!* online.

Emerging Technologies in Criminalistics

One of the most important advances in criminalistics in recent years involves DNA (deoxyribonucleic acid) fingerprinting (also termed DNA profiling). DNA is a nucleic acid found in the center of cells. It is the principal component of chromosomes, the structures that transmit hereditary characteristics between generations. Each DNA molecule is a long, two-stranded chain made up of subunits, called nucleotides, coiled in the form of a double helix. DNA fingerprinting makes use of human DNA for purposes of identification. Because of the fact that genetic material is unique to each individual (except in the case of identical twins or clones), it can provide a highly reliable source of suspect identification.

The DNA fingerprinting process, diagrammed in Figure 17-1, involves the use of a highly technical procedure called electrophoresis. Learn more about DNA fingerprinting, its current legal standing, and the important 1993 DNA-related U.S. Supreme Court decision in the case of *Daubert* v. *Merrell Dow Pharmaceuticals, Inc.*[1] (which established the well-known ***Daubert* standard**) at *CJNow!* online.

Cybercrime: The New White-Collar Crime

The flip side of high technology, as far as the justice system is concerned, is the potential it brings for committing old crimes in new ways, or for the commission of new crimes never before imagined. Because of the skill and knowledge required by their crimes, most, but not all, of today's high-tech offenders can aptly be labeled white-collar criminals. The term **white-collar crime** was coined by Edwin Sutherland in his 1939 presidential address to the American Sociological Society.[2] Sutherland later defined the term to include crimes committed by persons in authority during the normal course of their business transactions. White-collar crimes include embezzlement, bribery, political corruption, price fixing, misuse and theft of company property, corporate tax evasion, fraud, and money laundering (which obscures the source of funds earned through illegal activities, allowing them to enter the legitimate financial arena).

Criminologists were quick to realize that if persons of high socioeconomic status could commit crimes during the course of their business, then so could persons of lower social

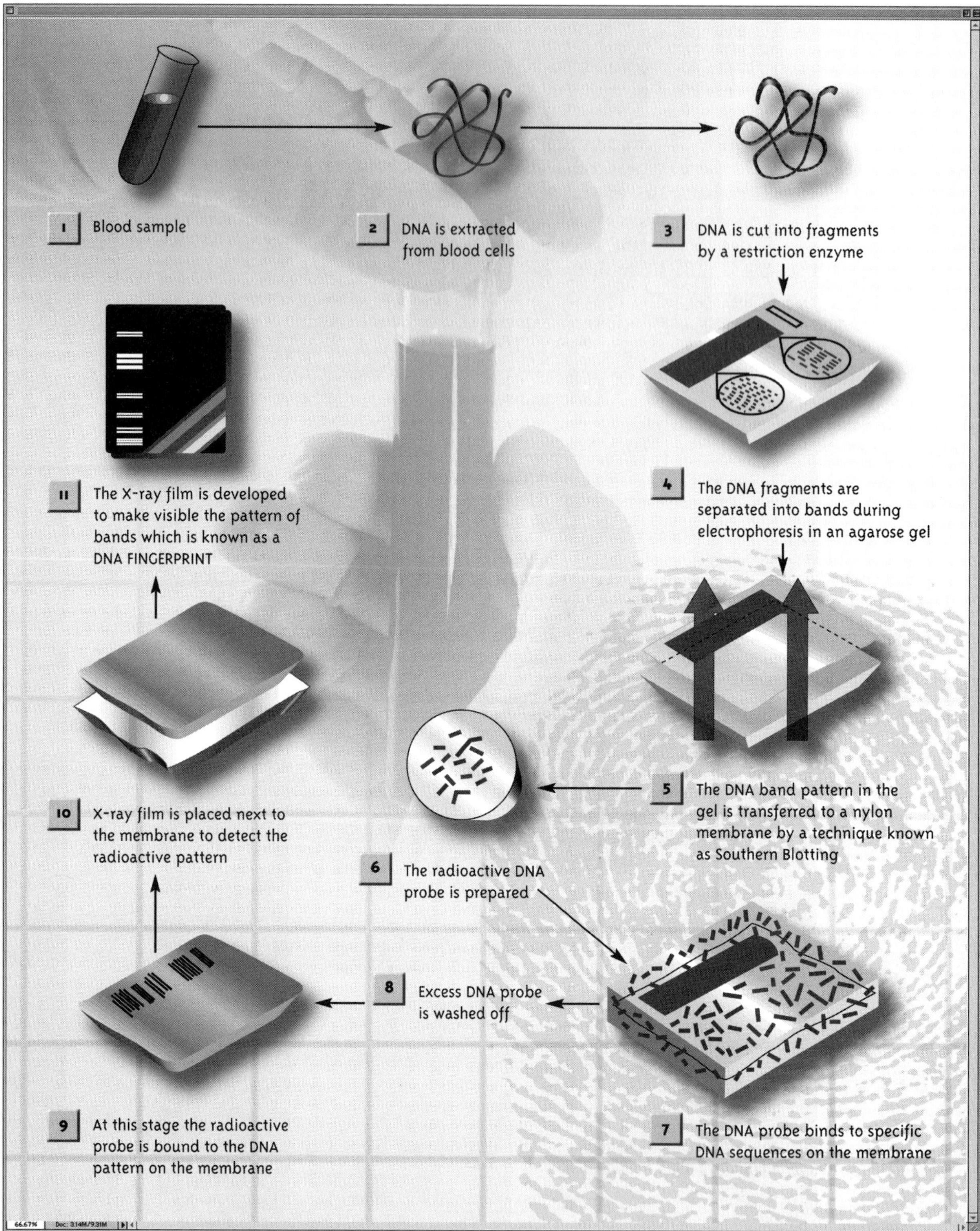

Figure 17-1 The DNA fingerprinting process. .Cellmark Diagnostics, Inc. Reprinted with permission.

standing. The term *occupational crime* was coined to describe the on-the-job illegal activities of employees. Thefts of company property, vandalism, the misuse of information, software piracy which occurs in the workplace, and many other activities come under the rubric of occupational crime.

Some authors maintain that occupational and **corporate crime** are a way of life in American businesses.[3] On May 20, 1999, for example, two companies, Hoffman-LaRoche, Ltd. and BASF AG, agreed to plead guilty to charges of fixing the prices of vitamins A, B2, B5, C, E and beta carotene. The companies agreed to pay a $500 million fine—the largest antitrust criminal fine ever imposed. They paid another $225 million as part of a plea bargain agreement.[4]

Computer crimes are rapidly becoming the white-collar crime *par excellence* in the modern world. **Computer crimes**, sometimes called **cybercrimes**, use computers and computer technology as tools in crime commission. Thefts of computer equipment, although sometimes spectacular, are not computer crimes, but are instead classified as larcenies. "True" computer criminals go beyond the theft of hardware, focusing instead on the information stored in computer systems and manipulating it in a way which violates the law.

Many of today's cybercrimes involve the theft of credit card or personal information, prostitution, child pornography, fraud, the theft of trade secrets, and copyright infringement. Some computer criminals offer to sell illegal goods and services through the Web. In 1999, for example, Diana Deveaux, 41, of Fort Smith, Arkansas, was arrested by an undercover police vice officer she had met on the Internet and charged with soliciting sex— a misdemeanor under state law. Deveaux, who advertised herself on her Web site as a "private escort," told police she had been meeting men through the Internet for a long time. Deveaux explained that she needed the money and had gotten the idea from other women on the Web.[5]

Another form of cybercrime, the unauthorized copying of software programs, also called **software piracy**, appears rampant. According to the Software Information Industry Association (SIIA), global losses from software piracy totaled nearly $11 billion in 1998.[6] According to the SIIA, 38% of all software in use in the world has been copied illegally. Learn more about computer and high-technology crimes, and what is being done to prevent them, at *CJNow!* online.

Terrorism

The technological sophistication of state-sponsored terrorist organizations is rapidly increasing. Handguns and even larger weapons are now being manufactured out of plastic polymers and ceramics. Capable of firing Teflon-coated armor-piercing bullets, such weapons are extremely powerful and impossible to uncover with metal detectors. Evidence points to the black market availability of other sinister devices, including liquid metal embrittlement (LME). LME is a chemical that slowly weakens any metal it contacts. It could be applied easily with a Magic Marker® to fuselage components in domestic aircraft, causing delayed structural failure.[7] Backpack-type electromagnetic pulse generators may also now be available to terrorists. Such devices could be carried into major cities, set up next to important computer installations, and activated to wipe out billions of items of financial, military, or other information now stored on magnetic media. International terrorists, along with the general public, have easy access to maps and other information which could be easily used to cripple the nation. The approximately 500 extremely high-voltage (EHV) transformers on which the nation's electronic grid depends, for example, are entirely undefended, but could be specified with extreme accuracy on easily available power network maps.

Equally worrisome are domestic underground survivalist and separatist groups and potentially violent special interest groups, each with its own vision of a future America. In 1993, for example, a confrontation between David Koresh's Branch Davidian followers and federal agents left 72 Davidians (including Koresh) and four federal agents dead in Waco, Texas.

Exactly two years to the day after the Davidian standoff ended in a horrific fire that destroyed the compound, a powerful terrorist truck bomb devastated the Alfred P. Murrah federal building in downtown Oklahoma City, Oklahoma. One hundred and sixty-eight people died and hundreds more were wounded. The fertilizer and diesel fuel device used in the attack was estimated to have weighed about 1,200 pounds and had been left in a parked rental truck on the 5th Street side of the building. The blast, which left a crater 30 feet wide and 8 feet deep and spread debris over a ten-block area, demonstrated just how vulnerable the United States is to terrorist attack.

Some experts believe that the Oklahoma City attack was modeled after a similar bombing described in the *Turner Diaries*, a novel used by extremist groups to map their rise to power.[8] Active fringe groups include those espousing a nationwide "common law movement," under which the legitimacy of elected government officials is not recognized.

In 1998 radical Muslim leader Osama bin Laden showed the world how easy it can be to strike at American interests abroad. Attacks on American embassies in Nairobi, Kenya, and Dar es Salaam, Tanzania, were apparently both planned by bin Laden and carried out by his henchmen. The attacks killed 257 people, including 12 Americans. Although American military forces responded by attacking some of bin Laden's reputed strongholds in Afghanistan, the terrorist leader remains at large as of this writing.

The current situation leads many observers to conclude that the American justice system of today is ill prepared to deal with the threat represented by domestic and international terrorism. Intelligence gathering efforts focused on such groups have largely failed. Military-style organization and training are characteristic of the groups that are known, making them difficult to penetrate. The armaments at their disposal include weapons of mass destruction, which the firepower and tactical mobility of law enforcement agencies could not hope to match.

Even more frightening is the prospect of nuclear terrorism. The collapse of the Soviet Union at the close of the 1980s led to very loose internal control over nuclear weapons and weapons-grade fissionable materials held in the former Soviet republics. Evidence of such lack of control continues to surface.

Another new kind of terrorism, called **cyberterrorism**, is lurking on the horizon. **Cyberterrorism** is a form of terrorism that makes use of high technology—especially computers, the Internet, and the World Wide Web—in the planning and carrying out of terrorist attacks. Cyberterrorism was first identified in a 1999 report by Rand Corporation that warned of an emerging "New Terrorism" which is being brought implemented by the way in which terrorist groups organize and use technology. The report warned of a coming "netwar," or "infowar," consisting of coordinated cyberattacks on our nation's economic, business, and military infrastructure.[9] Learn more about terrorism, the threat it holds for our nation and the world, and efforts being made to control it at *CJNow!* online.

Technology and Individual Rights

The Office for Technology Assessment of the U.S. Congress notes that "What is judicially permissible and socially acceptable at one time has often been challenged when technology changes."[10] When agencies of the justice system use cutting-edge technology, it inevitably provokes fears of a future in which citizens' rights are abrogated to advancing science. Individual rights, equal treatment under the law, and due process issues all require constant reinterpretation as technology improves. However, because some of the technology available today is so new, few court cases have yet to directly address the issues involved.

The online chapter considers the potential impact of emerging technologies on: 1) free speech rights embodied in the First Amendment (and includes discussion of the Communications Decency Act of 1996); 2) the Second Amendment's guarantee of the right to bear arms (and includes discussion of the Brady Handgun Violence Prevention Act of 1993 and other gun control legislation); 3) Fourth Amendment rights against unreasonable search and seizure (and includes discussion of "supersnoop" technologies); 4) developments in the social sciences and their effect on Fifth Amendment guarantees of due process (and includes discussion of psychological profiling and genetic manipulation); 5) the growing ability of today's mass media and expanding scientific jury selection techniques to abridge Sixth Amendment rights to public trial by an impartial jury; 6) the potential for the development of novel forms of cruel and unusual punishments (including hormone and gene therapy) in violation of eighth Amendment rights; and 7) Fourteenth Amendment guarantees to equal protection of the laws for all people (including the economically disadvantaged).

What You Should Remember

- Old concepts of criminality, and of white-collar crime in particular, have undergone significant revision as a result of emerging technologies. Science fiction-like products, already widely available, have brought with them a plethora of possibilities for new high-stakes crimes, including computer crimes and cybercrime.
- Tomorrow's law enforcement agencies will be seriously challenged to compete with technologically sophisticated criminals, and the ultimate outcome of future enforcement efforts is far from clear.
- Throughout the 1960s and 1970s, domestic terrorism was commonplace in the United States when groups like the Weathermen, Students for a Democratic Society, the Symbionese Liberation Army, the Black Panthers, and other radical groups challenged the authority of federal and local governments. Bombings, kidnappings, and shootouts occurred. During the 1980s, international terrorism came to the fore, and today's terrorist threats come from many quarters.
- Citizens of the future will regard as commonplace much of what is only fantasy today. Gradual lifestyle modifications will accompany changes in technology and will result in taken-for-granted expectations foreign to today's world. Within that changed social context the "reasonableness" of technological intrusions into personal lives will be judged according to standards tempered by the new possibilities technology has to offer. As a consequence, a complex tangle of legal and technological issues will confront law enforcement agencies of the future.

LIBRARY EXTRAS!

Library Extras! are suggested readings that are available digitally to readers of this guide. They may be accessed at the *CJNow!* Web site.

Library Extra! 17-1. *Convicted by Juries, Exonerated by Science: Case Studies in the Use of DNA Evidence to Establish Innocence after Trial* (NIJ, June 1996).

Library Extra! 17-2. *Improving the Nation's Criminal Justice System* (NIJ, December 1997).

Library Extra! 17-3. *Patterns of Global Terrorism 1994* (U.S. Department of State, 1995).

Library Extra! 17-4. *The Unrealized Potential of DNA Testing.* (NIJ, June 1998).

ENDNOTES

[1] *Daubert* v. *Merrell Dow Pharmaceuticals, Inc.*, 509 U.S. 579, 113 S.Ct. 2786 (1993).

[2] James William Coleman, *The Criminal Elite: The Sociology of White Collar Crime*, 2nd ed. (New York: St. Martin's Press, 1989), p. 2.

[3] William J. Chambliss, *Exploring Criminology* (New York: Macmillan, 1988), p. 64.

[4] "Vitamins Price-Fixing Antitrust Litigation," Web posted at http://www.lchb.com/vitamins.htm. Accessed January 5, 2000.

[5] Richard Zitrin, "Woman Charged with Online Prostitution," APB Online. Web posted at http://www.apbonline.com/911/1999/06/10/hooker0610_01.html. Accessed June 19, 1999.

[6] The Business Software Alliance, and the Software & Information Industry Association, *1999 Global Software Piracy Report*, Web posted at http://www.siia.net/news/releases/piracy/98globalpiracy.htm. Accessed June 19, 1999.

[7] Technological devices described in this section depend upon G. Gordon Liddy, "Rules of the Game," *Omni* Magazine (January 1989), pp. 43-47, 78-80.

[8] Michael E. Wiggins, "Rationale and Justification for Right-Wing Terrorism: A Politico-Social Analysis of the Turner Diaries," paper presented at the annual meeting of the American Society of Criminology, Atlanta, Georgia, October 1986.

[9] John Arquilla and David Ronfeldt, "The Advent of Netwar" (Santa Monica, CA: RAND, 1996).

[10] U.S. Congress, Office of Technology Assessment, *Criminal Justice: New Technologies and the Constitution: A Special Report* (Washington, D.C.: U.S. Government Printing Office, 1988), p. 51.